MENTAL ZOO

MENTAL ZOO

Animals in the Human Mind and Its Pathology

Edited by

Salman Akhtar and Vamık D. Volkan

Routledge
Taylor & Francis Group
LONDON AND NEW YORK

First published 2005 by International Universities Press

This edition published in 2014 by
Karnac Books Ltd

Published 2018 by Routledge
2 Park Square, Milton Park, Abingdon, Oxon OX14 4RN
711 Third Avenue, New York, NY 10017, USA

Routledge is an imprint of the Taylor & Francis Group, an informa business

British Library Cataloguing in Publication Data
A C.I.P. for this book is available from the British Library

ISBN: 9781782201670 (pbk)

To

the memories of
Allah-Rakkha, the cat; Ram-ji Lal's cow;
Dr. Waheed Mirza's menagerie; Jackie, the dog;

P.D., my son's beloved cat;
Buckwheat, my daughter's favorite horse;

my great uncle's pythons;
and
my grandfather's pet tiger

S.A.

To

the memories of
my grandfather's nameless donkeys,
true beasts of burden and important childhood friends;

Sultan, Roxelana, Tarçın and Napa,
our family dogs;

Rengin and Baby,
cats from different times of my life;

and
to the continuing companionship of Al,
my feline writing companion.

V.V.

TABLE OF CONTENTS

CONTRIBUTORS

D. Wilfred Abse, M.D., Clinical Professor of Psychiatry, University of Virginia School of Medicine, Charlottesville, Virginia; Faculty, Washington Psychoanalytic Institute

Salman Akhtar, M.D., Professor of Psychiatry, Jefferson Medical College; Training and Supervising Analyst, Psychoanalytic Center of Philadelphia, Pennsylvania

Jodi Brown, M.D., Instructor, Department of Psychiatry and Human Behavior, Jefferson Medical College; Candidate, Institute of the Philadelphia Association for Psychoanalysis, Philadelphia, Pennsylvania

Philip J. Escoll, M.D., Clinical Professor of Psychiatry, University of Pennsylvania School of Medicine; Training and Supervising Analyst, Philadelphia Psychoanalytic Institute, Philadelphia, Pennsylvania

Gregg E. Gorton, M.D., Assistant Professor of Psychiatry, Jefferson Medical College, Philadelphia, Pennsylvania

Dwarakanath G. Rao, M.D., Clinical Faculty, Department of Psychiatry, University of Michigan School of Medicine, Ann Arbor, Michigan; Faculty, Michigan Psychoanalytic Institute

John E. Schowalter, M.D., Albert J Solnit Professor of Child Psychiatry and Pediatrics, Yale Child Study Center; Past President, Group for the Advancement of Psychiatry; Faculty, Western New England Psychoanalytic Society, New Haven, Connecticut

Leonard Shengold, M.D., Training and Supervising Analyst, Psychoanalytic Institute at New York University, New York

Melitta Sperling, M.D., Clinical Professor of Psychiatry, State University of New York; Faculty, Downstate Medical Center, Division of Psychoanalytic Education, New York *(deceased)*

Vamık Volkan, M.D., Professor of Psychiatry and Director, Center for the Study of Mind and Human Interaction, University of Virginia, Charlottesville, Virginia; Training and Supervising Analyst, Washington Psychoanalytic Institute

ACKNOWLEDGMENTS

This book is an expression of our love for animals and for psychoanalysis. Both have taught us about the external and the internal worlds. To both, we are profoundly indebted. We are also thankful to the colleagues who have contributed to this volume. We sincerely appreciate their efforts, their sacrifice of time, and above all, their patience with our rigorous requirements, relentless reminders, and repeated requests for revisions. Drs. John Kafka and Eric Lager and Ms. Nishat Akhtar have drawn the pictures of the rat, the wolf, and the horse, respectively, for the jacket of the book and we wish to thank them here. Finally, we are grateful to Maryann Nevin for her outstanding skill and industry in the preparation of this book's manuscript. Her assistance in conducting library searches, maintaining correspondence with various authors, and her stylistic suggestions over the many years it took from the book's conception to its publication, deserve our very fond gratitude.

INTRODUCTION

Freud's deep and abiding love for his dogs is a matter of psycho-analytic folklore. This sliver of personal life was but one aspect of his regard for animals. Three of his "famous four cases"—Rat Man (1909a), Little Hans (1909b), and Wolf Man (1918)—involved human fantasies about animals. In discussing this clinical material, Freud elucidated the various ways in which animals symbolize our internal images and become reservoirs of our projections. In *Totem and Taboo* (1913), he traced the origins of parricidal impulses, guilt, and the associated incest barrier to pre-historic times and, in the process, highlighted the basis for certain ritualistic feasts in which an animal is consumed. He also eluci-dated the origins of idealized animal imagery in various religious motifs. Still later (1917), Freud emphasized the essential similar-ity between man and animals both in the physical and mental realms. Indeed, from a certain vantage point, it is possible to view his drive theory as largely a heuristic ordering of the animal na-ture of the human inner world. Freud thus offered a panorama of notions about the kinship between man and animals, the role of domesticated or wild animals in the mental development of a child, and the significance of animals in the evolution or amelio-ration of psychopathology. Later psychoanalysts, with the notable exception of Searles (1960), unfortunately did not advance this line of exploration in Freud's work, leaving a gap in psychoana-lytic theorizing and phenomenology.

This book fills that vacuum by offering a detailed and thor-ough perspective on the psychological meanings of animals to human beings and on their role in the development of the human mind and its psychopathology. More importantly, this book pres-ents a multitude of *new* observations on human interactions with animals and the influence of this kinship in various adaptive, maladaptive, and ameliorative psychopathological processes. The book is divided into three parts. The first part entitled "Concep-tual Backdrop" highlights the diverse ways animals give content to psychiatric symptomatology. It is against such a broad background that the second part of the book, "Freud's Menagerie," unfolds. It focuses on the animals that appear in the case histories of the Rat Man, Wolf Man, and Little Hans. These two parts of the book naturally lead to its third part, which devotes attention to certain other animals that have become an integral part of man's psychosocial existence, including cats, dogs, birds, snakes, and spiders. In thus discussing the role of animals in human psychopathology, these chapters weave a rich tapestry of mental illness and divers cultural impacts upon it, including those emanating from art, religion, literature, and cinema. A more detailed description of each part of the book now follows.

Part I is comprised of one chapter. In it, Salman Akhtar and Jodi Brown present a comprehensive review of the appearance of animals in the symptoms of the diagnostic categories of clinical psychiatry. These include psychotic delusions and hallucinations, obsessions, phobias, confusional states, sexual perversions, personality disorders, and childhood psychiatric conditions. The authors offer brief case reports to illustrate how the animals appear in each category. They also provide examples of how subtle yet explicit references to animals during intensive treatment contain manifestations of transference and countertransference and how a gentle inquiry regarding an individual's relationship with animals can significantly enhance the diagnostic interview in clinical psychiatry.

Part II of the book devotes individual chapters to three specific animals, namely the rat, the horse, and the wolf. Authored by Leonard Shengold, the chapter on rats illustrates the mental association of rats with intense sadism and omnivorous destructiveness in individuals who have been victims of severe abuse in childhood. Drawing upon etymological roots, literary sources, myth, history, human physiology, and poignant clinical material, Shengold convincingly demonstrates that individuals who suffered overwhelming stimulation to the extent of soul murder during childhood often employ rats as derivative expressions of their own cannibalistic impulses.

The next chapter is by John Schowalter and pertains to horses. Schowalter provides a fascinating commentary on the historical and cultural vicissitudes of man's actual and emotional relationship with the horse. His discourse ranges from prehistoric times through the Greek and Roman civilizations to the evocations of the animal in contemporary colloquialisms, theater, movies, and television. He also presents a detailed psychoanalytic case of a woman who was deeply involved with horses in an effort to resolve her intrapsychic struggles with her parents.

The last chapter of this section is about wolves. Written by Dwarkanath Rao, it offers a wide-ranging discourse on phenomenological, symbolic, mythic, and sociocultural aspects of man's psychic relationship to this terrifying animal. Critically reviewing the extensive post-Freudian literature on the Wolf Man case allows Rao conceptual space to add his own insights on this lasting clinical riddle. His contribution brings together anthropological observations on children raised by wolves, clinical descriptions of lycanthropy, psychoanalytic hypotheses regarding the implicit multilevel symbolism, and the place of the wolf in popular fiction and cinema.

Part III of the book is comprised of individual chapters on dogs, birds, snakes, spiders, and cats. The chapter on dogs is written by Philip Escoll. He provides a comprehensive historical and cultural perspective on man's relationship with dogs; his essay spans from the Egyptian dog-headed god Anubis to Richard Nixon's cocker spaniel Checkers. He describes psychiatric symptomatology as well as popular fiction and movies involving dogs. He also presents some personal experiences with patients of many age groups. Paying equal attention to the rampant anthropomorphization of dogs and their actual companionship value, Escoll presents a balanced discussion of the animal's adaptive as well as pathological valence in the psychic economy of human beings.

Next, Gregg Gorton provides a lyrical exposition on birds. His essay is more in the style of an existential meditation than a traditional scientific paper. Besides bringing a healthy dose of authenticity and a sudden air of stylistic freshness to the book, the chapter's format, with untitled subsections of uneven lengths, itself reminds one of a bird's flight. Gorton's essay is well grounded in history and language and yet capable of flying into imagination that enhances empathy with individuals whose lives are intertwined with birds. The portrayal of such individuals comes from literary, cinematic, and clinical realms.

The following chapter pertains to snakes and is written by Wilfred Abse. It offers a grand tour of the vast cultural terrain of man's involvement with snakes. Spanning thousands of years, Abse's contribution describes the ritualistic as well as mythopoetic elaboration of the snake by Paleolithic man, the ancient Greeks and Romans, the members of diverse African tribes, villagers in India, Chinese emperors, and the fundamentalist snake handlers of backwoods Appalachia. Abse also discusses the intense fear and fascination that snakes often stir up in human beings and deftly links the normal with the pathological and the average with the fantastic in this realm.

The next chapter of this part of the book is a reprint of the well-respected paper on spiders by the late Melitta Sperling. Originally published in 1971, the clinical material, comprised of eight cases, retains its phenomenological vivacity and technical virtuosity. Patients who used spider symbolism for the expression of their repressed perverse impulses are shown to reveal powerful anal fixations and unresolved preoedipal ties with their mothers. In the analytic situation, the spider symbolism was mostly indicative of an intense sadomasochistic mother transference. There also was a tendency for such symbolism to coexist with paranoid trends and psychosomatic vulnerabilities.

The last chapter is about cats and is authored by Vamik Volkan. After a brief autobiographical account of his involvement with cats and a quick sojourn through man's relationship with the animal throughout history, Volkan settles into a thorough clinical discussion of patients for whom cats played a central psychological role. He divides them into two groups. In the first group, cats were used as symbols either of psychosexual or aggressive objects or of the inner representation of one's siblings. In the second group, cats were used as protosymbols, that is, transitional objects unintegrated self-representations, or undifferentiated psychotic cores. It is to the group using cats as protosymbols that Volkan applies the term *cat people.*

This brief summary of the book's contents cannot do justice to its scope, depth, and richness. Written predominately, though not solely, by psychoanalysts, the book is actually interdisciplinary in approach. To be sure it relies heavily on clinical psychiatry and psychoanalysis but all its chapters also draw from history,

mythology, religion, anthropology, ethology, physiology, and lin-
guistics. There is also an ample sprinkling of material from fiction, poetry, art, and cinema. The book's range is panoramic and
goes from Freud's phylogenetic speculations to the endearing
antics of Lassie, from the animal gods in Indian temples to the
psychotic hallucinations of the Son of Sam, from the cockroach
in Kafka's *Metamorphosis* to the "cocaine bugs" in drug rehabilita-
tion clinics, from the life-saving scribblings of Charlotte the spider
to the gut-wrenching terror of lycanthropy, and so on. The effort,
in essence, is to demonstrate that our internal and external worlds
are inextricably intertwined and that animals play an important
role in both of them. To repudiate this is to send an integral part
of our true selves into exile. This book is aimed at preventing
such fragmentation of the human mental existence.

REFERENCES

Freud, S. (1909a), Analysis of a phobia in a five-year-old boy. *Standard
    Edition,* 10:1–147. London: Hogarth Press, 1955.
—— (1909b), Notes upon a case of obsessional neurosis. *Standard
    Edition,* 10:151–249. London: Hogarth Press, 1955.
—— (1913), Totem and Taboo. *Standard Edition,* 13:1–161. London:
    Hogarth Press, 1955.
—— (1917), A difficulty in the path of psycho-analysis. *Standard Edi-
    tion,* 17:135–144. London: Hogarth Press, 1955.
—— (1918), From the history of an infantile neurosis. *Standard Edi-
    tion,* 17:7–122. London: Hogarth Press, 1955.
Searles, H. F. (1960), *The Nonhuman Environment in Normal Development
    and Schizophrenia.* New York: International Universities Press.

Part I

Conceptual Backdrop

CHAPTER 1

Animals in Psychiatric Symptomatology

SALMAN AKHTAR, M.D., AND JODI BROWN, M.D.

While the celebrated case histories of the Rat Man, Little Hans, and the Wolf Man (Freud, 1909a,b, 1918) have immortalized the role of animals in human psychopathology, the fact is that animals have long roamed the terrain of diagnostic categories in clinical psychiatry. In the disrupted mind, the zookeeper leaves the cage doors ajar and lets the animals assume power over man by invading his thoughts and his body. Appearing as psychic hints and guesses, the animals wink at him mischievously in dreams; becoming cuddly maternal substitutes, they relieve loneliness and isolation. Turning cold blooded and vicious, animals terrify him or her by means of vague or explicit persecutory dreads and become receptacles of erotic emissions, soothing bodily tensions. Crawling under the skin and infecting the guts, they torture the individual from within. If the resulting chaos is intense, human identity becomes so fragmented that a person comes to believe or act as if he or she is transforming into an animal.

This chapter will offer a guided tour of this anguished, puzzling, scary, and, at times, darkly erotic mental zoo. It will cover a large terrain of psychiatric symptomatology involving animals, stopping at the scenic spots of (1) delusions and hallucinations; (2) confusional states; (3) lycanthropy; (4) culture-bound psychiatric syndromes; (5) obsessions and phobias; (6) personality disorders; (7) sexual perversions; and (8) childhood psychiatric disorders. The emphasis of this discourse will be descriptive and

3

its overall stance biopsychosocial with occasional forays into deeper psychodynamic issues involved in these symptoms.[1]

DELUSIONS AND HALLUCINATIONS

Psychotic symptomatology often involves animals. In 1977, the famous case of "Son of Sam," the New York serial killer David Berkowitz, felt commanded to commit murder by his neighbor's dog Sam, and the link between human madness and animals was brought to public awareness. Less dramatic delusions involving animals are, however, more common. The belief of having had sexual contact with them, for instance, is not rare among schizophrenics (Kraepelin, 1919); two in a sample of seventy-five schizophrenics studied in narcoanalysis (Norman, 1948) expressed such a delusion. However, the amytal-induced drowsiness is not a precondition for such delusions to surface, as was evident in the following case (Akhtar and Thomson, 1980).

Case 1

> A middle-aged chronic schizophrenic woman, relatively stable for two years, suddenly exhibited symptoms of frank psychosis after receiving a letter from her sister who stated that their father, a very regressed schizophrenic, had been indulging in sexual acts with a family dog named after the patient. On admission to the hospital, the patient had the delusional belief that she herself had had sexual activity with a dog named after her daughter. The fact that no such dog existed became clear only much later.

More frequent than such delusion is the syndrome in which the individual believes he or she is infested with parasites. While generally this "parasitosis" (Berrios, 1982; DeLeon, Antelo, and Simpson, 1992) involves ideas about alimentary infestation, sensations and fantasies about skin involvement are not infrequent.

---

[1] The clinical material presented here is disguised to protect the confidentiality of these patients. Cases 1, 2, 6, 8, 9, and 11 come from Dr. Akhtar's practice and cases 4, 5, 7, 10, 13, 14, 15, and 16 are from Dr. Brown's practice. Cases 3 and 12 have been kindly provided by Drs. Irene Dadson and Saif Abdullah respectively.

Worms, ticks, mites, and scabies thus enter the human psyche as delusions and hallucinations. The nosology, which varies from "Magnan's sign" (Magnan and Saury, 1889), and "Cocaine bugs" (Siegel, 1978), to Ekbom's syndrome (Ekbom, 1938), and Munro's (1982) "monosymptomatic hypochondriacal psychosis," offers both a historical perspective and—confusion. Terms like *acaraphobia* (Myerson, 1921) and *zoophobia* (Eller, 1929) are misnomers and have been replaced by *delusions of parasitosis.* The latter term correctly depicts the syndrome not as a "fear" but as a tenacious belief that insects are on or under the skin. Indeed, some patients carry "proofs" of such insects with them in a phenomenon called the "matchbox sign" of infestation (Morris, 1991). This is a good indicator of a primary psychiatric illness: either a delusional disorder (if confined to the single false belief system) or part of a depressive, manic, or schizophrenic psychosis (Berrios, 1982; Trabert, 1991; Mitchell and Vierkant, 1991; Morris, 1991; Jibiki and Yamaguchi, 1992; De Leon et al., 1992; Podoll, Bofinger, Von der Stein, and Stuhlman, 1993). Scratching behavior may also indicate the induced psychosis of folie à deux or folie partagée, for a significant percentage of patients do have a close relative with a similar delusional disorder (Mester, 1975; Siegel, 1978; Maier, 1987; Gieler and Knoll, 1990; Morris, 1991; De Leon et al., 1992; Bourgeois, Duhamel, and Verdoux, 1992; Gonsalez, Lastra, and Ramos, 1993). The literature debates whether the delusion of parasitosis is primary or secondary to real or hallucinated tactile sensations.[2] Moreover, the etiology of these conditions is viewed as multifactorial. While impaired vision, social isolation, and history of actual parasitic infestation in the past (May and Terpenning, 1991; Jibiki and Yamaguchi, 1992) might act as predisposing factors, deeper intrapsychic issues are invariably associated with such psychotic symptomatology. Thus, the literature is replete with references to "psychological precipitants" and "symbolic meanings" of insects (Hopkinson, 1973; Skott, 1975; Freinhar, 1984; Reilly, 1988).

---

[2] Using neuroimaging, Musalek et al. (1989) and De Leon et al. (1992) have explored anatomic location (limbic cortex versus prefrontal and associative areas) to understand further the etiology and pathogenesis of the delusions and hallucinations of animals under the skin.

Psychosexual conflicts contribute heavily to the onset of such a delusional state where the delusion functions to keep sexual and aggressive conflicts repressed (Paulson and Petrus, 1969; May and Terpenning, 1991; Horstein, Hoffman, and Joraschky, 1989). Obsessive-compulsive personality traits (Skott, 1975; Berrios, 1982; Reilly, 1988), paranoid defenses (Sizaret and Simon, 1976), and the "symbolic recuperation of loss" often lurk in the background (Sizaret and Simon, 1976; Horstein et al., 1989). Dynamic theories also offer reasons for the prevalence and significance of the insect in fantasies and delusions (Ostapzeff, 1975; Roux, 1988). "The insect's ephemericality, ubiquity, and ability to penetrate give it the ability to cross barriers of time and space, and are thought to be the reason for its special place in the subconscious of humans" (Roux, 1988, p. 1131). Ferenczi (1926) connects vermin to the unconscious phantasy of being pregnant, "of sheltering little things in and on the body," and notes that the German word for *worm* is applied to children as "an affectionate diminutive" (p. 361). Family dynamics have also been applied to delusions involving parasites (Verbeek, 1959; Macaskill, 1987; Reilly, 1988). In folie à deux involving animals, passive and dependent characteristics are commonly associated with the originally healthy partner (usually child or spouse) in which the delusion is induced. While this occurs in the setting of clear consciousness, some other symptoms involving animals depend upon a clouding of the sensorium.

CONFUSIONAL STATES

First and foremost, the delusions and hallucinations of parasitosis (either in the form of alimentary infestation or bugs crawling on or under the skin) often occur in association with a clouded sensorium. Cocaine or amphetamine intoxication, alcohol withdrawal, and certain states associated with vitamin B_{12} deficiency are especially associated with tactile hallucinations referred to as "formications" (Reilly, 1988; Mitchell and Vierkant, 1991; May and Terpenning, 1991; DeLeon et al., 1992). Differential diagnosis of such cases should also include organic causes such as medications, occult neoplasms, renal dysfunction, diabetes and neurologic conditions like Alzheimer's disease, cerebral infarction, or tumor (Berrios, 1982; Reilly, 1988; Marneros, Diester, and Rohde, 1988; Flynn, Cummings, and Scheibel, 1989; Trabert, 1991, Morris, 1991; Kanazawa and Hata, 1992). Second, the declining cognitive functions associated with dementia often lead to the neglect of pets. Hitherto loved animals go uncared for and become a source of concern to the family and neighbors. Finally, incomprehensible acts of violence toward pets can also result from a paroxysm of brain dysfunction during which the individual is completely confused. The following case reported by Akhtar and Brenner (1979) depicts one such occurrence.

Case 2

A young man was hospitalized after he bizarrely choked his dog to death, and could not recall doing it. He did, however, remember leaving home to walk his dog and a few hours later discovered himself on an unfamiliar road, his dog lying dead at his feet. Witnesses called the police and he was admitted for evaluation. Despite thorough interviewing, he did not reveal significant psychopathology and little symbolic significance to his act of violence could be detected. He was very perplexed and quite concerned about it also. There was no history of head trauma or seizures, but a nasopharyngeal EEG was consistent with temporal lobe epilepsy.

The dramatic quality of such epileptic fugue states is surpassed only by a syndrome in which the individual begins to claim that or act as though he has turned into an animal.

LYCANTHROPY

When disruption of the mind is so severe that projection can no longer prevent the dissolution of identity, man and animal merge in the syndrome known as "lycanthropy" (Campbell, 1989, p. 475). Lycanthropy is the belief that one can change into a wolf and the display of behavior suggesting such a belief. Those affected do not sleep, they go out at night, and wander until morning. They perceive themselves as evil and disgusting, ruminate on, and dream about wolves and believe themselves to possess satanic powers (Fahy, 1989). They yearn for raw flesh and might even hunt and devour small prey. At times, they seek sexual intercourse with cats and talk to animals (Kulick, Pope, and Keck, 1990). When they look in the mirror, they see the head of a wolf (Verdoux and Bourgeouis, 1993).

This syndrome has universal historic and mythic roots. Known also as "zoophilic metamorphosis" and "insania zooanthropia" (Fahy, 1989), lycanthropy derives its name from the Greek *Lycaon* who was turned into a wolf by Zeus for having deceitfully fed him human flesh. In the Middle Ages, hundreds of people were condemned to death in France for demonic possession in the form of lycanthropy. Among South American Indian tribes, animal metamorphosis was commonly recorded (Kulick et al., 1990). In the last two decades there have been almost twenty case reports of lycanthropy in the medical literature (Surawicz and Banta, 1975; Malliaras, Kossovitsa, and Khristodoulou, 1978; Coll, O'Sullivan, and Browne, 1985; Mellor, 1988; Keck, Pope, Hudson, McElroy, and Kulick, 1988; Benezech, DeWitte, Etchepare, and Bourgeois, 1989; Dening and West, 1989; Koehler, Ebel, and Vartzopoulos, 1990; Kulick et al., 1990; Rajna, Guillibert, Loo, and Debray, 1990; Rojo Moreno, Rojo Moreno, Baldemoro Garcia, and Rojo Siwerra, 1990; Verdoux and Bourgeois, 1993). From Spain, Canada, France, England, and the United States, patients present imitating and/or believing themselves to be wolves (as well as tigers, cats, dogs, rabbits, and birds). Today, lycanthropy is recognized as a nonspecific delusion, which can be understood through the varying perspectives of individual psychodynamics, disease state, and cultural and religious predisposition.

Intense frustrations and sadomasochistic object relations during early infancy and childhood at times lead to the internalization of a pet rather than a parent as the ideal self-object (Deutsch, 1951; Kulick et al., 1990). Projection of oral rage creates cannibalistic fears and intensifies castration anxiety. Thus there are also elements of identification with the aggressor in these instances. In cases where the onset follows sexual intercourse, lycanthropy serves as a defense against violent sexual urges (Rosenstock and Bincent, 1977; Jackson, 1978). Lycanthropic behaviors may represent the splitting-off of primitive drives and thus might be a bizarre escape mechanism from guilt (Surawicz and Banta, 1975; Keck et al., 1988). The wolf might also represent an archetypal symbol of sadistic behavior and an expression of primitive identity (Jung, 1954; Eisler, 1978). Dreams of werewolves may signify oral-sadistic or cannibalistic impulses condensed with oedipal conflicts (Fahy [1989] discussing Jones [1937]). Unlike the sphinx, the centaur, or the mermaid—where the amalgam of a man and animal leaves the nether regions to the animal half of the hybrid creature (Stone, 1992)—the werewolf is the metamorphosis of identity as a whole. In the former, man simply conceals his animal-like sexual and aggressive drives while in the latter, he becomes them.

Interestingly, lycanthropy has been seen in association with many medical and psychiatric disorders including drug-induced psychoses (Keck et al., 1988), temporal lobe epilepsy (Keck et al., 1988; Kulick et al., 1990), porphyria (Illis, 1964), schizophrenia (Surawicz and Banta, 1975; Coll et al., 1985; Keck et al., 1988), affective psychosis (Coll et al., 1985; Keck et al., 1988; Mellor, 1988; Dening and West, 1989; Verdoux and Bourgeois, 1993), borderline personality (Deutsch, 1942; Keck et al., 1988), antisocial personality (Benezech et al., 1989), and even factitious disorder (Keck et al., 1988). Removing themselves from the medical model, several authors (Merkur, 1981; Yellowlees, 1989; Fahy, 1989; Kulick et al., 1990) emphasize the effects of religion and culture on lycanthropy. The "culturally syntonic" animal-like behaviors, which led to increased tribal power for the shaman, were commonly ascribed to demonic possession and punished by death in the Middle Ages (Kulick et al., 1990). During a tribal religious ceremony before the hunt, Navajo Indians enact the behavior of the coyote. When "the psycho-hygienic function of the ritualism fails, hunting neurosis develops" (Merkur, 1981, p. 243) in which the guilt and horror of the hunt leads to delusional transformation of man into the coyote. Such culturally facilitated symptomatology involving animals is, however, not restricted to the syndrome of lycanthropy.

CULTURE-BOUND PSYCHIATRIC SYNDROMES

Psychotic symptoms involving animals cross not only the boundaries of skin and reality but also those of culture. In societies where animals are in closer contact with humans, they are perhaps more readily drawn into the psyche as projective containers for unacceptable sexual impulses, sadomasochism, guilt, fear, and shame. Three such culture-bound syndromes that involve animals are *amafufanyane, latah,* and *piblokto. Amafufanyane* (Kaplan and Sadock, 1989; Robertson and Kottler, 1993) is a psychosis of delusions and hallucinations seen in African men and women. One particular presentation is of a woman who awakens acting bizarrely and reporting that she is pregnant by a baboon. The belief surrounding the psychosis is that an evil spirit is sent to the patient through a baboon or a bird or some other creature. Symptoms also include sleep paralysis, abdominal pain, paralysis, blindness, shouting, sobbing, hysterical seizures, and amnesia. Thinly veiled symbolic enactments of sexual themes are invariably associated with these fits. *Latah* (Tseng and McDermott, 1981; Kaplan and Sadock, 1989) is a Malaysian or Indonesian cultural psychosis with symptoms of a startle response, echolalia, and echopraxia. Patients make inappropriate verbal and motor behaviors, frequently mimicking animals. Most accounts describe a frightened woman who begins to threaten and curse following a mild stimulus such as a sudden noise or some physical contact such as a slap on the back or tickling. Interestingly, the attack may follow a snake bite, seeing a snake, or dreaming of a snake. There is often an erotic character to many of the *latah* manifestations. *Piblokto* (Kaplan and Sadock, 1989), also called "Arctic hysteria," is an episode of psychosis or dissociation affecting Arctic Eskimos. Mutism may precede an attack in which a woman tears off her clothes and runs through the snow imitating the cry of some animal or bird. Periods of melancholic brooding may also herald an attack, which typically lasts for one to two hours. The afflicted person is believed to be possessed by evil spirits and observers remain at a distance. After the attack, the person gradually resumes normalcy while suffering amnesia for the episode.

Today, despite the prevalence of mental illness and drug abuse, animal metamorphosis is a rare syndrome, most commonly observed in traditional cultures[3] The modern werewolf stalks

---

[3] Increased use of computers and other electrical devices in developed countries has led to them forging their way between man and the animal world. As cultural determinants influence mental life (Akhtar and Byrne, 1983; Yellowlees, 1989), we are more likely to see delusions of being wired by the CIA through silver-plated fillings than of lycanthropy.

mainly the cinema and the literary imagination. While saved from this uncanny horror, modern man, however, cannot escape the more common fear of being victimized by animals invisible to the naked eye, that is, parasites and germs.

OBSESSIONS AND PHOBIAS

Although fleeting concerns involving animals may appear in all types of anxiety reactions, the anxiety disorder par excellence involving animals is simple phobia. In fact, animals have been identified as four of the five most common objects of phobias (Bourdon, Boyd, Dae, Burns, Thompson, and Locke, 1988). Snakes, spiders, mice, bugs, birds, and dogs (Marks, 1987; Bourdon et al., 1988) are perhaps the most commonly feared animals. Strikingly, while the "choice" of the dreaded animal varies from individual and region to region, these animal phobias occur with stability over culture and time (Arieti, 1974, pp. 114–120). In an attempt to understand the etiology of such fears, psychodynamic, learning, and biological perspectives have been evoked in the psychiatric literature.[4]

Animals also figure in the symptomatology of other anxiety disorders. Unlike childhood phobias, adult-onset phobias are usually precipitated by a relevant trauma such as a dog bite or a

---

[4] Modeling, vicarious learning, and observational conditioning have been discussed as alternative means by which animals have acquired their evocative potential (Wolpe and Rachman, 1960; Eysenck, 1965, 1976; Solyom, Beck, Solyom, and Hugel, 1974; Emde, 1984; Mineka, Davidson, Cook, and Keir, 1984; Cook and Mineka, 1987; Marks, 1987, pp. 372–442). This perspective reports cases of phobias arising after a child observes a parent responding fearfully to an animal (Solyom et al., 1974) or, as in Mineka et al.'s (1984) experiments, after lab-reared rhesus monkeys viewed wild-caught monkeys reacting fearfully to snakes. More recently, learning theory has been challenged and broadened by biological research in animal phobias (Mineka et al., 1984; Bennett-Levy and Marteau, 1984; McNally and Steketee, 1985; Davey, 1992; Davey, Forster, and Mayhew, 1993). This view suggests that learning is "biologically prepared" in that there are anatomic portions of the brain preprogrammed to perceive specific, fear-evoking animal movements much like the nondominant parietal lobe perceives faces. Sudden movement and speed are animal qualities of "stimulus configurations," which may cause certain animals to be "chosen" as fearful. Some of these authors have pointed to the fact that most animal phobias involve harmless (spider, cockroach, maggot, snake, and rat) rather than predatory animals (lions, tigers, sharks): they postulate that animal phobias correlate more with contamination and disgust rather than with fear. Together, these three etiological perspectives, namely modeling, vicarious learning, and observational conditioning along with consideration of potential hereditary determinants of fear and phobias (Delprato, 1980), might explain why specific animals have remained both "chosen" phobic objects and symbols in mythology in almost every culture.

bee sting (Friedman, 1966; Solyom et al., 1974; Marks, 1987). Symptoms of fearful preoccupation and recurrent nightmares lead to merging diagnoses of phobia and posttraumatic stress disorder (Marks, 1987). Similarly, individuals with obsessional neurosis might display behaviors such as compulsively searching for the feared animal, refusing to touch the feared animal or anything the animal may have touched (Marks, 1987). "Intrusive repetitive visual images involving sex with animals" occur, which are ego dystonic and may require psychopharmacological interventions (Hollander and Wong, 1995, p. 10). Such individuals might also suffer from hand-washing rituals enacted to relieve intrusive ruminations of contamination by the feared animal. Here the overlap between a specific animal phobia and obsessive-compulsive disorder becomes evident (Marks, 1987). Thus, through a mixture of unconscious fantasy, cultural learning, and biological evolution of the mind, the long-enduring association between man and animal becomes endowed with fear-inducing potential of a highly personal nature. Given a symbolically significant trigger from the external environment, this might become manifest as a recurrent nightmare, simple phobia, or obsessive-compulsive symptomatology.

Case 3

A 23-year-old single woman presented with a recent intensification of her obsessive-compulsive symptomatology. While she had always been detail oriented and orderly, it was only at age 16 that she had developed distressing ruminations regarding germs and contamination. Treatment with psychopharmacological means relieved her symptoms to a certain extent, though she continued to lead an inhibited social and sexual life. She lived with her mother, took occasional courses at a community college, and had few friends. Two months prior to her seeking consultation, she had developed a new concern. If she saw a housefly going into her bedroom, she would not be able to sleep there. She would spend that night in the living room, even if she had witnessed the fly exit her bedroom. She feared that the fly might have brought dirt from outside and deposited it on her bed.

The patient's parents were divorced when she was 5 years old and she had visibly suffered at the resultant distance from her father who left the marital home. He died when she was 12 and she was heartbroken. Passage through puberty and adolescence was difficult with much hostility toward the mother. She responded adversely to mother's dating, fearing that the mother might catch a venereal disease. She hated it when the mother had the lover stay overnight, especially because the mother asked her to clean the bathroom after the boyfriend had finished taking a shower there. For the past few months, the boyfriend had been staying over more often and it is around this time that the preoccupation with the fly entering her bedroom had started.

The potential links between the loss of father, inhibition of sexuality, anger at mother's psychosexual freedom, concern about mother's catching a venereal disease, exposure to the mother's boyfriend, and her own fears of contamination, together hinted at a complex unconscious fantasy with prominent regressive, anal elements. The fly, and the associated contamination fear, most likely represented the return of the repudiated wish for the father's (mother's boyfriend's) penis and his semen.

Just like the ordinary housefly, the phallic snake, the spermlike worm, and the free-flying bird acquire unconscious significance from the myths and totems of the past (Freud, 1913; Abraham, 1913) as well as from the unconscious conflicts of the present. As such, they serve as ready-made symbols for the displacement of internal anxiety onto relatively harmless external objects (Abraham, 1913; Domangue, 1985). In addition to a generalized or cultural meaning, the psychodynamic perspective also attributes phobic object choice to idiosyncracies of both individual experience and the associative process of unconscious mental life: thus, hens, millipedes, spiders, flies, cats, horses, frogs, butterflies, and locusts enter the phobic menagerie (Freud, 1895, 1909a; Abraham, 1913; Ferenczi, 1926; Sterba, 1935; English, 1945; Fenichel, 1945; Jones, 1948; Deutsch, 1951; Kolansky, 1960; Searles, 1960; Volkan, 1972; Arieti, 1974; Tyson, 1978; van der Hart, 1981; Domangue, 1985; Sperling, see chapter 9).

While both the descriptive and psychoanalytic literatures have focused upon symptomatic phobias, the fact remains that diffuse phobic tendencies that are assimilated in an individual's character are perhaps more common. Such a "phobic character" (Fenichel, 1945, pp. 163–204; MacKinnon and Michels, 1971; Akhtar and Byrne, 1983; Stone, 1992) is organized around the defenses of repression and displacement. The fearfulness of such an individual centers upon specific situations and objects. While resembling the dread experienced by a paranoid individual, the phobic constellation is actually quite different. Wurmser (1981) points out three differences between phobic and paranoid characters. In the phobic, the feeling is "It is a danger, but I do not know why. It may be for this or that reason," while in the paranoid it is, "It is a danger *and I know why,* namely, such and such is his or her intention" (p. 314; emphasis in original). In other words, the phobic character does not display the personalization and intentionality of the outside menace. Second, the leading affective reactions in the two conditions are different. In the paranoid personality, it is rage, hatred, contempt, and grudge, while in the phobic character it is anxiety, guilty fears, and their somatic counterparts. Third, the paranoid reacts by attack or provocation of attack, while the phobic reacts by avoidance and flight. The phobic organization is essentially a neurotic one while the paranoid leans toward the use of psychotic mechanisms. The phobic says that he is afraid of dogs while the paranoid maintains that dogs are out to get him!

PERSONALITY DISORDERS

Psychiatric symptomatology involving animals is also found in association with personality disorders. Though rarely included in standard interviewing techniques, questions regarding an individual's involvement with animals frequently reveal inflexible and maladaptive attitudes. Individuals with some personality disorders display intense involvements with animals. Those with a hidden psychotic core (e.g., schizotypal personalities) might develop split-off identifications with animals and might even behaviorally enact these identifications in private or in public; Volkan (1995) has reported the case of a young man whose clowning and dramatic identification with a dog brought him social acclaim underneath which a cauldron of anguish simmered. For less disturbed individuals, animals become narcissistic or exhibitionistic extensions (Mouren, Ohayon, and Tatossian, 1980) and they draw intense satisfaction from flattering comments about their pets. Schizoid patients often feel more comfortable with animals than with fellow humans and might carry on an intense imaginary dialogue with them. Yet another group of patients intensely involved with animals are those with borderline personality. They often use animals as transitional objects (Mouren et al., 1980; Akhtar, 1992) to ease the pain of separateness and aloneness. Such attachments can be striking.

Case 4

A middle-aged man with borderline personality disorder celebrated his birthday with a cake and candles shared only with his two dogs. He expressed a yearning to be valued by others and not used by them for his money or his willingness to do them special favors. At the same time, he felt unable to join in social activities and, feeling himself to be a misfit, would become silent and withdrawn. With his dogs, he felt needed and loved and did not experience the anxious detachment he felt with people. The company of his pets during his birthday celebration thus saved him from complete isolation.

Such reliance on the company of pets is usually characterological. However, this behavior is not uncommon in the elderly who, either missing their grown-up and alienated children or having been childless to begin with, refer to their pets as their "baby." At other times, it arises as a response to the disturbed equilibrium of a dependent transference during the course of psychotherapy.

Case 5

A 42-year-old woman with borderline personality disorder, was in twice a week psychoanalytic psychotherapy. Whenever our work was interrupted by my leaving, we would discuss how her anger toward me was directed at herself and how it was triggered by painful feelings of abandonment. Nevertheless, during my absence, she would threaten to take an overdose of her medication and require crisis intervention. She would experience me as "the best and only" doctor who could help her. All other doctors were "bad and cold." In the session preceding an interruption in the second year of treatment, the patient expressed a wish to hold onto me and keep me from leaving her. On my return, she came to my office and proudly told me she had not tried to hurt herself. She then described how she had purchased, cuddled with, and cared for "a little brown" guinea pig. This transitional object provided her with comfort at the same time as it allowed her to express her rage by devaluing her doctor "a little."

In view of borderline individuals' use of splitting and their propensity toward intense idealization and devaluation of others, relationships with animals provide them with a relatively peaceful avenue of connectedness. However, under states of stress, their pets might also become the targets of their intense rage (Volkan and Akhtar, 1979; Akhtar, 1994).

Case 6

A severely borderline young man with an exquisite sensitivity to rejection was seen in thrice-weekly, face-to-face, psychoanalytic psychotherapy. Once, early in his treatment, I informed him of an upcoming interruption in the schedule. He responded with a pained silence, gaze avoidance, and a noticeable drop in his voice. My empathic affirmation of this and encouragement of him to put his feelings into words met with little success. Later that evening (he told me amid sobs during the next session), the patient saw in his front yard a little frog that appeared sad and lonely to him. He picked up the frog, took it inside, and made a "home" for it in a little box. He tried to cheer up the frog by talking to it and giving it bread crumbs. The frog, however, jumped out of the box and soon was nowhere to be found. He looked for it all over his place. He repeatedly called for it, and with the absence of any response began to feel rejected and angry. This grew into rage. Then, suddenly, he saw the frog. Cursing loudly, he chased it around the room, damaging many of his belongings in the process.

In a fury, he caught the frog and repeatedly smashed it against the wall with all his might. Later, a dawning awareness that he was "committing murder" stopped him. He let the now badly injured frog out of a window.

The good frog/bad frog split, the shift from caretaker to murder self, the incapacity for ambivalence, and the flooding of the ego with raw aggression, are as explicit in this enactment as are the transference themes of feeling abandoned by the analyst (the bad frog), and the consequent loneliness and rage. Blum (1981) notes that in such cases because of the blurring of the self-object boundaries, the object's wish for independence is experienced as an agonizing, hence unforgivable, betrayal. Such anxious attachment to objects may even be maintained at the cost of mistreatment from them. This is especially characteristic of individuals with dependent personality disorder.

Case 7

A young woman in a relationship with a man who treated her quite cruelly struggled without insight *until* he threatened to leave her unless she gave away her cat. Identified with the cat who she viewed as "friendly, affectionate, and vulnerable" she began to be able to see that the way her boyfriend treated the cat was not dissimilar from the way he treated her. Her insight resulted in her telling her boyfriend that she could not move with him to another state. Yet, after the move, when the boyfriend agreed to her bringing her cat, the patient found herself more and more anxious to engage in the treatment. She expressed the feeling that the treatment might result in her leaving her boyfriend. Within several weeks, she opted to move with her cat to live with her boyfriend rationalizing that she knew that the way he would now treat both of them would be different.

Such struggles over autonomy often go back further and involve the primary objects of childhood while still manifesting within the matrix of neurotic symptomatology involving animals. The initially puzzling clinical picture turns out to be a phenomenological screen for the rapprochement subphase (Mahler, Pine, and Bergman, 1975) type push-pull for independent selfhood.

Case 8

A 27-year-old legal intern sought consultation with depressive complaints. For about a quarter of his first interview with me, he elaborated upon his apathy, anhedonia, and diminished sexual desire, relating their onset to the birth of his 6-month-old son. Then he abruptly stopped and said that while all he had said so far was true, there was something else that was troubling him even more. This "something" had been with him for many years and he had never revealed it to anyone. I responded by gently encouraging him to say more both about what this hidden problem was and also about the concerns that had led him to keep it a secret. After some hesitation, the patient revealed that he liked to chew upon cat's nails. He would frequent the homes of friends or acquaintances, and, at times, scout the neighborhood to find a cat. Holding the animal up in his arms, he would bite off a chip of its nails. He kept these bits and pieces in a little glass jar and chewed upon them at his leisure. As the interview progressed, a second interaction with cats emerged. He also liked to bring the cat's face very close to his own face and breathe in the air that came out of the cat's nostrils. Both these acts gave him deep gratification though he also worried about their apparent oddity and did not quite know what to make of them.

In the second interview, while describing his family background, the patient came upon the topic of his mother. He sighed, saying, "You don't want to know about her. She is so controlling, so intrusive that I can't begin to describe it. She lives about a thousand miles from here but I constantly feel her claws on my arms." As he said this he grabbed the upper part of his left arm with his right hand, making the latter appear like a claw, and dug his nails into the skin. Seeing the connection between the biting off of a cat's nails and the alleged claw of his mother on his arm, I said: "Did you notice what you just said?" He was puzzled. I said "What do you make of your saying *claws*? And, how do you connect them with *nails*?" He was at first dumbfounded and then become somber and began to talk about his chronic difficulty in maintaining an optimal distance from his mother. To my mind, the biting off of the cat's nails and breathing the air of cats' nostrils were two sides of his distance-closeness conflict. Why a cat was chosen to symbolize mother was to come up much later in the course of his treatment.

A relatively less noticeable psychopathological use of animals is the practice of grotesquely decorative exhibitionism involving pets (Mouren et al., 1980). Such behaviors are thinly disguised forms of self-aggrandizment in less sophisticated, often rural, narcissistic and histrionic patients. On the more severe end of psychopathology are two other forms of involvement with animals. The first refers to animal sacrifice in satanic rituals. Though cultural factors might play a role here too, such animal abuse should raise the suspicion of a sadistically tinged paranoid personality disorder. The second form of involvement with animals is sexual contact with them.

SEXUAL PERVERSIONS INVOLVING ANIMALS

"Bestiality," or sexual contact with animals, usually occurs in association with predisposing cultural factors[5] (Kinsey, Pomeroy, and Martin, 1948; Schneck, 1974), lower levels of education (Kinsey et al., 1948), and schizoid tendencies. However, the use of animals for sexual purposes is not restricted to direct tactile contact with them.[6] Indeed, Krafft-Ebing (1892), the pioneer in the descriptive classification of sexual perversions, distinguished two syndromes of erotic interest in animals: *zoerastia* and *zoophilia*. The former involves sexual acts with animals in lieu of human partners. The latter involves the use of an animal (e.g., via petting and stroking) to enhance sexual desire for human partners. Stolorow and Grand's (1973) description of an individual who used little bugs to terrify women as an erotic precondition for masturbation belongs in this latter category, though it may at times be difficult to separate the conditions of zoerastia and zoophilia. Psychoanalytic literature generally does not make this distinction and employs bestiality as an overarching concept. In any case, the reports pertaining to this matter are few and far between. Greenacre (1951)

---

[5] The sprinkling of "sheep jokes" in the usual repertoire of obscene humor nearly always reflects such cultural distribution of bestiality.

[6] At times the erotic element of physical contact with animals remains unconscious. In certain tribes of central Australia, for instance, one may observe a woman with a baby feeding at one breast and a puppy at the other. Similarly, in New Guinea, it is not uncommon to come across a woman suckling a pig (Roheim, 1943). Such practices, while culturally sanctioned, do contain aim-inhibited zoophilia at their base.

described the case of a girl who became very attached to her dog during puberty and engaged in sexual play with it. The dog represented the transitional object of her early childhood. Shengold (1967) found many instances of sexual contact with dogs in his "rat people." Rappaport (1968) reported on two analytic cases with significant sexual contact with animals. One was that of a young man who had been adopted as a child and had suffered many other losses while growing up. Upon becoming an adult, he slept with a cat, encouraging the animal to lick his hand or to engage in a sham fight with him. This gave him an erection and subsequently led to masturbation. However, his perversion was not limited to cats. Habitually, he broke into stables and would try to squeeze the neck of a horse between his legs, at the same time masturbating the horse's penis. The second case involved a man whose zoerastic abuse of a cat was a reenactment of primal scene memories and fantasies generated in him by witnessing his mother's adultery. Most recently, Daniel Traub-Werner (1986), using the term *bestophilia*, described a case in which a young man had sexual intercourse with a dog as well as with a variety of farm animals. Strikingly, the patient had trained the dog to reverse the active-passive positions, and, on occasion, practiced bestial fellatio as well. This activity subsided in late adolescence when he became aware of, and frightened by, a powerful homosexual fantasy. The patient had a history of torturing little animals during his childhood and his central masturbatory fantasy of adolescence revolved around his father's dog. This animal stood for the primal parental figure imbued with cannibalistic powers with whom the wish for and dread of reunion was repeatedly enacted in a libidinized manner. The animal also served as a fetish and sustained the fantasy of the phallic mother. Viewed from either perspective, the element of sadomasochism was prominent in this patient's symptomatology. This element, while always lurking in the background of such perversions, at times comes to occupy the center stage.

Case 9

Once every two or three months, a tall, handsome, highly affluent middle-aged, married businessman had his sadomasochistic, erotic encounter with the family pet. All dressed up to go to work, he would suddenly announce to his wife—herself a lawyer, and ready to leave for the office—that he was not feeling well and would perhaps go to work a bit late. Deftly overcoming her protests, he would convince his wife that she need not delay her departure. With her gone, he would find himself alone with their cat in a large, sprawling, and now suddenly very quiet suburban house. Their game would begin.

He would retrieve a ball of yarn, hidden in the metallic underside of his bed. One by one, he would tie each of the cat's legs to four different chairs. Pouring himself a scotch in a short stubby glass, snugly fitting in his large confident hand, he would put on some classical music. Sipping his drink, he would begin to walk around the four chairs gently pushing the chairs a bit farther apart. Soon the cat would be stretched and start making noises of pain. Its anguished shrieks would give the man an erection and he would now circle the chairs more rapidly and push them even further apart from each other. The cat would scream. The man would get more aroused. Soon, he would masturbate with an intense orgasmic release. Exhausted, he would then take a brief nap. By evening, his wife would come back and things would return to the humdrum routine of an affluent suburban life. This serenity would last for two or three months until the macabre dance would be staged again.

Not surprisingly, this patient had a background of severe frustrations in childhood. He grew up in a small one-family dwelling in an ethnic neighborhood. His father was an alcoholic and his mother a hypochondrical, chronically sighing housewife. There was much primal scene exposure as well as inappropriate physical closeness between the mother and the child. Growing up, he felt idealized for his academic talents but neglected as a person in his own right. He hated his home but he felt trapped there. The sexual perversion of his adulthood reflected the continuation of this hatred, symbolic enactment of primal scene fantasies, as well as a profuse libidinization of the sadomasochistic object relations of his early childhood.

CHILDHOOD PSYCHIATRIC DISORDERS

The "average expectable environment" (Hartmann, 1958) necessary for a harmonious psychological growth consists not only of reliable parents and siblings but also a consistent inanimate world. Animals thus enter and exit the evolving psychological structure of a child. Emotions and fantasies not verbalized with the human figures in the environment are often mastered through enactments with animals (Searles, 1960). In societies where the man–animal separation is less pronounced than in the West, such growth-facilitating role of animals may be greater. In any case, children "have no scruples in allowing animals to rank as their full equals. Uninhibited as they are in the avowal of their bodily needs, they no doubt feel themselves more akin to animals than to their elders, who may well be a puzzle to them" (Freud, 1913, p. 127). In the child's eye, animals are less able to fit into the rules of adult life (Schowalter, 1983). Animals may also represent power and courage for the child. That they bite, bark, sting, claw, and devour, makes animals ready recipients for conflict-ridden aggressive drives (Freud, 1909a,b; Fenichel, 1945; Schowalter, 1983). Because their sexual organs and reproductive lives are often more visible to children (Jelliffe and Brink, 1917), animals may also become the objects of libidinal derivatives. Because many animals are warm, soft, and available on an as-needed basis, they come to be substitutes for emotionally absent parents.

While a child's use of an animal may be part of normal development, at times the bars of normality bend a little too far or are broken right through. Unleashed into the unconscious, the animal may now transform into a hallucination, or a delusional representation of self. It may creep into the patient's current life as either a captive object of the compulsion to repeat cruelty or as a feared one.

Case 10

> A 4-year-old girl was hospitalized for one week after awakening one night with the sensation and belief that spiders were crawling over her legs and stomach. She tried to scratch and brush them off. A complete medical workup was negative. Later it was learned that the mother's boyfriend had frightened the girl with a fake spider on the day prior to the onset of her psychosis. Further inquiry revealed that the nature of the boyfriend's play with this oedipal-age child was often overstimulating and involved frightening the child. Intervention included parental guidance regarding

the differences between types of play that help children work toward mastery and those that may result in symptomatology by overwhelming the child's ego. The hallucinations recurred at nap and bedtimes for the next month. Whenever the hallucinations occurred, the parents learned to comfort the child by verbal reassurance and to allow the child to talk about feeling frightened. Following these interventions, the symptoms resolved in one month. It is interesting that the child's hallucination of sensations of crawling were restricted to the lower half of the body. The original scare by the boyfriend was only visual and did not involve touching. Since no further treatment was requested by the patient or her family, the exact meaning of the hallucination remained unknown, and, with its resolution, sank further into the depths of the unconscious.

The hidden presence of animals in such recesses of the mind may not be revealed until the child grows up and enters analysis as an adult. An apt transference stimulus might then evoke pertinent memories of childhood enactments with animals.

Case 11

A 42-year-old, well-mannered but explosive attorney, who had grown up from age 5 onwards with a bedridden mother, tyrannical father, and four other siblings, got extremely enraged when I told him at relatively short notice that I had to take a week off from our analytic work. Feeling a bit remorseful the next day, he rambled on until he stumbled upon a disturbing episode of his childhood.

He came from an affluent family which lived in a rural area and had many animals. As a child the patient was extremely fond of the pigeons the family owned. Once when he was 10, a stray cat killed one of the pigeons. The patient got so furious that he picked up the cat, carried it some distance in the fields, and threw it in a dry well on the property. With the cat pacing on the well's floor, he returned to the main house, played with his siblings, ate supper, and went to sleep. However, at midnight, he woke up in anxiety. What was the cat doing right now? Was it still alive? Had he killed the cat? Nauseated with remorse, he woke up his 16-year-old brother and pleaded with him to help rescue the cat. The brother said that he would go out with him but would not get into the well itself. An agreement was struck between them whereby the patient put on his raincoat, galoshes, gloves, and a hat and was lowered into the dark well by a rope by the older brother. There he picked up the now furious cat in his arms and then released it upon being pulled up to the ground. Only after the rescue, could he go to sleep. The patient sobbed bitterly as he told me this anecdote. The transference implications of this recall (my "killing" a week; his angry attack, his subsequent remorse) were explicated only later.

The fact that this deliberate act of hurting an animal was followed by intense remorse suggests the existence of intrapsychic conflict. The two sides of this conflict (hurting the cat/rescuing the cat), however, took control of the consciousness alternately in a fashion reminiscent of borderline splitting (Kernberg, 1975). In children whose psychic structures are organized at a higher level, aspects of such intrapsychic conflict remain deeply unconscious. As a result, unintended acts of neglect of a pet happen more or less accidentally with a concomitant (not subsequent) sense of horror and guilt.

Case 12

A 13-year-old, in psychotherapy for depression and delicate self-cutting, would frequently complain that there was "no food in my house." Her affluent background and specific questioning regarding the contents of the family refrigerator suggested that this was not factually true. The complaint seemed to represent her sense of inner depletion which, in turn, emanated from her not feeling loved and supported by her mother. The patient described her mother as not having "a life" of her own, as being "no fun," always duty-bound, self-absorbed, hypochondriacal, miserly, and unempathic. She could not recall a single attempt by her mother to instruct her about bodily care, makeup, sexuality, what boys were about, and how to handle them. She had a better relationship with her father who took note of her talents, encouraged her, and regarded her with warmth. However, she could not utilize him for the maternal support she needed at this crucial transition from childhood into adolescence.

As psychotherapy proceeded, the patient obtained a pet rabbit. She wanted the rabbit to stay in her room but the mother,

citing its "bad smell," sternly objected to this. Father's gentle protests in support of his daughter's position went unheeded and the
mother quickly bought a cage for the rabbit to be placed in the
backyard. Each afternoon after school, the patient had to go out
of the house to play with the rabbit and feed it.

A few weeks later, the patient came in very, very upset. The
rabbit had died. Apparently, busy running track after school hours,
the patient had forgotten to feed the rabbit for four or five days.
Her father had been away for a professional conference and her
mother too had failed to feed the pet. Indeed, the mother sarcasti-
cally said that this is why she was always opposed to pets since she
would end up with all the responsibility of taking care of them. As
the patient told all this in the midst of much crying and sobbing,
I asked her: "What do you think the rabbit would be saying to
himself again and again in his last few days?" She looked at me,
eyes filled with tears, pleading with me to continue. I said, "The
rabbit must be saying, 'There is no food in my house. There is no
food in my house.' "

Unlike such conflicted and guilt-ridden enactments, re-
morse-free cruelty toward animals almost always suggests a serious
conduct disorder of childhood. Indeed, such "cruelty to animals"
is the only other time, besides the description of simple phobias,
that the DSM-IV (APA, 1994) refers to human involvement with
animals. This symptom usually represents an identification with
the aggressor as the ego's way of discharging hostile impulses
toward parents. Difficulties of metabolizing parental introjects are
clearly evident here with the consequent disturbances of superego
formation. Not surprisingly then, children who are cruel to animals are at a higher risk for developing antisocial personality
disorder in adulthood. They have not internalized those "Jim-
miny-Cricket"-like aspects of the superego which help to "always
let your conscience be your guide." By hurting a helpless animal,
the child gives vent to his sadism, turns passivity into activity, and
replaces narcissistic mortification by manic triumph.

Case 13

In a psychiatric residential treatment center for 9- to 12-year-old
boys, six boys caught a fish. They brought the fish into their facility

and proceeded to torture it for close to an hour. They kicked it, threw it into the air, and laughed at it before flushing it down the toilet. They reported how they enjoyed watching the fish squirm and thrash against the toilet bowl before disappearing.

The boy who was most active in this fish torture and who thought of using the toilet as the final sadistic chamber was often "the butt" of his peers' jokes. His early life was a history of repeated acts of neglect by his mother who was addicted to drugs and physical attacks by her boyfriends. He as well as the other boys in the facility had a tortured past. In days prior to the fish torture, his "friends" had been particularly cruel to him, teasing him about his mother dying of AIDS. When asked his feelings about his mother and her illness, he had remained silent as tears rolled down his face. He was unable to express the hurt and shame she had caused him nor the anger he felt regarding multiple abandonments including her dying. When asked what made him want to torture the fish, he again was silent and tearful and reexperienced the affect he felt in relation to his mother. Like the fish, he felt abused by his peers, his parents, and life circumstances. Earlier in his life, he had attempted to commit suicide. The episode of fish torture was a shift in the direction of expressed hostility from self to other.

When the humiliation and helplessness felt by a child is less intense, its externalization upon an animal does not lead to deliberate cruelty but unintended neglect of a pet. In such cases, the interpretation of the underlying dynamics usually leads to the resolution of the problematic behavior.

Case 14

A 16-year-old girl with symptoms of posttraumatic stress disorder and feelings of intense anger was dissuaded from running away from home when her parents agreed to buy her a puppy. In this case, the animal walked literally into the treatment as the child insisted on bringing her to sessions. Along with the new arrival came a revival of early childhood memories of having been laughed at for an episode of "wetting" herself in front of her family. Though responsible for training the dog, the girl found it difficult to wake up early enough to walk the dog before she went to school, and frequently, the dog would wimper and then wet itself. She stopped bringing the pet to sessions saying that she was afraid it might wet itself.

The dog then became aggressive and the veterinarian told the patient that unless she spent extra time with her pet, the dog's aggression might become so severe that it would have to be put to sleep. Interestingly, the girl began struggling with sleepiness during sessions and had requested to come to therapy less often. An interpretation identified the puppy with the patient and further stated how the patient was shaming and neglecting her puppy as she herself felt she had been shamed and neglected by her family. Her sleepiness was discussed as a way she tried not to feel the shame, hurt, and anger of her situation. She was able to verbalize her feelings and started taking better care of her dog and herself.

Children's symptomatic involvement with animals can at times be a way station to healthier adjustment. In such instances neurotic symptoms and seemingly provocative acting out serve to ameliorate a developmental crisis, putting the child ahead in the game of psychosocial mastery.

Case 15

A 12-year-old boy's unremitting daily pleading with his parents to allow him to take his uncle's German shepherd to school with him, resulted in his coming for treatment. He described how he wanted to bring the dog because he could not defend himself against the aggressive teasing of his peers. Despite his age-appropriate physical build, he was frightened and uncomfortable with healthy aggressive impulses. While avoidant of other children due to feeling unable to defend himself, the boy was quite comfortable with animals. He began to use animals to display his fearlessness to other kids and also to frighten them with snakes, iguanas, and large attack dogs. Eventually, however, he began to use dogs as a metaphor for talking about his feelings of vulnerability and passivity which were associated with a discomfort with the seductive behavior of his mother. He recalled how his father had a little dog when he was a boy and how little dogs can protect themselves by strategic biting. As he developed internal confidence, the insistence on bringing a dog and other various creatures to school diminished. After animals had been used to overcome inhibition with normal aggressive drives, the boy came to the office, seated himself, and suddenly unzipped his coat to flash me with a now barking Chihuahua. Animals had finally come into the transference and had begun to serve as a means of expressing sexual impulses!

The dog–penis equation here was unmistakable. This use of animals to represent body parts might extend to an overall identification with them (Kupferman, 1977). At times, such transient identifications are the child's way of sorting out inner conflicts of identity while passing through a stormy developmental phase.

Case 16

A 15-year-old girl, who was born with a mild facial palsy, sought treatment for depression. All of her life she had felt painfully different from others. Through latency and preadolescence, she was teased by peers. She coped by withdrawing into a menagerie of pets including exotic birds, lizards, mice, snakes, and a very special rat. Absorbed in playing with her pets, she escaped ridicule and feelings of alienation. In weekly sessions, she began first to talk about her rat. She explained that people were always frightened of rats and that rats were very misunderstood. They were not animals of attack but gentle creatures with the powerful attribute of being survivors. She talked about not wanting to be seen and having a wish to be nocturnal like her rat. With continuing psychotherapy, she began to recognize that she too was a survivor and how this was an attractive quality to her adolescent peers. Gradually she shifted her sense of self-esteem by making a virtue of her difference.

All in all, animals hover on the border between the psychically savage and civilized in the lives of children. They might facilitate normal development or press against the bars of the ego and break through them into neurotic or borderline symptomatology. Such symptoms might be transient and serve as developmental bridges. Or, they might be fixed and hence harbingers of problematic outcome in adulthood. Deliberate and ruthless cruelty toward animals is the example par excellence of such childhood psychic pathology.

CONCLUSION

Psychiatric symptomatology involves animals in myriad ways. These range from frank delusions and hallucinations through sequestered sexual perversions to subtle obsessions and phobias. Some animals seem to occur with a greater frequency than others in the terrain of psychopathology. Our own cases, while certainly involving other animals, largely focus upon dogs, cats, and spiders. Such distribution might be due to the inherent capacities of these creatures to evoke or contain intrapsychic projections as well as cultural factors. Thus, in societies where man–animal contact extends widely, other animals might figure more often in psychiatric symptoms. Another thing to be noted is that animals appear in the psychiatric symptoms of both children and adults. Their involvement in adult psychopathology, however, has remained less recognized. Underscoring it serves to remind clinicians to include a question or two about animals in their diagnostic interviews. A simple inquiry like "Tell me something about the role of animals in your imagination or actual life" might lead to important clinical data that could otherwise be withheld.

Animals also make their appearance in the course of psychotherapy and psychoanalysis. The most readily noticeable, and perhaps the most frequent, manner in which they enter the treatment situation is by way of language and metaphor. Projecting their own deviousness, patients refer to the analyst as a sly fox; angrily, they call him a son of a bitch; wanting to accompany the analyst on vacations, they evoke the image of a baby kangaroo in its mother's pouch; yearning for his penis, they dream of snakes; fearing entrapment, they suffer dark visions of spiders; celebrating the mending of their hitherto split-off libidinal and aggressive self-representations, they refer to themselves as zebras (see the case of Ms. H in Akhtar, 1994), and so forth.

At times, however, matters go beyond metaphor. Actual pets are talked about in great detail during treatment sessions. These might be current pets or those from the patient's childhood. In either case, the pet often signifies an unassimilated self-representation of the patient as well as aspects of an unacknowledged transference configuration. The border between allusion and reality is narrow here. The resulting "animal transferences" might contain reactivation of early object relations with animals (containers of still deeper layers of parent–child relations) as well as metaphorical molding of the analyst into a "new" animal, rather like a "new object." Countertransference experience might also involve complementary (Racker, 1957) phenomena whereby the analyst comes to feel toward a regressed patient as he might have done toward a pet of his own. The analyst might also develop feelings of envy and jealousy vis-à-vis the patient's real or imaginary, past, or current, relationships with a pet.

Pets might also be acquired for the first time during the course of treatment. This can serve as a resistance to further exploration of the internal world in the here and now of the transference–countertransference axis. More often, it is a developmentally progressive step in a patient's moving on to greater capacities for commitment, tolerance of ambivalence, and identification with the (maternally) caring aspects of the analyst. The pets might be actually brought into the office. While child patients more frequently do so, this practice is not restricted to them.[7] This is not entirely surprising. After all, relationships with real and imagined animals play a big role in hiding and expressing childhood concerns and curiosities, matters that persist well beyond the beginning years of life, and give shape to adult psychopathology. Wishes, dreams, fantasies, and fears of childhood are what underlie the grown-up psychiatric patients' sense of foreboding and misery anyway. If animals are the child's internal objects

---

[7] This is different from a deliberate use of animals by the therapist in "pet therapy" (Jenkins, 1986; Redefer and Goodman, 1989; Hoffman, 1991) which might provide companionship, solace, and psychic relief to elderly and terminally ill patients. In this connection, it is interesting to note that many state hospitals have a dog, usually a pet of a senior staff member, that is friendly to (hence psychically used by) its patients. More striking is the fact that the founder of psychoanalysis himself had his dogs present while conducting sessions with his patients. Perhaps, they diminished his loneliness and distress while encountering his patients' psychic suffering!

then they are also the adult's internal objects. Indeed it might only slightly stretch matters to paraphrase Freud here and conclude by saying that "the mind is first and foremost an animal mind!"

REFERENCES

Abraham, K. (1913), Restrictions and transformations of scoptophilia in psycho-neurotics; with remarks on analogous phenomena of folk psychology. In: *Selected Papers*. London: Hogarth Press, 1927, pp. 226–234.
Akhtar, S. (1992), *Broken Structures: Severe Personality Disorders and Their Treatment*. Northvale, NJ: Jason Aronson.
—— (1994), Object constancy and adult psychopathology. *Internat. J. Psycho-Anal.*, 75:441–455.
—— Brenner, I. (1979), Differential diagnosis of fugue-like states. *J. Clin. Psychiatry*, 40:381–385.
—— Byrne, J. P. (1983), The concept of splitting and its clinical relevance. *Amer. J. Psychiatry*, 140:1016–1018.
—— Thomson, J. A. (1980), Schizophrenia and sexuality: A review and a report of 12 unusual cases. Part I. *J. Clin. Psychiatry*, 41:123–143.
American Psychiatric Association (1994), *Diagnostic and Statistical Manual of Mental Disorders*, 4th ed. (DSM-IV). Washington, DC: American Psychiatric Press.
Arieti, S. (1974), *American Handbook of Psychiatry*. New York: Basic Books.
Benezech, M., DeWitte, J., Etchepare, J. J., & Bourgeois, M. (1989), A case of lycanthropy with deadly violence. *Annales Medico-Psychologiques*, 147:464–470.
Bennett-Levy, J., & Marteau, T. (1984), Fear of animals: What is prepared? *Brit. J. Psychol.*, 75:37–42.
Berrios, G. E. (1982), Tactile hallucinations: Conceptual and historical aspects. *J. Neurol. Neurosurg. Psychiatry*, 45:395–403.
Blum, H. (1981), Object inconstancy and paranoid conspiracy. *J. Amer. Psychoanal. Assn.*, 29:789–813.
Bourdon, K., Boyd, J., Dae, D., Burns, B., Thompson, J., & Locke, B. (1988), Gender differences in phobias: Results of the ECA Community Survey. *J. Anxiety Disorders*, 2:227–241.
Bourgeois, M. L., Duhamel, P., & Verdoux, H. (1992), Delusional parasitosis: Folie à deux and attempted murder of a family doctor. *Brit. J. Psychiatry*, 161:709–711.

Campbell, R. J. (1989), *Psychiatric Dictionary*, 6th ed. New York: Oxford University Press.

Coll, P. G., O'Sullivan, G., & Browne, P. J. (1985), Lycanthropy lives on. *Brit. J. Psychiatry*, 147:201–202.

Cook, M., & Mineka, S. (1987), Second order conditioning and overshadowing in the observational conditioning of fear in monkeys. *Behav. Res. & Therapy*, 25:349–364.

Davey, G. (1992), Characteristics of individuals with fear of spiders. *Anxiety Res.*, 4:299–314.

Davey, G., Forster, L., & Mayhew, G. (1993), Familial resemblances in disgust sensitivity and animal phobias. *Behav. Res. & Therapy*, 31:41–50.

DeLeon, J., Antelo, R. E., & Simpson, G. (1992), Delusion of parasitosis or chronic tactile hallucinosis: Hypothesis about their brain physiopathology. *Comprehen. Psychiatry*, 33:25–33.

Delprato, D. (1980), Hereditary determinants of fears and phobias: A critical review. *Behav. Therapy*, 11:79–103.

Dening, T. R., & West, A. (1989), Multiple serial lycanthropy: A case report. *Psychopathology*, 22:344–347.

Deutsch, H. (1942), Some forms of emotional disturbance and their relationship to schizophrenia. *Psychoanal. Quart.*, 11:301–321.

——— (1951), *Psychoanalysis of Neuroses*. London: Hogarth Press.

Domangue, B. (1985), Hypnotic regression and reframing in the treatment of insect phobias. *Amer. J. Psychotherapy*, 39:206–214.

Eisler, R. (1978), *Man into Wolf.* Santa Barbara, CA: Ross-Erikson.

Ekbom, K. A. (1938), Der presenile dermatozoenwahns. *Acta Psychiatrica et Neurol. Scand.*, 13:227–259.

Eller, J. J. (1929), Neurogenic and psychogenic disorders of the skin. *NY Med. J.*, 129:481–485.

Emde, R. (1984), The affective self. In: *Frontiers of Infant Psychiatry*, ed. J. D. Call, E. Galenson, & R. L. Tyson. New York: Basic Books, pp. 38–54.

English, O. (1945), *Emotional Disturbances during the Phallic Period: Emotional Problems of Living.* New York: W. W. Norton, pp. 119–127.

Eysenck, H. J. (1965), *The Causes and Cures of Neurosis.* London: Routledge & Kegan Paul.

——— (1976), The conditioning model of neurosis. *Behav. Res. & Therapy*, 14:251–267.

Fahy, T. A. (1989), Lycanthropy: A review. *Roy. Soc. Med.*, 82:39–39.

Fenichel, O. (1945), *The Psychoanalytic Theory of Neurosis.* New York: W. W. Norton.

Ferenczi, S. (1926), *Theory and Technique in Psychoanalysis.* London: Hogarth Press.

Flynn, F. G., Cummings, J. L., & Scheibel, J. (1989), Monosymptomatic delusions of parasitosis associated with ischemic cerebrovascular disease. *J. Geriat. Psychiatry & Neurol.*, 2:134–139.

Freinhar, J. P. (1984), Delusions of parasitosis. *Psychosom.*, 25:47–53.

Freud, S. (1895), Obsessions and phobias: Their psychical mechanism and their aetiology. *Standard Edition*, 3:69–82. London: Hogarth Press, 1962.

———— (1909a), Analysis of a phobia in a 5-year-old boy. *Standard Edition*, 10:1–147. London: Hogarth Press, 1955.

———— (1909b), Notes upon a case of obsessional neurosis. *Standard Edition*, 10:151–249. London: Hogarth Press, 1955.

———— (1913), Totem and Taboo. *Standard Edition*, 13:1–161. London: Hogarth Press, 1955.

———— (1918), From the history of an infantile neurosis. *Standard Edition*, 17:7–122. London: Hogarth Press, 1955.

Friedman, D. (1966), Treatment of a case of dog phobia in a deaf mute by behavior therapy. *Behav. Res. Therapy*, 4:141–150.

Gieler, U., & Knoll, M. (1990), Delusional parasitosis as "folie à trois." *Dermatologica*, 181:122–125.

Gonsalez, S., Lastra, M., & Ramos, V. (1993), Parasitic delusions: Literature review and report of new cases. *Actas Luso-Espanolas de Neurologia, Psyiquiatria y Ciencias Afines*, 21:52–62.

Greenacre, P. (1951), Respiratory incorporation and the phallic phase. *The Psychoanalytic Study of the Child*, 6:180–205. New York: International Universities Press.

Hartmann, H. (1958), *Ego Psychology and the Problem of Adaptation*. New York: International Universities Press.

Hoffman, R. G. (1991), Companion animals: A therapeutic measure for elderly patients. *J. Gerontolog. Soc. Work*, 18:195–205.

Hollander, E., & Wong, C. (1995), Body dysmorphic disorder, pathological gambling, and sexual compulsions. *J. Clin. Psychiatry*, 56:7–12.

Hopkinson, G. (1973), The psychiatric syndrome of infestation. *Psychiatria Clin.*, 6:330–345.

Horstein, O. P., Hoffman, P., & Joraschky, P. (1989), Delusions of parasitic skin infestation in elderly dermotologic patients. *Zeitschr. Hautkrankheiten*, 64:981–989.

Illis, L. (1964), On porphyria and the aetiology of werewolves. *Proc. Roy. Soc. Med.*, 57:23–26.

Jackson, P. M. (1978), Another case of lycanthropy. *Amer. J. Psychiatry*, 135:134–135.

Jelliffe, S. E., & Brink, A. B. (1917), The role of animals in the unconscious, with some remarks on theriomorphic symbolism as seen in Ovid. *Psychoanal. Rev.*, 4:253–271.

Jenkins, J. L. (1986), Physiological effects of petting a companion animal. *Psycholog. Reports*, 58:21–22.

Jibiki, I., & Yamaguchi, N. (1992), A case with delusion of parasitosis as a reactive psychosis following scabies infection. *Europ. J. Psychiatry*, 6:181–183.

Jones, E. (1937), *On the Nightmare*. London: Hogarth Press.

——— (1948), The theory of symbolism. In: *Papers on Psychoanalysis*, 5th ed. London: Bailliere, Tindall & Cox, pp. 87–144.

Jung, C. G. (1954), *The Development of Personality*. London: Routledge & Kegan Paul.

Kanazawa, A., & Hata, T. (1992), Coexistence of the Ekbom syndrome and lilliputian hallucination. *Psychopathology*, 25:209–211.

Kaplan, H., & Sadock, B. (1989), *Comprehensive Textbook of Psychiatry*, Vol. 5. Baltimore, MD: Williams & Wilkins, pp. 844–845.

Keck, P. E., Pope, H. G., Hudson, J. I., McElroy, S. L., & Kulick, R. (1988), Lycanthropy: Alive and well in the twentieth century. *Psycholog. Med.*, 18:113–120.

Kernberg, O. F. (1975), *Borderline Conditions and Pathological Narcissism*. New York: Jason Aronson.

Kinsey, A., Pomeroy, W., & Martin, C. (1948), *Sexual Behavior in the Human Male*. Philadelphia: W. B. Saunders.

Koehler, K., Ebel, H., & Vartzopoulos, D. (1990), Lycanthroup and demonomania: Some psychopathological issues. *Psycholog. Med.*, 20:629–633.

Kolansky, H. (1960), Treatment of a 3-year-old girl's severe infantile neurosis. *The Psychoanalytic Study of the Child*, 15:261–285. New York: International Universities Press.

Kraepelin, E. (1919), *Dementia Praecox and Paraphrenia*, tr. R. M. Barclay & G. M. Robertson. Edinburgh: Livingstone.

Krafft-Ebing, R. (1892), *Psychopathia Sexualis with Special Reference to Contrary Sexual Instinct: A Medico-Legal Study*. Philadelphia: Davis.

Kulick, A., Pope, H. G., & Keck, P. E. (1990), Lycanthropy and self-identification. *J. Nerv. & Ment. Dis.*, 178:134–137.

Kupferman, K. (1977), A latency boy's identity as a cat. *The Psychoanalytic Study of the Child*, 32:363–385. New Haven, CT: Yale University Press.

Macaskill, N. D. (1987), Delusion parasitosis: Successful non-pharmacological treatment of a folie-à-deux. *Brit. J. Psychiatry*, 150:261–263.

MacKinnon, R. A., & Michels, R. (1971), *The Psychiatric Interview in Clinical Practice*. Philadelphia: W. B. Saunders.

Magnan, V., & Saury, M. (1889), Trois cas de cocainisme chronique. *Comptes rendes. Séances et Memoires Soc. Biologique*, 41:60–63.

Mahler, M. S., Pine, F., & Bergman, A. (1975), *The Psychological Birth of the Human Infant.* New York: Basic Books.

Maier, C. (1987), The problem of parasitosis delusions. *Nervenarzt,* 58:107–115.

Malliaras, D. E., Kossovitsa, Y. T., & Dhristodoulou, G. N. (1978), Organic contributors to the intermetamorphosis syndrome. *Amer. J. Psychiatry,* 135:985–987.

Marks, I. M. (1987), *Fears, Phobias, and Rituals.* New York: Oxford University Press.

Marneros, A., Deister, A., & Rohde, A. (1988), Delusional parasitosis. *Psychopathology,* 21:267–274.

May, W. W., & Terpenning, M. (1991), Delusional parasitosis in geriatric patients. *Psychosomatics,* 32:84–94.

McNally, R. J., & Steketee, G. S. (1985), The etiology and maintenance of severe animal phobias. *Behav. Res. & Therapy,* 23:431–435.

Mellor, C. S. (1988), Depersonalisation and self perception. *Brit. J. Psychiatry,* 153(Suppl):15–19.

Merkur, D. (1981), The psychodynamics of the Navajo Coyote ceremonial. *J. Mind & Behav.,* 2:243–257.

Mester, H. (1975), Induced acaraphobia. *Psychiatria Clinica,* 8:339–348.

Mineka, S., Davidson, M., Cook, M., & Keir, R. (1984), Observational conditioning of snake fear in rhesus monkeys. *J. Abnorm. Psychology,* 93:355–372.

Mitchell, J., & Vierkant, A. D. (1991), Delusions and hallucinations of cocaine abusers and paranoid schizophrenics: A comparative study. *J. Psychology,* 125:301–310.

Morris, M. (1991), Delusional infestation. *Brit. J. Psychiatry,* 159(Suppl.):83–87.

Mouren, M., Ohayon, M., & Tatossian, A. (1980), Animals and their masters. Psychological and psychopathological aspects. *Annales Medico Psychologiques,* 138:543–557.

Munro, A. (1982), *Delusional Hypochondriasis: A Description of Monosymptomatic Hypochondriacal Psychosis,* Monogr. series 5. Toronto, Canada: Clarke Institute of Psychiatry.

Musalek, M., Podreka, I., Walter, H., Suess, E., Passweg, V., Nutsinger, D., Strobl, R., & Lesch, O. M. (1989), Regional brain function in hallucination. A study of regional cerebral blood flow with 99m-Tc-HMPA)-SPECT in patients with auditory hallucinations, tactile hallucinations, and normal controls. *Comprehen. Psychiatry,* 30:99–108.

Myerson, A. (1921), Two cases of acaraphobia. *Boston Med. & Surg. J.,* 184:635–638.

Norman, J. P. (1948), Evidence and clinical signs of homosexuality in 100 unanalyzed cases of dementia praecox. *J. Nerv. & Ment. Disorders*, 107:484–489.

Ostapzeff, G. (1975), Parasitism. *Perspectives-Psychiatriques*, 53:296–302.

Paulson, M. J., & Petrus, E. P. (1969), Delusions of parasitosis: A psychological study. *Psychosomatics*, 10:111–120.

Podoll, D., Bofinger, G., Von der Stein, B., & Stuhlmann, W. (1993), Delusional parasitosis in a patient with endogenous depression. *Fortschritteder Neurroligie Psychiatrie*, 61:62–66.

Rachman, S. (1977), The conditioning theory of fear-acquisition: A critical examination. *Behav. Res. & Therapy*, 15:375–387.

Racker, H. (1957), The meanings and uses of countertransference. *Psychoanal. Quart.*, 26:303–357.

Rajna, D. D., Guillibert, E., Loo, H., & Debray, Q. (1990), A case of bird metamorphosis delusion in a buddhist schizophrenic. *Annales Medica-Psychologiques*, 148:539–542.

Rappaport, E. A. (1968), Zoophily and zoerasty. *Psychoanal. Quart.*, 37:565–587.

Redefer, L. A., & Goodman, J. F. (1989), Pet-facilitated therapy with autistic children. *J. Autism & Development. Disorders*, 19:461–467.

Reilly, T. M. (1988), Delusional infestation. *Brit. J. Psychiatry*, 153 (Suppl.):44–46.

Robertson, B. A., & Kottler, A. (1993), Cultural issues in the psychiatric assessment of Khosa children and adolescents. *S. African Med. J.*, 83:207–208.

Roheim, G. (1943), *The Origin and Function of Culture*. New York: Nervous & Mental Disease Monographs.

Rojo Moreno, J., Rojo Moreno, M., Baldemoro Garcia, C., & Rojo Siwerra, M. (1990), The delusion of lycanthropic transformation. *Actas Luso-Espanolas de Neurologica, Psiguiatria Y Ciencias Afines*, 18:327–331.

Rosenstock, H. A., & Bincent, K. R. (1977), A case of lycanthropy. *Amer. J. Psychiatry*, 34:1147–1149.

Roux, G. (1988), Images of insects and psychosis. *Psychologie Medicale*, 20:1129–1136.

Schneck, J. M. (1974), Zooerasty and incest fantasy. *Internat. J. Clin. & Experiment. Hypnosis*, 4:299–302.

Schowalter, J. (1983), The use and abuse of pets. *J. Amer. Acad. Child Psychiatry*, 22:68–72.

Searles, H. F. (1960), *The Non-Human Environment in Normal Development and Schizophrenia*. New York: International Universities Press.

Shengold, L. (1967), The effects of overstimulation: Rat people. *Internat. J. Psycho-Anal.*, 48:403–415.

Siegel, R. (1978), Cocaine hallucinations. *Amer. J. Psychiatry,* 135:3.

Sizaret, P., & Simon, J. P. (1976), Presenile delusion of parasitosis. *Encephale,* 2:167–175.

Skott, A. (1975), Delusions of parasitosis (parasitophobia) or Ekbom's syndrome: A literature survey. *Nordisk Psykiatrisk Tidsskrift,* 29:115–131.

Solyom, L., Beck, P., Solyom, C., & Hugel, R. (1974), Some etiological factors in phobic neurosis. *Can. Psychiatric Assn. J.,* 19:69–78.

Sterba, E. (1935), Excerpts from the analysis of a dog phobia. *Psychoanal. Quart.,* 4:135–160.

Stolorow, R. D., & Grand, H. T. (1973), A partial analysis of a perversion including bugs. *Internat. J. Psycho-Anal.,* 54:349–350.

Stone, J. (1992), A psychoanalytic bestiary: The wolf woman, the leopard, and the siren. *Amer. Imago,* 49:117–152.

Surawicz, F. G., & Banta, R. (1975), Lycanthropy revisited. *Can. Psychiatric Assn. J.,* 20:537–542.

Trabert, W. (1991), Epidemiology of delusional parasitosis: Psychotherapeutic engagement. *Nervenarzt,* 62:165–169.

Traub-Werner, D. (1986), The place and value of bestophilia in perversions. *J. Amer. Psychoanal. Assn.,* 34:975–992.

Tseng, W., & McDermott, J. (1981), *Culture, Mind, and Therapy: An Introduction to Cultural Psychiatry.* New York: Brunner/Mazel.

Tyson, R. (1978), Notes on the analysis of a prelatency boy with a dog phobia. *The Psychoanalytic Study of the Child,* 33:427–458. New Haven, CT: Yale University Press.

van der Hart, O. (1981), Treatment of a phobia for dead birds: A case report. *Amer. J. Clin. Hypnosis,* 23:263–265.

Verbeek, E. (1959), Le délire dermatozoaire et le problème de l'hallucinose tactile chronizue. *Psychiatrie et Neurologie,* 138:217–233.

Verdoux, H., & Bourgeouis, M. (1993), A partial form of lycanthropy with hair delusion in a manic-depressive patient. *Brit. J. Psychiatry,* 163:684–686.

Volkan, V. (1972), The birds of Cyprus. *Amer. J. Psychotherapy,* 26:378–383.

——— (1995), *The Infantile Psychotic Self and Its Fates: Understanding and Treating Schizophrenic and Other Difficult Patients.* Northvale, NJ: Jason Aronson.

——— Akhtar, S. (1979), The symptoms of schizophrenia: Contributions of the structural theory and object relations theory. In: *Integrating Ego Psychology and Object Relations Theory,* ed. L. Saretsky, G. D. Goldman, & D. S. Milman. Dubuque, Iowa: Kendall/Hunt, pp. 270–285.

Wolpe, J., & Rachman, R. (1960), Psychoanalytic evidence: A critique based on Freud's case of Little Hans. *J. Nerv. & Ment. Dis.*, 131:135–148.

Wurmser, L. (1981), Phobic core in the addictions and the paranoid process. *Internat. J. Psychoanal. Psychother.*, 8:311–335.

Yellowlees, P. P. M. (1989), Werewolves down under—Where are you now? *Med. J. Australia*, 151:663–665.

Part II

Freud's Menagerie

CHAPTER 2

Rat People

LEONARD L. SHENGOLD, M.D.

The compulsion to repeat dominates the lives of people who have been seduced or beaten by psychotic and psychopathic parents. In my book *Soul Murder* (1989), I have stressed the importance for these people of fixation on the cannibalistic level of libido development and regression to it, with concomitant maldevelopment and regression of the ego and superego. Overstimulation continues to be a central problem in the lives of these people, and therefore also in their analytic transferences.

The clinical conditions I have been describing as the effects of soul murder sometimes appear in combination with a preoccupation with rats. Obviously not all soul murder victims are rat people, and whether all people who are preoccupied with toothed creatures and rodents have suffered actual overstimulating experiences as children must also be subject to doubt. But such a preoccupation, evidenced by the frequent appearance of rats in analytic associations, should alert the observer to the possibility of soul murder. All the rat people I have described in my book were victims of soul murder, and my generalizations about them are applicable to other victims.

I view the image of the rat as a kind of hallmark indicating cannibalistic impulses and the presence of too-muchness (having had to bear the unbearable), and I will try to illustrate this in the clinical material of this chapter and in such works of literature as Orwell's (Nineteen Eighty-Four) and others. The rat is one of the principal symbolic mental images (imagos) of cannibalism—probably by virtue of the impact on the human mind of the rat's propensity for murdering and devouring members of its own species, of its omnivorous destructiveness, and perhaps above all of its remarkable teeth. On reviewing Freud's case of the Rat Man (1909), one sees that the rat can stand for subject or object of any stage of libidinal development but is particularly associated with eating and being eaten and with anal erogeneity.

RATS, CANNIBALISM, AND OVERSTIMULATION

A literary quotation that connects rats, oral sadism, and overstimulation comes from the novel *Torture Garden* (1899) by Octave Mirbeau, which I believe to be the source of the story that obsessed Freud's famous patient known in psychoanalytic circles as the Rat Man (Freud, 1909). This story, the Rat Man told Freud, was related to him by the sadistic Captain N, who " 'had *read* of a specially horrible punishment used in the East . . . the criminal was tied up . . . a pot was turned upside down on his buttocks . . . some rats were put into it . . . and they . . .'—he got up again and was showing every sign of horror and resistance—'*bored their way in* . . .'—'into his anus,' I [Freud] helped him out" (1909, p. 166; the Rat Man is speaking and the hesitations are his; emphasis in original).[1]

The difficulty of saying "into his anus" is demonstrated by its not being specifically stated in Mirbeau's story either. I think this evasion marks the special resistance evoked by the cannibalistic vulnerability of the anal zone and especially the anal sphincter. The psychological importance of the anal sphincter has to do with its resonance in the body ego's and subsequently the psychic ego's control of intense, early (primal) drive-derived affects and body feelings (Shengold, 1985). In my clinical experience, the anal and perianal area of erogeneity seems to be the principal intrapsychic site for the overwhelming stimulation (experienced as being eaten into and eaten up) that can lead to ego dissolution.

---

[1] Freud's "help" is cited by Kanzer (1952) as evidence of his countertransference. He verbally performs a penetration.

Torture Garden was published in Paris in 1899, seven years before the Rat Man's encounter with Captain N. During those years the book was widely read in Europe and acquired notoriety for being pornographic; it is, however, the work of a serious artist (Wilson, 1950). The book's climactic episode is about a rat torture; the Garden is in China ("the East"), the torturer is Chinese, and the heroine, Clara, obsessed by torture, asks him:

> "What is this torture of the rat? . . . Can you describe it to us?" [The torturer answers:] "You take a condemned man, charming lady, a condemned man, or anybody else . . . you take a man, as young and strong as possible, whose muscles are quite resistant; in virtue of this principle: the more strength, the more struggle—and the more struggle, the more pain! Good! You undress him. Good! And when he is stark naked . . . Yes, milady? You make him kneel, his back bent, on the earth, where you fasten him with chains . . . Good! I don't know if I'm making myself understood? Then in a big pot, whose bottom is pierced with a little hole . . . a flowerpot, milady . . . you place a very fat rat whom it's wise to have deprived of nourishment for a couple of days,[2] to excite its ferocity. And this pot, inhabited by this rat, you apply hermetically, like an enormous cupping-glass, to the back of the condemned by means of stout thongs attached to a leather girdle about the loins. A ha! Now the plot thickens!" He looked maliciously at [her] out of the corners of his lowered lids, to judge the effect his words were producing. "And then?" said Clara, simply. "Then, milady, you introduce into the little hole into the pot . . . guess what!" "How should I know?" The good fellow rubbed his hands, smiled horribly, and then continued: "You introduce an iron rod, heated red hot at the fire of a forge . . . and when the iron rod is introduced, what happens? Ah, ha ha! Imagine what must happen, milady. . . ." "Oh, come on, you old gossip!" . . . "A little patience, milady. . . . Well, you

---

[2] In the version that the Rat Man told to Freud one rat becomes "some rats." We do not know if this is his distortion or Captain N's. (According to Freud's notes [p. 291], the Rat Man at one point remembered Captain N's mentioning two rats.) What does this multiplication signify? There are many possible meanings, in two categories: defensive (for example, obfuscation) and revelatory (for example, *some* could connote *two* [female symbol] or *three* male symbol]; the two categories can also coexist). According to one defensive meaning, the one rat is the biting phallus from which one must keep away. The Rat Man speaks of both "the rat punishment" and "the punishment of the rats" but when the rat becomes singular it is clearly phallic: "When he was wishing Constanze the rats he felt a rat gnawing at his own anus and had a visual image of it" (Freud, 1909, p. 308).

introduce into the pot's hole, an iron rod, heated red-hot at the fire of a forge. The rat tries to escape the burning of the rod and its dazzling light. It goes mad, cuts capers, leaps and bounds, runs around the walls of the pot, crawls and gallops over the man's flesh, which it first tickles and then tears with its nails and bites with its sharp teeth, seeking an exit through the torn and bleeding skin. But there is no exit. During the first frenzied moments, the rat can find none. And the iron rod, handled cleverly and slowly, still draws near the rat, threatens it, scorches its fur. What do you think of this for a beginning?" [pp. 191–193].

At the beginning of the torturer's narrative there are many hesitations, similar to those in the Rat Man's concise retelling. For the Rat Man whose predominant involvement is with the passive victim, these interstices are simultaneously attempts at isolation and a supplying of holes to be penetrated. (Freud responded to this when he interjected the words *into his anus.*) For the torturer, who boasts that he invented the torture of the rat, the making of interrupting "holes" is predominantly in the service of tormenting the impatient Clara. Once arrived at, the nearly climactic penetration of the "pot's hole" by the phallic, red-hot iron rod, the torturer's narration becomes an unimpeded gush. This is peristaltic language, the halts and rushes in the service of overexcited passion. The torturer's description continues:

"Its great merit lies in the fact that you must know how to prolong this initial operation as much as possible, for the laws of physiology teach us that there is nothing more horrible to the human flesh than the combination of tickling and biting. It may even happen that the victim goes mad from it. He howls and struggles; his body . . . heaves and contorts, shaken by agonizing shudders. But his limbs are firmly held by the chains, and the pot, by the thongs. And the movements of the condemned man only augment the rat's fury, to which the intoxication of blood is often added. It's sublime, milady!" "And then?" said Clara . . . "Finally . . . for I see you're anxious to know the climax of this wonderful and jolly story; finally . . . threatened by the glowing rod and thanks to the excitation of a few well-chosen burns, the rat ends by finding an exit, milady. Ah ha ha!" "How horrible!" exclaimed Clara. "Ah, you see . . . I'm proud of the interest you take in my torture. But

wait! [With Clara's increasing impatience, the Torturer has re-
sumed his hesitations.] The rat penetrates the man's body, widening with claws and teeth the opening he madly digs, as in the
earth. And he croaks, stifled, at the same time that the victim
who, after a half-hour of ineffable, incomparable torture, ends
by succumbing to a hemorrhage . . . when it isn't from too much
suffering . . . or even the congestion caused by a frightful insanity.
In all cases, and whatever the final cause of this death . . . you can
be sure it's extremely beautiful" [pp. 193–194].

The anal eroticism and oral and anal sadomasochism that
are associated with the obsessions of the Rat Man are set forth
here, as are the connotations of overstimulation and cannibalism.[3] First the rat is overstimulated with the red-hot iron rod (the
danger throughout is that of a penetrative, mainly anal invasion
by a phallus equipped with flesh-destroying, flesh-eating power).
The rat "goes mad" and tears and bites at the man's flesh, finally
making a cannibalistic anal penetration after unbearably overstimulating the victim with the "prolonged" and "horrible . . . combination of tickling and biting." Both rat and victim are trapped
and helpless in the face of increasing torment. Both are overstimulated and die. The basic story of the victim's being eaten and
anally penetrated by the rat is also present in displacement in
relation to the glowing rod and the rat (here as victim); symbolically, it is presented through the heated iron rod and the flower-
pot with the hole in its bottom; in attenuation the theme is
repeated by way of the torturer's teasing method of telling his
story to the enthralled, overexcited, impatient Clara.[4]

THE RAT AS CARRIER OF THE TOOTH

The words *rat* and *rodent* are derived from the Latin *rodere*: to
gnaw, consume. Related roots are *radere* (Latin), to scratch, and
radona (sanskrit), tooth.

---

[3] The Rat Man told Freud of having a dream in 1906 involving Oriental torture—before the meeting with Captain N.

[4] Robert Fliess (1956) calls impatience "the cannibalistic affect" (p. 107). Mirbeau
describes in an earlier part of *Torture Garden* Clara's fascinated curiosity about details of
literal cannibalism (pp. 92–100).

The rat imago appears as a leading motif in the study of oral sadistic and masochistic phenomena (tooth phenomena).[5] The rat is a tooth carrier, endowed with the power to creep back and forth from level to level of libidinal development, from one erogenous zone to another, biting and being bitten. It is among the most common of many imagos that are first of all cannibalistic: carriers of the destructive tooth. These include the wolf, snake, and spider, which are found in nature, and the monstrous sphinx, vampire, and werewolf. These are biting, sucking, tearing, devouring creatures.[6]

Remains of rats and men have been found together in fossils of the Pliocene and Pleistocene periods (Zinsser, 1935). There are no references to rats as such in classical or biblical literature; for Greeks and Hebrews, the term for *mouse* was used to indicate both kinds of animals.[7] Herodotus mentions field mice, and according to Zinsser (1935): "in ancient Palestine, the Jews considered all seven mouse varieties . . . unclean, and as unsuited for human nourishment as were pigs" (p. 191). The special designation for the rat was adopted in European languages only after the great invasions from Asia by the black rat in the twelfth and thirteenth centuries. The black rat probably exterminated the prevailing indigenous rats and brought with it the devastating medieval plagues (*Encyclopedia Britannica*, 14th ed.). The brown rat, *mus norvegicus*, swept over Europe in the early eighteenth century and in its turn killed off the black rat in most parts of the world.

The resemblance between men and rats has often been pointed out, usually in connection with their adaptability, their

---

[5] Lewin (1950) refers to the regression seen in pharmacothymic stupors: "The wish to be eaten sometimes makes its appearance starkly in the delirious hallucination of menacing animals, large and small"(p. 123). Rats are especially common in the hallucinations of delirium tremens.

[6] We get to look upon the child's fear of being devoured, or cut up, or torn to pieces . . . as a regular component of its mental life. And we know that the maneating wolf . . . and all the evil monsters out of myths and fairy stories flourish and exert their unconscious influence in the phantasy of each individual child" (Klein, 1933, p. 268).

[7] Some patients make no differentiation between mice and rats; more frequently, the mouse has more benevolent (or less destructive) connotations. For example, it is used as a symbol of pubic hair and in some languages as a term of affection. Often the mouse is the rat-as-victim; for example, in the Witch's song in Act 3 of Humperdinck's *Hansel and Gretel*, "Kommt kleine Mauslein, kommt in mein Hauslein" (Come little mousie, come into my housie); see also the clinical example below.

success as species in proliferating and occupying territory, and their similar intraspecific destructive competitiveness. Lorenz (1963) notes "the collective aggression of one community [of rats] against another" (p. 134) as a model of what now threatens mankind. Both creatures demonstrate murderous aggressiveness within the species: "The gradual, relentless progressive extermination of the black rat by the brown has no parallel in nature so close as that of the similar extermination of one race of man by another" (Zinsser, 1935). "There are other similarities: the difficulties of combatting the most successful biological opponent to man, the brown rat, lies chiefly in the fact that the rat operates basically with the same methods as those of man, by transmission of experience and its dissemination within the close community" (Lorenz, 1963, p. 137).

The rat is usually described in literature as evil and is detested; it persecutes and is persecuted. "Rats are, indeed," wrote the mild-mannered Charles Lamb (1799), "the most despised and contemptible parts of God's earth. I killed a rat the other day by punching him to pieces and I feel a weight of blood on me to this hour" (p. 41). The series of quotations that follows illustrates the rat's connection with overstimulation and cannibalism.

The Rat Is Destructive, Voracious, Omnivorous

By the fourteenth century [the rat] was well enough established in Northern Europe that rat-transmitted *Pasteurella pestis*, the organism causing bubonic plague, managed to kill some 25 million people, more than a quarter of the European population, during the Black Death. Rat-borne diseases have resulted in the deaths of more people during the last 5000 years than the combined casualties of the wars taking place over those years (Barker, 1951, p. 114). Most rats kill birds or animals for their flesh and blood; others simply have a lust for killing (Mills, 1959). Their diet is omnivorous; they eat anything, including human flesh . . . when driven by hunger they are so ravenous that neglected babies have been killed and eaten by them . . . [There are] a few cases of able-bodies men who have suffered a like fate when attacked by hordes of rats (*Encyclopedia Americana*, 1957, Vol. 23). It eats anything that lets it, and—like man—devours its own kind, under stress [Zinsser, 1935, p. 195].

The Rat Is Fecund so That if Left Unchecked It Can Overwhelm Other Species

The terrible rate at which the rat increases explains the slow process of extermination, despite the vast sums expended. It has been calculated that two rats, if left unchecked, would in the course of three to four years multiply into 20 million (Protheroe, 1940). They are able to breed at three to four months and can produce up to seven litters a year, each containing 6 to 22 young [*Encyclopedia Britannica*, 1985, Vol. 9, p. 950].

By 1910, Norway rats outnumbered humans.

The Rat Is Especially Ferocious and Destructive Toward Its Own Kind

They change into horrible brutes as soon as they encounter members of any other society of their own species . . . what rats do when a member of a strange rat-clan enters their territory . . . is one of the most horrible and repulsive things which can be observed in animals . . . with their eyes bulging from their sockets, their hair standing on end, the rats set out on the rat hunt. They are so angry that if two of them meet they bite each other. . . . [The strange rat] is slowly torn to pieces by its fellows. Only rarely does one see an animal in such desperation and panic, so conscious of the inevitability of a terrible death, as a rat which is about to be slain by rats. It ceases to defend itself [Lorenz, 1963, p. 139].

This description of the "rat hunt" notes both the sadistic fury and the terrified masochistic submission that can be evoked by the rat.

The Rat, Like All Rodents, Has Amazing Teeth

[They] have a set of fierce looking gnawing teeth . . . [these] incisors sharpen themselves to chisel-like points as they are used. The owner gradually grinds down these teeth with incessant gnawing,

but they never wear out. A rodent's incisors continue to grow as
the fingernails of people do (Hegner, 1942). The rat's incisors
grow at the rate of five inches a year [Mills, 1959].

The Rat Must Not Lose an Incisor or His Teeth Can Cause Death

Should a member of this group have the misfortune to break a
chisel tooth, he is often doomed to death. The broken tooth fails
to meet the tooth opposite; both teeth grow unhindered. Since
they are no longer ground off against each other, they grow wildly,
sometimes circling the victim's face, locking his jaws, and causing
starvation [Hegner, 1942; see also Schour and Masser, 1949].

The rat is a fit object on which to project cannibalism. It is
particularly linked with anal erogeneity because of its association
with dirt and disease. Man has had to deal continually with the
rat because of its omnipresence, destructiveness, and great fecundity; the last has made the rat's extermination necessary but ineffectual. The problem of the continual increase in the number of
rats, emphasized by the historical invasions of rats on a grand
scale (with accompanying cataclysmic, deadly plagues), makes the
rat particularly suited to represent, by allusion, overstimulation
(too-muchness). And cannibalism is invoked. The linkage of rats,
teeth, and biting is evidenced by folklore from all parts of the
world (see below). As for the rat's remarkable teeth, one may say,
paraphrasing Freud, that they must use them to bite others or
they will literally bite themselves.

MEANINGS OF THE RAT TO THE RAT MAN

The Rat Man came to Freud complaining about an obsession
and compulsive actions that had begun when he was on military
maneuvers, after the sadistic Captain N told him about the rat
punishment. On the same occasion the Captain had said something about paying back money that was owed to a third person.
The violent symptomatic reaction that followed was analyzed by
Freud: "In the short interval between the captain's story and the
request . . . to pay back the money, rats had acquired a series of

symbolic meanings, to which, during the period that followed, fresh ones were continually being added" (p. 213). Rats, Freud said, are associated with anal eroticism. They are connected with dirt (feces, money), infection (venereal disease), and cruelty and sadism. Rats mean teeth and biting and cannibalism (the Rat Man felt that a rat was feeding off his father's corpse). There is a condensation of meanings from the oral sadistic and anal sadistic developmental phases. Most rat phenomena of the Rat Man (and of other rat people too) can be schematically conceived of in terms used by Fliess (1956): the erogeneity involved (where the bodily excitement is) is anal, but the libido is oral sadistic (the energy of the instinctual drives is seen as derived from the latter half of the oral developmental period and possessing certain qualities of it). The instinctual aim is destructive and ultimately cannibalistic; if turned against the self, the aim is to be destroyed and eaten, and anal erogeneity implies that the anal region is the site for destruction.

The rat was equated by the Rat Man with the penis, especially in relation to anal (anal sadistic) intercourse. Here phallic power is equated with cannibalistic penetration: the penis has teeth and can bite (for example, the rat was linked by the Rat Man with syphilis, which eats into the body). Not only is the rat as a phallic symbol destructive (as are such symbols as the knife, spear, club, and gun) in contrast to more benign phallic symbols such as the stick, necktie, umbrella, and balloon, but it is also specifically cannibalistic.

Like the penis (the little one) rats can represent children, but these are dirty, biting, raging children. As vermin, rats can symbolize unwanted siblings or unwanted children who evoke rage.[8] The law of talion applies to rats—if they bite, they can be bitten: "but rats cannot be sharp-toothed, greedy and dirty with

---

[8] As in *The Pied Piper of Hamelin* or in Ibsen's play *Little Eyolf.* Eyolf is an unwanted child, like Oedipus crippled by his parents' selfishness. He is covertly resented by both parents, regarded as a guilt-producing sibling rather than as their child. He bites at his parents' conscience like a rat, and is finally lured to his death by the Rat Wife, a mysterious old lady, the embodiment of death wishes toward unwanted creatures, who had introduced herself prophetically by asking, "I humbly beg pardon—but are your worships troubled with any gnawing things in your house . . . for it would be such a pleasure to me to rid your worships' house of them" (1894, p. 19). Many of the ambiguous meanings of the rat for the Rat Man can also be found in Ibsen's play.

impunity; they are cruelly persecuted and mercilessly put to death by men" (Freud, 1909, p. 216). If the rat equals the penis, destructivity toward the rat involves castration. If the rat equals the child, destructivity toward the rat involves child murder.

I want to underline the ubiquitous oral sadism and masochism in all these meanings that Freud and his patient attach to rats: rats bite into the anus; the rat-penis has teeth; rat-children bite and are bitten. The basic fantasy of castration is the biting off of the penis; intercourse is a biting into the cloaca.

The rat can represent subject or object, part-subject or part-object; that is, it can refer to oneself or to another, or to part of oneself or part of another. The Rat Man, "a nasty little wretch who was apt to bite people when he was in a rage" (p. 216), was also subject to the rat: he remembered being "fearfully punished" (p. 216) by his father at the age of 3 or 4 "because he had bitten someone" (p. 206), and this he had taken as a castration threat. The father, here playing the role of rat as persecutor, is in the fantasy of the adult Rat Man eventually eaten by a rat, in his grave. Father, mother,[9] and analyst can all be rats who bite and are bitten.

Implicit in Freud's clinical material and explicit in the rat torture is the association of overstimulation and rage with rats.

CLINICAL MATERIAL: PATIENTS' EXPERIENCES OF OVERSTIMULATION

The rat people discussed in this section suffered experiences of overstimulation when they were children that made them victims of soul murder. The traumas endured included sexual seduction by an adult (frequently a parent), often involving penetration or defloration; repeated, extensive exposure to adult exhibitionism, especially to the primal scene; and being beaten often and severely. These events had occurred at the beginning of the phallic phase of development or during it (ages 3 to 6). In these patients,

---

[9] "The real objects behind those imaginary terrifying figures (evoking cannibalism) are the child's own parents, and those dreadful shapes . . . reflect the features of its father and mother" (Klein, 1933, p. 268).

one has the sense of dealing with recurrent themes in their analytic and therapeutic associations irrespective of their diagnoses. These themes are sounded repeatedly by patient after patient.

Much of the patients' material (fantasies, dreams, phobias) involves a cannibalistic animal, frequently the rat. Unlike the Rat Man, most of these patients do not talk of mice and rats constantly. Rats appear in the material as derivative expressions of activated cannibalistic impulses, usually in relation to anal erogeneity. Some patients grind and gnash their teeth like rodents (often during sleep). The rat imago is both subject and object, with the ambiguity and multiplicity of meaning that can be seen in the case of the Rat Man; this involves both an identification with the rat as torturer and a relationship to the rat as victim.

Because of the compulsion to repeat, traumas in childhood lead to reenactments—usually with people not originally involved (Greenacre, 1960). As with other victims of soul murder, one finds that most frequently a really traumatic experience is avoided by identification with the aggressor, as the once passive and masochistic child now appears in the role of active sadist: rat-victim becomes rat-torturer. The terrifying wish for the passive role is great, and passivity is allowed under carefully controlled conditions, or in circumstances making for attenuation. The frightening passive wishes, usually involving anal erogeneity, come out strongly in the fairly safe repetition circumstances of the analysis, with the analyst appearing as the rat-torturer who is to be made into the rat-victim. The adult maintains the chronic state of overstimulation, partly by repeating the original traumas in conjunction with others, partly by continuing relations with the original, overstimulating soul murderer, and, most important, by identifying with the soul murderer.

The effects of the traumas, defenses, and fantasies, and the means the child took to try to deal with them, are also subject to the unconscious compulsion to repeat. For example, it would seem that a child subjected to repeated seduction by an adult cannot discharge the resulting state of chronic overstimulation, because most children are incapable of orgasm (Kramer, 1954). The child may faint (I have seen one patient, unfortunately insufficiently studied, who continued to do this into adult life), or attempt to obtain discharge by urinating or defecating. According to Fliess, urination is a regular method for releasing cannibalistic impulses (I have found this true for defecation, too). Ferenczi (1915) describes how urination can calm the distressed and frightened (that is, overstimulated) child, and says this may be because "it provides for the child a *sudden* relief" (p. 317; emphasis added).[10] Like all who have been overstimulated, like the victims of soul murder, these rat people are particularly afraid that nothing is going to happen—that they will be left in a state of terrible overexcitation. This makes the analytic requirement for frustration of action and gratification more difficult for them. For example, once a transference neurosis has been established, the analyst's vacation, which arouses feelings of being left, is often experienced as almost intolerable. Also, in life and in analytic transference, the unbearable feelings of overstimulation frequently lead to rage of a cannibalistic intensity.

Even after past traumas are brought out of repression by hard analytic work, the patient attempts to treat them as never having happened, and this denial is especially needed if the seduction or beating was at the hands of a parent. The great need not to know what has happened is often supplemented by a direct order from the seducer (the psychic murderer) not to tell about it. The not knowing is accomplished by massive isolation, transient ego splits ("She is naughty, I am good," said one nonpsychotic patient about herself),[11] and chronic autohypnotic states. Frequently a combination of these is present, with a resultant (partial) impairment of intellectual functioning that remains in part instinctualized (Keiser, 1962). The brainwashing that creates denial implies a compromised identity.

The stories of rat people again show that when the seducer or torturer is a parent, the child victim usually can seek rescue and the fulfillment of basic needs only from the person who has

---

[10] Often attacks on the child begin with a sudden change in the adult assaulter and end with equal suddenness. The child frequently fears and expects abrupt shifts in mood followed by a sudden onslaught. One musical patient broke into a cold sweat when hearing the words "And suddenly" in the *Messiah* of Handel or in Bach's *Christmas Oratorio*.

[11] These vertical ego splits are often denoted by the patient's switching from the first to the second or third person; this also involves defensive generalization. An example: "I felt very excited about the size of his penis. I said to myself, 'You are not interested in that. Only homosexuals are interested in penis size They get excited by other men's penises. One sometimes has thoughts like that, but they go away.' " In the course of his last four sentences, the patient's "I" also went away.

brought about the child's distress. This is poignantly presented in Orwell's *Nineteen Eighty-Four* when Winston Smith, tortured by rats, ends up loving Big Brother. In patients one finds a similar delusional insistence on the goodness of the destructive parent who is "loved." This is not only to deny the terrible experiences: the tormented, overstimulated child desperately needs a loving parent ("Who else would have buttered my bread?" was one patient's explanation of why she could never inform on her seducing mother). Most urgent is that loss of the parent leaves the child in danger of being pushed beyond the stimulus barrier toward ego dissolution; the loss of the parent is felt as unbearable.

Parents, especially if they have assaulted their children during acute psychotic episodes, are experienced as lost during the abusive attacks; they are transformed by their loss of emotional control. The patients often describe what happened in terms of a feral alteration ("Suddenly [again!] mother would become a wild beast"), usually into a cannibalistic creature (especially rat, wolf, or tiger; sphinx, witch, werewolf, or vampire). Many myths and stories about these creatures involve transformations. The good parent becomes a destructive, alien presence who does not recognize the child's identity or kinship; the child is treated as a need-fulfilling part-object, an extension of the parent's own body that can be discarded after use. The child denies loss of the good parent who must be there to make everything all right, and insists on the parent's goodness. A loving parent is desperately needed and must be fabricated by delusion. Like poor Winston Smith, the children can turn only to their tormentor for rescue: "[Winston Smith] opened his eyes and looked up gratefully at O'Brien. . . . He had never loved [O'Brien] so deeply as at this moment, and not merely because he had stopped the pain. . . . O'Brien had tortured him to the edge of lunacy, and in a little while, it as certain, he would send him to his death. It made no difference. In some sense that went deeper than friendship, they were intimates" (Orwell, 1948, p. 256).

The intimate relation of O'Brien to his victim is illuminated by a remark of Freud to Fliess about the confessions of those supposedly possessed by the devil that were extracted under torture during the Inquisition. He traced this back to their seduction as children by adults, by parents; the torture and torment, the leading questions of the inquisitor, and the compliant answers of the accused: "Thus victim and torturer alike recall their earliest youth" (Freud, 1887–1902, p. 188).

The presence of another, healthier parent, so important as a source of identification for the healthier aspects of the patient, does not help the child if (as is often the case) that parent either does not know or must deny what is going on with the soul-murdering spouse. The brainwashing that is produced by the child's denial of the overstimulating experiences easily develops into characterological lying (often most pronounced on an unconscious level, and involving lying to oneself). Lying makes easier the experiences that are repetitive of the traumas. Paradoxically, the insistent need for a protective parent becomes part of the motivation for repeating the traumatic events, in the delusional insistence that "this next time it won't be allowed to happen."

Soul murder means damage to the child's conscience: a severity evidenced by a strong, unconscious need for punishment coexists or alternates with an overpermissiveness that allows for psychopathological behavior in identification with the parent, who is frequently psychotic and usually (at least intermittently) psychopathic. If the seducer-torturer is not a parent, the effect is similar but diluted.[12] As in Freud's cases of the Rat Man and Wolf Man, one finds in the associations of these patients the regressive expression of oedipal conflicts in oral-sadistic terms. In addition to this, I emphasize the actual state of overstimulation and its characteristic rage—the experience of feeling passive and having active cannibalistic strivings.[13]

---

[12] See Klein (1948) on the effects of the superegos of children seduced by adults, and Simmel (1944) on the "multiple superegos" created in children seduced by parents, as seen in alcoholics.

[13] "The idea of being devoured by the father is typical age-old childhood material. It has familiar parallels in mythology (e.g., the myth of Kronos) and in the animal kingdom. Analytic observation shows that the idea of being devoured by the father gives expression, in a form that has undergone regressive degradation, to a passive, tender impulse to be loved by him in a genital erotic sense. Is it, moreover, a question merely of the replacement of the psychical representative by a regressive form of expression or is it a question of a genuine regressive degradation of the genitally-directed impulse in the id?" (Freud, 1926, p. 105). Freud felt that the latter description applies to the Wolf Man. I think it is also true of my patients whose fantasy life means regressing to the cannibalistic *experience* of overstimulation and fixating on it.

CLINICAL MATERIAL

Patient E

Over a few previous sessions E, a young male homosexual whose symptoms included a phobia of mice and rats, had fully remembered having been pressed against the genitals of his psychotic mother when he was a child, apparently while she had an orgasm. This had begun with the mother exposing herself to the 5-year-old boy, using her hands to open her vagina fully, so that the shock of castration was especially great. E began the next session as follows:

> I don't want to ferret around in the past today like yesterday. Ferret is a kind of rat, I think. You know I hate rats; once one fell into a wastebasket, and I had to call someone else to throw it out—as if I were a woman. Rats bite; I think of their teeth, as if one would bite into the base of my penis. Fur—one touch, and I can't stand it. They burrow. I think of the strawberry color of my mother's genitals; I think of rubbing against it, like against a rat's muzzle. . . . I can't stand it [the patient seems most anxious and writhes on the couch]—her spread white thighs—punish me! Fuck me to death!

This is said as the patient is working through the experience he has brought out of repression. The state of overstimulation is characteristic, although the terrible intensity has been brought out by the memory. E would go to an older homosexual who would slowly and discreetly stimulate E's genitals "for hours," teasing and tormenting him and keeping him from orgasm, which he would finally achieve, as he could not in childhood.

The cannibalistic animal is present. The rat stands for the maternal *vagina dentata* connected with the experience the patient has just remembered, and for the mother's penetrating finger that gave anal stimulation during other sexual assaults in childhood. The mother is and has the rat, and by way of primal scene observations is also subject to the rat, which stands for the invading father and his penis. E himself, despite his passive longings, usually played the role of the sadistic rat. He was characteristically sarcastic and coldly masterful toward the men he picked up and with whom he played the active role sexually. He was always seeking but never allowing himself to find a sadistic older man to "fuck him to death" anally. This meant simultaneously repeating the childhood experience with his mother and obtaining a castrative punishment by his father. He was most afraid of this destructive wish involving both parents, sensing (probably rightly) that it would bring on intimations of ego dissolution, and so he had always avoided the compelling but terrifying experience.

E was very intelligent, yet his intellectual functioning and identity were impaired by his inability to hold to a conviction for any length of time. Everything had to be made hypothetical in the service of denying and not knowing about the incestuous contact with his "good" mother. This effect of the soul murder was revealed in the analysis in the great difficulty and shame with which the patient told me of his oral-anal sexual activities. These intimacies, routine in his homosexual contacts (this was before the era of AIDS), evoked the greatest transference resistance as he began to fantasize about me. This was because of an even deeper repression resistance: the mother was the original object, and the past must not be remembered. He told me at this time of how without knowing why he did it he was wont to whisper into the ear of his dog, who came into his bed to lick his face in the morning, "We have a secret." He consciously identified with the dog, which seemed to him to represent predominantly an orally and anally excited child. At the same time he was literally repeating his mother's words from the past sexual scenes. Before his analysis he used to masturbate in the presence of the dog, not allowing himself to acknowledge fully that he wanted and was excited by the dog's looking on. He was thus repeating the past, but he could not know the past or consummate the knowledge of it. This confusion and contradiction spilled over into his working life, where he found it necessary to borrow the convictions of others; this was done "secretly"; that is, without any acknowledgment to his "leader," whom often he would later let down and betray.

One aspect of E's intellectual malfunctioning was that he had trouble reading "good" books, although he could easily read mystery stories, popular novels, and especially magazines and

newspapers; I have found this to be characteristic of reading difficulties in such patients. "Good" books seem particularly
charged (as symbols) with incestuous meaning. E as an adolescent
frequently had erections when reading in public libraries—he
associated the open book with his mother's spread thighs. He
said, "I have difficulty only when I really respect what I'm reading
and want to know and remember what I have read." He would
usually read the beginning and then the end of a worthwhile
book, but not the middle, revealing the castration anxiety he felt
when dealing with his mother in this symbolic and allusive form
that repeated past experiences. Another patient (also a rat person) found himself completely unable to read the hardcover edition of a classic novel that had been assigned in a college course.
He had no trouble when he found a used, underlined (that is,
dirty) paperback edition of the book. As might be guessed, he
suffered from a compulsion to split his affection and sexuality in
what is often called the madonna–whore complex.

Patient F

A young woman had been repeatedly overstimulated sexually as
a child by her mother. Under the pretext of guarding against or
treating a supposed infection in the child, the mother would
regularly "clean out" the girl's vagina. This was but the most
frequent of many seductive contacts. The rather gentle rubbing
the mother performed was not described as frightening or cruel;
it became cannibalistic and expressible in rat imagery because of
the teasing, mounting excitement that evoked an unbearable
need for discharge—a need the child could not fulfill. Although
children (particularly girls) may be capable of some kind of orgastic experiences, these do not appear to effect an adequate discharge of the overstimulation evoked in prepubescents by an
adult's sexual excitement and seductive contact.
    During the session preceding the one I will deal with at
length, F had told me of her feeling of revulsion on seeing "a
swollen, foul-smelling rat." She had seen it when in the company
of a person she characterized as "looking like a vampire," with
teeth that "gleam like a rodent's." She continued: "I feel as if *I*

am rotten and swollen somehow, with vaginal and rectal odors—as if I were that rat."

In the waiting room before the next session, F had a fantasy of performing fellatio on the analyst: "I pictured it, but I had no real sexual feeling about it." This showed her characteristic isolation of affect, which she maintained in part by autohypnotic states. "I felt like sinking into a trance,'' she said, and then reported this dream: "Our positions were reversed. I was sitting and you were lying down. As you talked, I turned into a sphinx. I couldn't control my mouth. It kept opening and closing, like a lion's." Associations led to a telephone conversation that she had had with her mother before going to sleep the preceding night. She had been "ferociously angry" with her mother and felt like telling her she never wanted to see her again (that is, she wanted to lose control of her mouth and do something destructive with it). She had not told her mother anything of the kind, realizing that it was not true that she did not want to see her and sensing that she really wanted to provoke her mother to a retaliatory verbal attack (to bite her back). I interpreted, "That would have intensified things, while it would have appeared, falsely, that you wanted to be rid of her." F agreed. The falseness consisted of her fooling herself—a kind of dishonesty that had made her unaware that her consistent rebelliousness was a disguise for the symbiotic relationship with her mother.

When F was dreaming, she had felt like ripping and tearing with her teeth, and in the session now began to feel this way again (the autohypnosis was lifting). "I feel my mouth; it is the only part of me that feels fully alive"—the oral excitement was being experienced. I interpreted that her fantasy in the waiting room of fellatio was apparently connected with an impulse to bite my penis. "Yes, I have a feeling as if my two front upper teeth were very large and were stiffening my upper lip, making it immobile, *like a rodent's.*" Here F had become the rat. Then she commented on a noise in the room: "It sounds as if you are moving in your chair. I feel as if you are writhing." Then, after a pause: "*You* said writhing," and she realized she had made a slip of the tongue—she had meant to say, "*I* said writhing." (The slip of the tongue is a "doing something wrong with the mouth"; see Yazmajian [1966]). I responded that it was she who had the desire

to writhe and that twice, directly and in the slip, she had tried to
attribute it to me (the dream had reversed historical roles and
made me, the parent figure, the object of a cannibalistic attack).
The interpretation seemed valid—F started to feel her overexcite-
ment. She went on to tell me about her sadistic sexual teasing;
making men writhe, or trying to. The reversal of roles in the
dream represents F's characteristic attempt to become the Sphinx
(devouring, bisexual) or an oral-sadistic castrative animal like the
rat. In the dream the analyst is the victim. F's overstimulated state,
evaded at the beginning of the session by hypnosis, came out as
she associated to the dream, so that finally she was able to become
aware that it was she who felt like writhing. As the feelings began
to flow, there was as usual a reciprocal lifting of the hypnotic
defensive state.

As a child, F had repeatedly teased male dogs. She was taking
the role of the overstimulating adult who whether man or woman
is always endowed with a penetrative, cannibalistic phallus. She
would stroke the dog's penis to erection, but, if she could not
help it, not enough to let him ejaculate. She would also get the
dog excited by letting him sniff her genital area (and sometimes
lick it, paralleling the mother's "cleaning her out"). She was
especially gratified if the dog would get so excited by the smelling
that he would ejaculate onto the floor, without his penis being
touched. Making the male ejaculate with a humiliating loss of
control meant conquering and castrating him. As an adult, F repeated the performance with susceptible men.[14] Sensing the nature of her excitement, one man asked her early in his
relationship with her, "Do you want me to tease you?" She complained of him: "He touches [my clitoris] and lets me subside,
not letting me quite reach climax. It goes on and on, so I feel

---

[14] Three of the patients discussed in this book, one man and two women, had fantasies
of a man ejaculating without being touched, having been overstimulated by teasing. The
male patient would carry out the passive role in his fantasy while "masturbating" by lying
on his back and, without touching it, pushing his penis up "against the air" (see chapter
8). Among its other meanings were those of anal movement and sensation, and an unconscious identification with the passive, feminine position—paralleling the role that this
woman patient (F) assigned to her victim-dog (an anal creature). The male patient was
also unable to bear the stimulation and usually had to ejaculate by using his hand vigor-
ously. Thus the passive role seemed to predominate up to a point, then the active—although there was throughout a split that enabled him to impersonate both partners in
fantasied anal intercourse (the air was associated to farting).

tortured for want of satisfaction." But predominantly it was F, a present-day version of Mirbeau's Clara, who teased in many ways, all leaving the man in a state of overexcitation. She almost always had an orgasm, or at least sadistic satisfaction, but seldom allowed her partner to climax, or made him, like the dog, ejaculate onto the floor without having his penis touched. She would also tease him by "lightly touching and rubbing" his penis, again preventing him from coming to orgasm, like the dogs from her childhood. She had fantasies of "tormenting men sexually to the point of unbearable sensations—so that the man would go into an *arc de cercle* with the torment."

AUTOHYPNOSIS

In addition to F's portrayal in her dream of the analyst as the victim of a cannibalistic attack that was revealed in her associations, she assigned to him a contrasting role of causing her to change into a sphinx under his hypnotic control. I quote from the dream as F wrote it out after the session: "I was watching and listening to you. You were saying, among other things, that I was a sphinx. As you spoke I became conscious of my arms which projected from my shoulders like the forelegs of a lion . . . [there was] a growing feeling that my arms had paws and claws. As you continued speaking the feeling of being a maneating animal grew . . . I felt that your voice was bringing out my true nature and activity. I felt like biting." Here the analyst became the overstimulating parent, making the patient into a ferocious, maneating animal by arousing the rage of overstimulation. The session had begun with F's feeling she was "in a trance"; she was in a state of autohypnosis characteristically used to evade her sexual excitement.[15]

One of F's associations to the sphinx was Baudelaire's poem *La Beauté*, in which beauty is personified as a stone sphinx: "I reign in the azure like a sphinx beyond all understanding (*Je trone*

---

[15] Most of the patients cited in this chapter are subject to autohypnotic states; I believe that if I had known about hypnotic defense at the beginning of my practice I would have found it in all of them. I think it is a universal human defense phenomenon, but its frequency of use, depth, and pervasiveness are greater in victims of soul murder.

dans L'axur comme un sphinx incompris) against which poets hurl
and bruise themselves." It is to these poets that the sphinxlike
Beauty refers when she says, "to hypnotize my enslaved lovers"
(*pour fasciner mes dociles amants*). F's love affairs involved a continual kind of playacting intended to fascinate and hypnotize her
lovers, most of them masochistic. Being subject to autohypnotic
states was characteristic; this had become clear in the course of
her analysis. Hypnosis was used not only as a defense to deal with
the erogeneity, excitement, and rage involved in her predominantly sadomasochistic fantasies, but also to bring about in attenuation repetitions of the past traumas. She could do with others
and to others what had previously been done to her, and in addition to the defense of identifying with the past aggressor could
more successfully evade the approach to overstimulation by using
autohypnosis. The defensive use of hypnosis seems most important, but hypnosis can also provide gratification without responsibility in service of the compulsion to repeat past traumatic
experiences; this prompts me to use the term *hypnotic facilitation*
to complement what Fliess calls hypnotic evasion—the pair constituting a kind of symptomatic state.

At another time, F remarked that before going to bed she
"was so sexually excited I was beside myself." (I omit material
that shows the anal erogeneity aroused, except to report that she
was afraid she would lose control and soil the sheets.) She
dreamed that a favorite dog from childhood had been caught by
a frightening, evil man, who "demanded that my dog submit to
an immediate rape by members of his family and held him immobile and exposed—as though they might even take him sexually
while he was being held . . . at this point, my ability to see what
was happening disappeared, and I understood that the dog was
partially or wholly eaten by the family."

While telling the last part of this dream of impatient sexual
urgency, F said that she felt "great relief at the speed and completeness with which the dog's suffering was ended." Before this,
during the narration of most of the dream, she had felt as if she
would "lose control and urinate in a broad stream the entire
contents of my body." This represented an attempt to pass off
the overstimulation involved in the rape scene, this time by urination. The wish-fear was for an explosive discharge that is really

cloacal—the discharge would end an unbearable forepleasure. At the same time such a discharge involves the terrifying feeling of losing sphincter control, and its incipient evocation of ego dissolution (Shengold [1988]; F had also been subjected to traumatic enemas as a child). The feeling of relief about "the speed and completeness with which the dog's suffering was ended" refers not only to the need for discharge but to F's penis envy, which for her was definitely colored by a cannibalistic impulse (biting off the penis).

Both male and female children who have been overstimulated tend to see the adult penis as an organ that can effectively discharge cannibalistic overexcitation and can bite. The mothers in these cases seem always to be predominantly phallic mothers for the children—mothers who have or who have stolen the paternal penis. These patients frequently have fantasies of *penis dentatus* as well as of *vagina dentata*. F identified with the phallic adult who can have orgasm, or tried to, with her body as a phallus. The wish for an explosive discharge that can relieve the painful tension and destroy the object also means the possibility of ego dissolution (emptying out "the whole body contents") and must of course be defended against. The wish lives on, in nonpsychotic patients, through introversion in their fantasies, and in some instances these explosive fantasies are enacted in attenuation, or under carefully controlled conditions.

EGO REGRESSION AND EGO SPLITS IN RAT PEOPLE

Freud used the case of the Rat Man to describe the dynamic antecedents and the symptoms and defenses of obsessive-compulsive neurosis. I have stressed the intensity and massiveness of the isolating defenses used by people who were subjected to soul murder—defenses needed to split off and contain their traumatic, overstimulating experiences. In the case of the Rat Man, Freud described two kinds of isolation. There is disconnection between idea and idea, which is one mechanism that can bring about the more defensively fundamental disconnection between thought and affect. "Repression is effected not by means of amnesia but by a severance of causal connexions brought about by a withdrawal of affect that appears to persist in some kind of shadowy form . . . and they are thus transferred, in a process of projection, into the external world, where they bear witness to what has been effaced from consciousness" (1909, pp. 231–232; emphasis added).

The disconnection between thoughts can also be accomplished by "inserting a time interval" between them (Freud, 1909, p. 246). Where such isolation is massive and intense, as with the victims of soul murder I am calling rat people, vertical splits occur in the mental apparatus, making possible those mental processes that Orwell calls doublethink (and his definition includes the use of autohypnosis). Doublethink was conditioned, in part, by the use of rat-torture, onto the victim and hero of *Nineteen Eighty-Four*. Freud says that the Rat Man "went on to say that he would like to speak of a criminal act, whose author he did not recognize as himself, though he quite clearly recollected committing it." The Rat Man then paraphrased to Freud the saying of Nietzsche quoted above: " 'I did this,' says my Memory. 'I cannot have done this,' says my Pride and remains inexorable. In the end—Memory yields' " (Freud, 1901, p. 184). But for the Rat Man, "yielding" still leaves the memory in the "shadowy" form described by Freud, and he goes on to relate this to Freud. The shadowy memories make for two kinds of knowing: "For he knows [things] in that he has not forgotten them, but he does not know them in that he is unaware of their significance" (1909, p. 196).

The result of this is an "as if" knowing, and for some people this can involve an as if part of their personality—small, considerable, or as one woman remarked, "but I really can't feel it." Freud describes this in a way that shows the centrality of feelings for "owning" one's convictions and characteristics. (For me this implies the crucial clinical and human importance of some theoretical concept of drive energy—what Freud called economic considerations—that is implicit in our emotions.) "[The Rat Man] could not help believing in the premonitory power of dreams, for he had several remarkable experiences to prove it. Consciously he does not really believe in it (the two views exist side by side, *but the critical one is sterile*)" (1909, p. 268; emphasis added). Freud gives another example in his early work *Studies on Hysteria* (Breuer and Freud, 1893–1895), quoting the following dialogue between himself and his patient Miss Lucy R. Freud has asked about her relationship with her employer—he knew that an unconscious incestuous attachment was involved, though she did not.

[Freud:] But if you knew you loved your employer, why didn't you tell me?
[Lucy R:] I didn't know—or rather I wanted to drive it out of my mind and not think of it again, and latterly I believed I had succeeded [p. 117].

In a footnote apparently written somewhat later, Freud adds, "I have never managed to give a better description than this of *the strange state of mind* in which one knows and does not know of a thing at the same time. It is clearly impossible to understand it unless one has been in such a state oneself" (1893–1895, p. 117; emphasis added). The "strange state of mind" is for me an alteration of consciousness. This predominantly defensive autohypnosis is universally used (we have all "been in such a state" ourselves) and is such a striking feature of those who have had to ward off soul murder.

Freud goes on to tell about the "very remarkable experience of this sort" that he himself had once had (p. 117), ending with a memorable metaphoric phrase appropriate to the future discoverer of the Oedipus complex, to Oedipus himself, and to everyone: "I was afflicted by that *blindness of the seeing eye* which is so astonishing in the attitude of mothers to their daughters, husbands to their wives and rulers to their favourites" (p. 117; emphasis added). For Freud, this was an occasional, exceptional experience, but for the victim of soul murder and for rat people it represents a kind of thinking that can dominate their mind and their world—as it does in *Nineteen Eighty-Four*, where doublethink is aimed at abolishing the *memories* of the past.

By means of isolation and autohypnosis, vertical splits of the ego take place. A major one is inherent in the intense isolation of affect—the split between the cognitive and the experiencing ego (Shuren [1967]; Shuren's formulation is based on clinical material similar to mine). A functioning of the ego necessary for the subjective feeling of identity, the ability to feel what is there to be felt,[16] is disrupted by this split; the personality is compartmentalized in a vertical split of the ego (like the Rat Man's), usually not completely but in a partial and "shadowy" fashion (mentioned by Freud). It is "as if" there are provisional and alternating personas that can take over with slight alterations of consciousness. Freud twice describes the compartmentalization in the Rat Man. In the published case history he notes his

> [I]mpression that [the Rat Man] had, as it were, disintegrated into three personalities: into one unconscious personality, that is to say, and into two preconscious ones between which his consciousness could oscillate. His unconscious comprised those of his impulses which had been suppressed at an early age and which might be described as passionate and evil impulses. In his normal state he was kind, cheerful and sensible—an enlightened and superior kind of person—while in his third *psychological organization* he paid homage to superstition and asceticism. Thus he was able to have two different creeds and two different outlooks upon life [1909, p. 248; emphasis added].

This is more succinctly put, without the "topographical" explanation, in the case record not meant for publication: "He is made up of three personalities—one humourous and normal, another ascetic and religious and a third immoral and perverse" (p. 278). In my patients' "hypnoid states," alterations of consciousness, and autohypnosis keep separate these "psychological organizations," between which these people can shift. This disrupts the consummation of feeling what there is there to be felt (preconsciously) that is ordinarily taken for granted. For example, a patient says: "I know that I hate you and I want to bite off your penis but that part of me is wrapped in cellophane." When the patient is fully "awake" (the hypnotic wrapping dissolved), these feelings can be acknowledged: the patient can know experientially that she hates. When analysis works for such people, the

---

[16] The complete absence of the split is seen in Walt Whitman's well-known affirmation of identity when one takes his statements in reverse order: "I am the Man; I suffered; I was there" (1855, p. 76).

autohypnotic symptomatology is given up, and the synthetic function of an ego really able to know and own feelings is free to blend the disparate "personalities" and contradictory trends.

TEETH AND TEETHING

I have presented the rat as a psychological image that derives much of its emotional power from being the carrier of the tooth: the rat as biter. There is much folklore connecting rats, mice, and teeth. As will be seen, these rodents are portrayed as having a special relationship to the losing of teeth. I mention this here to underline the impact of the rodent's amazing teeth on human psychology, where these teeth figure as an element in the external world that is used to express what is going on in the individual's mind and body. The teeth have acquired a symbolic significance in the Freudian sense: become a part of our cultural inheritance (and as Freud would have us add, our phylogenetic inheritance).

In describing the second oral state of libido development, Abraham (1924) points out that the development of the teeth coincides with an influx of sadism:

Undoubtedly the teeth are the first instruments with which the child can do damage to the outer world. For they are already effective at a time when the hands can at most only assist their activity by seizing and keeping hold of the object . . . the teeth are the only organs [small children] possess that are sufficiently hard to be able to injure objects around them. One has only to look at children to see how intense the impulse to bite is. This is the stage in which the cannibalistic impulses predominate [p. 451].[17]

Abraham quotes a comment of van Ophuijsen, who believes "that certain neurotic phenomena are due to a regression to the age when teeth were being formed" (1924, p. 451). Despite much that has been written on biting and oral sadism, the phenomenon

---

[17] Painful teething usually takes place between the ages of 6 and 18 months. This fits in with Abraham's timing. Teething accompanies all the stages of libido development, however; the last baby teeth to come in, the second molars, usually erupt in the first half of the third year. The permanent teeth begin to come in when the child is about 6 (Spock, 1957).

of teething has since been strangely neglected in psychoanalytic literature. An exception is an article of Kucera (1959), which points out that pleasure in sucking is interfered with by teething, and that this intensifies the sadistic effect on the infant of the coming in of the teeth. Kucera notes further that the *"experience* which is regularly provoked during teeth eruption can be looked upon as the key situation for the origin of primary masochism, as its physiological organic foundation" (p. 289; emphasis added). Without going into the moot question of the origin of primary masochism, I will deal with the *experience* of teething, and its experiential link with aggressive phenomena.

As the teeth painfully force their way through the mucosa of the gum, infants can be said to bite themselves (and experience being bitten) before they can bite anything or anyone else; this occurs both during and of course after the eruption of the tooth. Tooth eruption produces the experience of being simultaneously the subject and object of biting for the owner of the tooth and surrounding mucosa. One cannot of course empathize with the infant, for the ego at the initial time of teething is in a rudimentary state, with incomplete differentiation of subject and object, of inside and outside. As part of the development of body ego and ego, this differentiation is taking place during the time of teething, which corresponds in our theory to the oral-sadistic phase of libido development. During this phase the infant has to deal with an instinctual access of aggression, which must be modified by libido, and of primal affects (see Fliess, 1956; Shengold, 1988). To deal with the frustration of need satisfaction and with overstimulation, a loving mother is needed to counteract the danger of a breakthrough of the stimulus barrier at the time the aggressive instinct is burgeoning (Hoffer, 1950; Mahler, 1952). Active discharge of the aggressive drive takes place by way of the teeth and the body musculature—by biting and eventually by locomotion. Passive oral masochism is also experienced in the body (registering therefore in the forming body ego that is fundamental to the psychic ego), in part by way of the teeth and their adjacent mucosa. The phylogenetic significance of the teeth and the teething experience is probably much greater than the ontogenetic. A look at animal life with evolution in mind, or at what Tennyson calls "nature red in tooth and claw," certainly suggests this. (The continuously teething rat may also epitomize a primal, common ancestor for man.) I do not know that children have been sufficiently "observed" teething. The change of what has hitherto been predominantly a pleasure-giving erogenous zone to a source of tension and unpleasure, at a time when the ego is beginning to coalesce, may be very significant. Perhaps we have avoided its significance because of primal anxieties and concomitant resistances.

CANNIBALISTIC WISHES, INFANTILE EXPERIENCES, AND TEETHING

Teething might furnish an ontogenetic root for the subjective reality of the cannibalistic act. The existence of the act is questioned by Fliess (1956), who says that the second oral phase is the only phase of libido development when direct instinctual gratification is denied. Although children do not discharge their oral impulses by eating flesh from the breast, they do bite themselves when they are teething, and the breast when they have teeth. Most analysts would agree that autocannibalism stems from the time when the mother's breast is still regarded as part of the body ego of the child—a time when "The breast is a part of me—I am the breast" (Freud, 1938, p. 299). Lewin (1950) pointed out that the infant's wish to be devoured is not based on direct infant observation but is "a heuristic fiction . . . a construction based on inference" (p. 104). Klein (1933) asserted that the fear of being eaten is experienced during the first year of life, and that this is due to the projection of active oral-sadistic wishes onto the parent. Simmel (1944) spoke of cannibalistic fears and wishes as associated with the infant's identification with food. The food that is incorporated becomes a part of the baby's ego, and the baby might be considered as eating itself. About the baby at the breast during this period, alternately chewing at its fingers and toes, "one may say, with license, that it indulges thereby in an act of autocannibalism" (Lewin, 1950, p. 107). I would ask the same license for my formulation that teething involves autocannibalism; it supplements rather than supplants the other constructions.

TEETHING AS A PHYSIOLOGICAL PROTOTYPE OF PROJECTION

Teething also provides an experience of discharge of painful tension in the infant's first year (with an experiencing ego present):

Fell sorrow's tooth doth never rankle more
Than when it bites but lanceth not the sore
[*Richard II*, Act 1, scene 3, lines 301–302].

But when the tooth actually breaks through the mucosa of the gum, tension is discharged and the sore is lanced.[18] Perhaps this experience conditions some of the fantasies of explosive cannibalistic penetration, passive and active, that one finds in patients who have undergone experiences of overstimulation, and who compulsively and repetitively crave a discharge of tension, as if they were addicts. They seek out any kind of destructive penetration as a means of getting rid of the overstimulation. (One recalls the patient who wanted to be "fucked to death" to discharge his terrible, overstimulated state.)

After tooth eruption, the infant can bite others as well as bite itself. Aggression can be turned outward and also projected onto the environment, so that a tension felt within becomes "outside" and "other." The eruption of the tooth is a physiological prototype, especially meaningful for what starts out as a body ego, like a material projection onto the environment. When the psychic capacity for projection becomes possible, not only can the tooth be used against others, but others can be endowed with it by the mind. Freud (1920) said of internal stimuli (like the drive representatives of oral masochism): "There is a tendency to treat them as though they were acting, not from the inside, but from the outside, so that it may be possible to bring the shield against stimuli into operation as a means of defence against them. This is the origin of projection" (p. 29). The eruption of the teeth

---

[18] There is at least one instance in literature in which rats deliver the victim from a traumatic and unendurable situation (that is, they discharge tension): rats bite through the ropes to release the prisoner in Poe's story *The Pit and the Pendulum*. I am grateful to Mark Kanzer for pointing this out.

may make for an experiential impetus for this early defensive operation.

TEETH AND CASTRATION ANXIETY

There is much in the psychoanalytic literature about teeth and the phallic phase of libido development—for example, tooth dreams interpreted as referring to masturbation (Freud, 1900). These tooth phenomena usually involve the falling out of the teeth rather than their eruption, and invoke castration anxiety. I believe it is also because the teeth can connote the terrors of oral destruction as well that they can evoke the "surprise . . . [of] strong resistance" pointed out by Freud (1900, p. 385). Freud is referring mainly to castration anxiety. The developmentally earlier danger situations that give rise to preoedipal anxiety are connected with the tooth experience that precedes the falling out of teeth: the biting and being bitten associated with tooth eruption. The two levels of anxiety can of course coalesce: Fliess (1956) wondered whether castration is not at its most frightening level conceived of as effected through biting.

The phenomena related to teething have also been surrounded by a surprisingly "strong resistance," and not only by psychoanalysts whose very few contributions I have already mentioned. The fact of physiologically painful teething, familiar to any parent, had been minimized and even denied by generations of dentists and pediatricians (Kucera, 1959).

THE OBJECT ENDOWED WITH A TOOTH

Fliess (1956) has pointed out how oral-sadistic libido is regularly discharged in subsequent stages of libido development in situations both normal and pathological, so that an erogenic zone can be infused with cannibalistic libido. Any combination of a sudden access of defused aggression and ego regression involves an impending loss of control of the instinctual access, and means a return to traumatic, passive, cannibalistic terror if it goes far enough. In relation to the anal stage, for example, the Rat Man's terror concerns the rat biting its way into his body through his anus. (This threatens to undo the power of the anal sphincter, so much needed for the anal defensive foundation of feelings of control; see Shengold [1988].) I have reviewed the many meanings of the rat for the Rat Man: the animal is above all the carrier of the tooth and thereby gains its full terrifying power. This is illustrated by Abraham (1922) in his explication of another symbol that can be endowed with a tooth, the spider. Abraham implicitly stratifies the symbolic meanings of the spider, with each added statement bringing in more terrifying connotations. The spider symbolizes the destructive phallic mother. It also symbolizes her destructive phallus, which can castrate. Abraham quotes Nunberg, who says that the spider sucks blood, and finally Freud, who adds that some female spiders devour their mates after sex: they eat cannibalistically and so castrate by biting. The symbol for the phallic mother becomes terrifying when the phallus is endowed with teeth that can castrate and devour.

The tooth equips, accompanies, and is the prototype for penetrative, devouring objects at any stage of libidinal development, and in relation to any erogenic body zone that discharges oral-sadistic libido. Differentiated objects that can be tooth carriers include: the penetrative, castrating phallus of the parent (father or phallic mother) and the fecal mass of the second anal stage that is clearly "not-me." The fecal stick that is simultaneously me and not-me and the breast-mouth are the earlier, not completely differentiated subject-objects that can be charged with cannibalistic libido. So both subject and object, self and other, can be equipped with teeth. The fantasies can take many forms, involving erogenous zones that are part object and part subject: breast with teeth, vagina dentata, *rectum dentatum, urethra dentata* (Keiser, 1954), phallus equipped with a mouth (Fliess, 1956). "The mouth of this [second oral] stage is transferable on to all subsequent dominant erogenic zones" (Fliess, 1956, p. 86). Subject, object, and erogenous zone can all be represented by cannibalistic creatures like the rat, which will appear in analysis in the associations of patients who have had traumatic overstimulating experiences, who have been subject to attempts of soul murder.

MATERIAL FROM MYTHS AND FOLKLORE ILLUSTRATING THE ENDOWMENT OF OBJECTS WITH A TOOTH

Many myths show the connections among the teeth, the projection of cannibalistic aggression, and mice and rats.

> Thus in many parts of the world it is customary to put extracted teeth in some place where they will be found by a mouse or a rat, in the hope that through the sympathy which continues to exist between them and their former owner, his other teeth may acquire the same firmness and excellence as the teeth of these rodents. In Germany it is said to be almost a universal maxim that when you have a tooth taken out, you should insert it in a mouse's hole. To do so with a child's milk tooth . . . will prevent the child from having toothache [Frazer, 1890, pp. 31–32].

Lewis (1958) quotes folklore about mice and rats and the loss of teeth from Russians, Germans, Costa Ricas, Oceanians, and Polish Jews; Frazer has examples from Jews, Germans, Sinhalese, and Americans.

In this folklore the tooth is projected upon the rodent (literally), as in earlier development aggression is projected upon the mother to form the bad mother and bad "not-me." To put it genetically, the breast is endowed with teeth: this is the basic meaning of the rat (into whose hole the lost tooth is to be inserted). The bad, toothed breast is a projected part of the self at first, invested with narcissistic libido—part-self, part-object. After the establishment of object relations and a sense of the self, the danger of being eaten and the sources of overstimulation are felt clearly as coming from outside. This is eventually evidenced by the castration fear of the oedipal period; expressed and disguised in regressive terms, this fear has an important role in these myths about losing teeth. The parent will not castrate the child if the child loses the penetrative tooth that can symbolize the penis, or has it knocked out (as in puberty initiation rites). At a more regressive level, these myths are about refraining from biting to avoid being bitten: the rat has the tooth, not I.

REFERENCES

Abraham, K. (1922), The spider as dream symbol. In: *Selected Papers.* London: Hogarth Press, 1949, pp. 326–332.

—— (1924), The influence of oral erotism on character formation. In: *Selected Papers.* London: Hogarth Press, pp. 393–406.

Barker, W. (1951), *Familiar Animals of America.* New York: Harper.

Baudelaire, C. (1861), La Beauté. In: *Poems,* ed. F. Scarfe. Baltimore: Penguin, 1961.

Breuer, J., & Freud, S. (1893–1895), Studies on Hysteria. *Standard Edition,* 2. London: Hogarth Press, 1955.

Encyclopedia Britannica, 14th ed., s.v. "Rat."

Ferenczi, S. (1915), Micturition as a sedative. In: *Further Contributions to the Theory and Technique of Psychoanalysis.* New York: Basic Books, 1952, p. 317.

Fliess, R. (1956), *Erogeneity and Libido.* New York: International Universities Press.

Frazer, J. G. (1890), *The New Golden Bough,* ed. T. Gaster. New York: Criterion, 1959.

Freud, S. (1887–1902), *The Origins of Psychoanalysis: Letters, Drafts and Notes to Wilhelm Fliess.* New York: Basic Books, 1954.

—— (1900), The Interpretation of Dreams. *Standard Edition,* 4&5. London: Hogarth Press, 1953.

—— (1901), The Psychopathology of Everyday Life. *Standard Edition,* 6. London: Hogarth Press, 1960.

—— (1909), Notes upon a case of obsessional neurosis. *Standard Edition,* 10:151–244. London: Hogarth Press, 1955.

—— (1920), Beyond the Pleasure Principle. *Standard Edition,* 18:1–64. London: Hogarth Press, 1955.

—— (1926), Inhibitions, Symptoms and Anxiety. *Standard Edition,* 20:75–172. London: Hogarth Press, 1959.

—— (1938), Findings, ideas, problems. *Standard Edition,* 23:299–300. London: Hogarth Press, 1964.

Greenacre, P. (1960), Regression and fixation. *J. Amer. Psychoanal. Assn.,* 8:703–823.

Hegner, R. (1942), *A Parade of Familiar Animals.* New York: Macmillan.

Hoffer, W. (1950), Oral aggressiveness and ego development. *Internat. J. Psycho-Anal.,* 31:156–160.

Ibsen, H. (1894), Little Eyolf, tr. W. Archer. In: *Last Plays of Henrik Ibsen.* New York: Bantam, 1962, pp. 1–70.

Kanzer, M. (1952), The transference neurosis of the Rat Man. *Psychoanal. Quart.,* 21:181–189.

Keiser, S. (1954), Orality displaced to the urethra. *J. Amer. Psychoanal. Assn.*, 2:263–279.

——— (1962), Disturbances of ego function of speech and abstract thinking. *J. Amer. Psychoanal. Assn.*, 10:50–73.

Klein, M. (1933), Early development of the conscience in the child. In: *Contributions to Psycho-Analysis*. London: Hogarth Press, pp. 267–278.

——— (1948), A contribution to the theory of anxiety and guilt. *Internat. J. Psycho-Anal.*, 29:113–123.

Kramer, P. (1954), Early capacity for orgastic discharge and character formation. *The Psychoanalytic Study of the Child*, 9:128–141. New York: International Universities Press.

Kucera, O. (1959), On teething. *J. Amer. Psychoanal. Assn.*, 7:284–291.

Lamb, C. (1799), Letter to Robert Southey. In: *The Selected Letters of Charles Lamb*, ed. T. S. Matthews. New York: Farrar, Straus & Cudahy, 1956, pp. 40–42.

Lewin, B. (1950), *The Psychoanalysis of Elation*. New York: W. W. Norton.

Lewis, H. (1958), The effect of shedding the first deciduous tooth upon the passing of the Oedipus complex. *J. Amer. Psychoanal. Assn.*, 6:5–37.

Lorenz, K. (1963), *On Aggression*. New York: Harcourt, Brace.

Mahler, M. S. (1952), On child psychosis and schizophrenia. *The Psychoanalytic Study of the Child*, 7:286–303. New York: International Universities Press.

Mills, R. (1959), *Rats: Let's Get Rid of Them*. U.S. Dept. of the Interior, circular no. 22. Washington, DC: U.S. Government Printing Office.

Mirbeau, O. (1899), *Torture Garden*. New York: Citadel, 1948.

Orwell, G. (1948), Letter to Julian Symons. In: *The Collected Essays, Journalism and Letters of George Orwell*, Vol. 4, ed. S. Orwell & I. Angus. New York: Harcourt, Brace & World, 1968, pp. 415–417.

——— (1949), *Nineteen Eighty-Four*. New York: Harcourt, Brace.

Protheroe, E. (1940), *New Illustrated Natural History of the World*. New York: Garden City Press.

Schour, I., & Masser, M. (1949), The teeth. In: *The Rat in Laboratory Investigation*, ed. E. J. Farris & J. Q. Griffith. Philadelphia: J. B. Lippincott, pp. 104–160.

Shakespeare, W. (1593), Richard II. In: *The Oxford Shakespeare*, ed. W. J. Craig. New York: Oxford University Press, pp. 437–469.

Shengold, L. (1985), Defensive anality and anal narcissism. *Internat. J. Psycho-Anal.*, 66:47–73.

——— (1988), *Halo in the Sky*. New York: Guilford Press.

——— (1989), *Soul Murder: The Effects of Childhood Abuse and Deprivation*. New Haven, CT: Yale University Press.

Shuren, I. (1967), A contribution to the metapsychology of the preanalytic patient. *The Psychoanalytic Study of the Child,* 22:103–138. New York: International Universities Press.

Simmel, E. (1944), Self preservation and the death instinct. *Psychoanal. Quart.,* 13:160–185.

Spock, B. (1957), *Baby and Child Care.* New York: Duell, Sloan.

Whitman, W. (1855), *Leaves of Grass.* New York: Modern Library, 1921.

Wilson, E. (1950), In memory of Octave Mirbeau. In: *Classics and Commercials.* New York: Farrar, Straus, pp. 471–485.

Yazmajian, R. (1966), Verbal and symbolic processes in slips of the tongue. *J. Amer. Psychoanal. Assn.,* 14:443–461.

Zinsser, H. (1935), *Rats, Lice and History.* New York: Little, Brown.

CHAPTER 3

Horses and Horsewomen

JOHN E. SCHOWALTER, M.D.

Man has always been fascinated by the creatures around him. In the animistic and pantheistic religions all life is seen as a unity, although in the Hebraic creation only man is made in God's image. The domestication of animals for social reasons is very ancient, and there is archaeological evidence of pre-Neolithic, Mesolithic peoples living with dogs (Zeuner, 1963). At present, more than 50 percent of families in the United States have pets.

There is an early psychoanalytic literature on the uses and intrapsychic meanings of animals, but then interest waned until recently when there has been an upsurge of medical, psychiatric, and psychoanalytic research on the impact of animals on humans.

In the psychoanalytic literature the two earliest descriptions of the treatment of children, Little Hans (Freud, 1909) and Little Chanticleer (Ferenczi, 1913), both involve youngsters who used animals (horses and fowl) as objects to which they had displaced their sexual interests leading to subsequent phobic fears. In academic psychology, Watson and Raynor (1920) used Little Albert to show how conditioning could cause animal fears. In 1913 Freud commented on the closeness children feel with animals when he stated, "Children have no scruples over allowing animals to rank as their full equals. Uninhibited as they are in the avowal of their bodily needs, they no doubt feel themselves more akin to animals than to their elders, who may well be a puzzle to them" (p. 127). Anna Freud (1936) has noted that "substitution of an

animal for a human object is not in itself a neurotic process"
(p. 74), but she also comments on and gives examples of how
commonly animals are used by children for neurotic symptom
formation.

I have reviewed (1983) the sparse child psychiatry literature
and through clinical vignettes described the more common ways
that interactions with animals influence children's behavior and
development. In greater depth, Mahon and Simpson (1977) discuss how 3-year-old nursery school children struggled with their
mourning following the death of the class's pet guinea pig. Kupferman (1977) described in detail the analysis of a 7-year-old by
who imitated a cat, in large part as a defensive denial of his identity as a human being. Sherick (1981) detailed a girl's use of
various pets during her three-year analysis and how these changes
chronicled gains in her treatment and her psychosexual maturation.

CULTURAL AND MYTHOLOGICAL ASPECTS OF HORSES

The wild horse, along with mammoths, bears, and lions, is among
the animals most commonly depicted in man's earliest drawings.
For example, horses are sketched frequently in the cave discovered in 1994 in the village of Vallon-Pont-d'Arc in France. These
drawings date to the Paleolithic age, some 17,000 to 20,000 years
ago. According to Zeuner (1963), the horse was probably domesticated relatively late in the agricultural phase of man's development, after sheep, cattle, and pigs. Horses were not domesticated
for eating, but used by secondary nomads for transportation and
for labor. Horses were therefore the responsibility of the males,
and this association has always been important.

The power and sexuality of the horse symbol was portrayed
in Peter Shaffer's play, *Equus* (1973). The centaur was portrayed
in myth as sexual, but more reliable and less lustful than the satyr.
The same can be said for that American centaur, the Western
cowboy, whose strong, gallant exploits have been promulgated
through generations of novels, short stories, and films (Rappaport, 1968).

Horses were considered a source of power, both brute and
financial, in ancient Greece. A man's wealth was measured by the

number of horses he owned. By this time horses were formidable fighting vehicles. At the time, the effectiveness of a horseman against a foot soldier was the equivalent today of a tank against a jeep. Horses were power. We still speak in these terms when we say someone or some group "does not have the horses to compete." Shakespeare has Richard III cry pleadingly, "A horse! A horse! My kingdom for a horse!"

It is therefore also not surprising that the horse for the common man became a symbol of death and destruction. In the Book of Revelations, chapter 6, we read what the world will face at the time of the apocalypse. There will be four horses, white, red, black, and pale. On them will ride Conquest, Slaughter, Famine, and Death. Our own fathers remembered Grantland Rice's stirring self-same description of the unstoppable 1924 Notre Dame back-field, "The Four Horsemen." Parenthetically, their line blockers were given the less grand description of "The Seven Mules." Greek warriors were not only effective on a horse, but, in the case of the Trojan Horse, were effective inside a horse.

The Greek notion of the power of a horse was true for sexuality as well as for aggression. Centaurs were a mythic race of creatures, part horse and part man. Centaurs were usually depicted as models for man's animal passions. They raped, they fought, they pulled the chariot of the wine god Dionysus, and they were ridden by Reos, the god of love. A centaur exception to prove the rule was Chiron. He was famous for his patience, wisdom, and healing skills. Chiron was also the most popular of tutors and he instructed a veritable heroes' hall of fame, which included Asclepius, Achilles, Jason, and Heracles.

Finally, from Greek mythology, was the winged horse Pegasus who sprang from the blood of Medusa when she was beheaded by Perseus. Pegasus was also associated with death, but his unsuccessful attempt to escape up to heaven with the pure Bellerophon on his back has long served as a metaphor for trying to gain immortality through the soaring spirit of the arts.

Perhaps the most famous horse in ancient Rome was Incitatus. In the first century C.E., the Emperor Caligula proposed, perhaps only in jest, but his jest could be deadly serious, that his horse Incitatus become Consul of Rome. This was one of Caligula's whims that was not carried to fruition.

Because there is such a strong bond between horse and rider, many popular sayings have arisen which allude to various aspects of these relationships. Knights rode large horses and they were also often arrogant. Today to say someone is "on his high horse" indicates that he or she is acting superior or putting on airs. In chess, the knight is also called the horse. Horses, however, are not so terrible when they are out of their element. A horse on the water is like a duck out of water. In the eighteenth century, horse soldiers were sometimes transported by ship to where they were going to fight. While on board, the sailors laughed at the soldiers' naiveté about their awkwardness on ships. The sailors dubbed them horse marines. A common expression of disbelief by sailors was "tell that to the horse marines," since presumably a sailor would not be so gullible as to believe it. A song which captured this degree of foolishness described Captain Jinks of the Horse Marines who fed his horse on corn and beans.

Horses may be considered handsome, smart and perhaps a man's best friend. For example, Sylvestor Stallone likes to be called The Italian Stallion. To be called a "stud" is to be admired for male virility. "Horse sense" represents a laudable variant of common sense. The closeness of horse and rider was celebrated repeatedly around the mid-twentieth century in a plethora of movie westerns, also known as horse operas or even as oaters. Some of the cowboys kissed their horses instead of their sweethearts, and others never had sweethearts because they could not or would not two-time their horses.

Horses can also be symbols of the opposite of the above. To call someone a horse can label him as plain, ugly, stupid, slow, or all of the above. Hoss is a more lovable nickname which softens the insult. Hoss Cartwright of television's *Bonanza* is a good example of the big, slow, but lovable "horse." An opposite of talking horse sense is to talk horse shit, or in more polite company, to talk horse feathers or hooey. Horse shit, of course, not infrequently comes from a person known as a horse's ass. In fact since the invention of the horseless carriage, there are probably now more horse's asses in the country than there are horses.

A horse and a woman who is mounted for sexual congress have long been associated. To horse around is to be involved in sexual play or activity. A horse and a whore are both ridden. To be back in the saddle may mean having gotten up again after fallen off a horse, but it also can refer to one having renewed sexual activity or ability. In all cases, it means that things have been brought back to normal. A whore who has been too oft ridden may be called a harridan or a hack. A harridan has been so worn out that she has lost her horse sense and has become a nag. A hack is short for a hackney horse which in turn was the term for a rented-out saddle horse. Just as now with rental cars, hackneys were overused and not always returned in the best of condition. A hack became a name for horseless carriages for rent, taxicabs, but also for old and tired rented women. Worn-out, often rented, writers may also be called hacks.

CLINICAL ASPECTS

I have been struck by a relatively common but not much studied phenomenon, the horse-crazy girl. The girl will often begin by wanting to buy horse figures or horse pictures. She may well gravitate together with other horse-crazy girls to exchange dreams and wishes with one another. They discuss what kind of horse they like best, how they will buy it (perhaps requiring winning the lottery), which are the best stables in the area, and how they can arrange their lives so they will always be around horses. These obsessions may have all of the qualities of a "crush," except the girls usually begin younger than do their classmates who will only develop crushes on boys. Occasionally the obsession can get in the way of the girl's schoolwork or general social development. It is only then that they come to the attention of clinicians. More often, a love of horses is only a distraction, but one that is likely at times to also drive parents to distraction.

It is important to note that this specific type of obsession is not only a modern occurrence. It was instrumental in the development of Britain's Society for the Prevention of Cruelty to Animals, a template for this country's National Society for the Prevention of Cruelty to Children (Turner, 1964). The SPCA became Royal (RSPCA) because Queen Victoria had become interested in protecting horses and had been an SPCA patron before her accession to the throne. Angela (later, Baroness) Burdett-Coutts was devoted to horses as a young girl and when she later became the richest heiress in England, in 1870 she founded and lavished her wealth and attention on the Ladies Committee of the RSPCA. The latter in 1889 inspired 40,000 essays from schoolchildren which extolled the virtues of the horse and other animals and pleaded for their humane treatment.

The modern horse-crazy girl is less exalted but no less committed to her interest. Although I am not suggesting homogeneity, most come from the urban or suburban class. The interest in horses usually begins during latency or early adolescence and is often sparked by a book, a movie, or an opportunity to ride. There may then be a compulsion to do more reading, to collect figures, pictures, or other horse memorabilia, to take horseback riding lessons, and to own a horse. For some girls these interests last for only weeks or months while for others it lasts a lifetime, although a tapering off of interest is common in late adolescence or early adulthood. Riding academy owners state that a similar high level of involvement with horses by boys is relatively rare.

The development of intense interest in horses is by no means necessarily pathological. Indeed, during a study of oedipal-age children's interests in dinosaurs (Schowalter, 1979), I was struck by how many of the same issues of control, fear, and love of a seemingly overwhelming parent were present in the mostly male dinosaur fanatics. Children who are enraptured by dinosaurs, unless it becomes an obsession, usually develop very well, if not precociously. Most girls who are horse crazy also do fine, and in these there is seldom the opportunity to study the meanings of their interest. One young woman's brief period in analysis, however, afforded the opportunity to observe close at hand some of what the horse meant for her. While her analysis was not directly focused on this issue, her revelations may well, in exaggerated form, suggest why horses are so important for a subpopulation of young women.

CASE REPORT

CZ was a 20-year-old junior at a nearby college when she was referred for analysis at the suggestion of a psychoanalyst who practiced in her hometown. Although she was doing quite well academically, she did not seem to know what to do with her life, was a binge eater, and had recently attempted suicide with a relatively small amount of aspirin.

She was an attractive, tall young woman with auburn hair who tended to wear bluejeans and plaid shirts. She managed to convey both a boyish quality, through her quick, deft movements, and an aura of little-girl confused helplessness. Some days she wore her hair tightly tied and close to her head, at other times flowing long and free.

She was the youngest of four sisters who were considerably older than she. Although she could not help but wonder whether she was a wanted child, her parents had always assured her she was. Both of her parents were successful professionals, and although her mother was careful to spend time with the children, the patient's earliest memories involved fears about being abandoned. She could remember being terrified that her parents would not return when they left to go out in the evening. She also remembered vividly her older sisters leaving home for college and thinking that she herself would never be so self-sufficient. It was in this context that she mentioned that many people mispronounced her name. As a young child, the Oz books were read to her and she later read them herself—her name was the same as one of the characters. Some of the Oz books featured a sawhorse whose main quality is indefatigability. He could run forever without tiring. In the stories, she said, the horse would be used to carry the children away from impending danger.

She had periods of school avoidance in kindergarten and again in first and third grades. She remembered her mother being gentle but forceful to get her out of the house and to school, but at the time it seemed like cruel coercion. She recalled hoping that her father would save her by giving her a reprieve, but to her great disappointment he remained passive and unavailable. In school she felt unliked by her peers and throughout grade school had few or no friends. During this time, she filled her spare time with reading and music, but she was dissatisfied and believed she would be happier if she were a boy. Toward this end she became interested in sports, asked for tailored clothes, and soon was known in the neighborhood as a tomboy. She had a long-standing interest in horses, but first began riding lessons at age 11, "when some of the other girls began to 'change.' " Riding and then showing horses were described as the most exhilarating experiences of her young life.

She claimed she never thought of herself as a sexual person. Indeed, in the almost a year of once-a-week psychotherapy she had had before seeing me, she contended that sex was never brought up by her or the therapist. When she did think of sexuality, it was in idealized and sanitized terms of "roses and romance." She put her menarche at age 16 when she was a junior in high school, but could not recall breast development until the following year, which was also the time she first began dating. In fact, this memory must have been distorted, since breast formation occurs routinely two years prior to menarche. She denied ever having masturbated. Since her senior year in high school, she had had a few short-lived sexual relationships, including orgasms, but denied there had been much of an emotional bond. She dreaded getting close and breaking up.

Although her weight was always within normal limits, her bulimia began about the time of her menarche. She had had no severe gains or drops in weight, but had experienced brief periods of amenorrhea. Her weight was very much tied up with her riding and showing, because she believed that the horses performed better and that she looked better to the judges when her build was slight. She would tend to binge when she felt alone and ignored. Binges often took place in the early morning hours after a previous day of careful control. She was conscious of "a battle of wills within myself" and hated herself when she gave in to her appetite. To try to offset her lapses of overeating, she would run, lift weights, and row crew (all things she associated as masculine), and occasionally use laxatives and force herself to vomit (things that seemed to her feminine). The former were more ego syntonic and provided a certain pleasure in "pushing myself through pain." They were experienced as the antithesis of bingeing, while the purging, although palliative, was linked with the bingeing as a weakness.

Her thoughts about her parents encompassed strong feelings of both closeness and distance. In the abstract she felt that they were caring and loving, but her predominant affects were terror and anger because they were untrustworthy and inconstant. Her sisters were so much older than she that they remained relatively shadowy creatures, something akin to additional, but even less caring, parents. Often during her childhood she believed her parents hated her, not because of any cruel actions on their part, but because they did not give her the time and attention she craved. Her burgeoning interests in music and sports, she recalled, were efforts to please her mother and father. She had particular problems when her parents went away. Because of this they generally abstained from vacations without her, but she found even short absences terrifying. Both incidents of her taking overdoses of aspirin (neither serious) coincided with her parents' being out of the country on brief holidays while she was in college.

She agreed with her parents that she should enter analysis. She had liked the psychotherapist she had been seeing, but she did not believe anything had been accomplished. She felt her life had little focus, that no one really cared about her, and that she would probably eventually kill herself if these things did not change. What she said she hoped to get out of psychoanalysis were direction and a better sense of who she was.

Following the initial interviews, we agreed to begin a trial analysis five times a week. She lay on the couch initially with some misgivings, noting that it made her feel very vulnerable, but she came regularly and on time. The first clear theme and the one that remained most crucial was her belief that no one cared for her. Early memories emerged of her mother telling her she was too old to have another child and did not have the energy to raise her. Very early in life (she dated it to preschool age) she already felt that she was unwanted. Although her parents said they wanted all of their children, she developed the opposite persuasion. As a little girl she decided she would not be a good mother and should not have children herself. While growing up, she had a frequent fantasy of being a nun. An especially appealing part of the fantasy at the time was that nuns sleep alone. As she became older, it occurred to her that being a nun and sleeping alone were tied with her wish not to have children.

It was toward the end of the first month of analysis that her interest in horses came to the fore. She said they were the most important thing in her life and, because of this, she assumed I would believe this involvement was unhealthy. When I asked why, she said she sometimes felt that way herself, but that her interest in horses was what gave stability to her life. At this time vivid memories returned of having no friends in elementary school, feeling unwanted by her parents, and longing to love and be loved. Besides the sawhorse in the Oz books, she could at first recall little that was specific about how horses became hypercathected. She did know that she daydreamed about them often and that there were two specific types of fantasies. One fantasy—which later became less important—had to do with a baby horse that was the only baby cared for by a group of horses. The second fantasy involved her caring for a horse that was large, powerful, and "sort of king" of all the other horses. It was clear that in these two fantasies she could satisfy both her pregenital dependency longings and her phallic and oedipal wishes.

Simultaneously with the discussion of horses in her hours, she began occasionally to be late or miss a session, usually because of a transportation problem associated with her riding lessons. After the second such occasion, I asked about a possible connection. She said it was quite by happenstance, and this was the occasion of her first flare of irritation with me. This irritation did not, however, inhibit her desire to discuss the meaning of horses.

She described her home always having been clean, neat, and sterile. By contrast, the stables exuded rich smells of sweat, leather, liniments, feed, and manure. While at home emotions were not shown, the people at the stable were passionate and always seemed excited about their relationships with the horses and with each other. The size of the horses was important. The ability to control an animal so much bigger than herself gave her a sense of awe and wonderful power. It was, however, not only gratifying in a physical sense; the caring for, riding, and showing of the horse also represented the mastery of a world that was completely mysterious to the uninitiated. This aspect of being special was reminiscent of the preschool boys for whom knowing better than their parents or teachers the names, sizes, or habits of dinosaurs represented a major impetus for their continuing interest (Schowalter, 1979). For my patient the stable became a separate, "better," and more controllable home.

It soon became apparent that she wanted me to understand her feelings about horses, but the more she told me the more fearful she became that I would be angry or turn against her. When asked about her parents' responses to her interest in horses, she initially said that they had always been supportive. This, indeed, seemed to have been the case, but it became increasingly clear that she believed they would or should be jealous. There was a considerable difference in what she expected each parent's reaction to be. Her main fear was that her mother would suddenly "take them away." At times she thought of her interest as something she secretly shared with her father, but there was the danger that her mother would "force" him to join her in saying that CZ was overinterested and should cut back or stop her riding and showing. It was at the time of this disclosure that she somewhat overdramatically announced she had added another riding lesson per week to her crowded schedule, which I understood as a clear expression of a wish to provoke a maternal transference reaction from me. In response to my interpretation, she described how important caring for the horse was for her. Although she never owned "a really good" horse and was now renting one, she found the grooming of the horse very satisfying. She would make the horse look "as good as possible." The idea that she was treating the horse as she wished to be treated was close to consciousness. It was also her way, even as a young girl, of having a "child" and probably made it easier for her to say she did not want or need children when she grew up.

By the third month of analysis, the patient's life had settled down remarkably. She was getting along better with the fellow students with whom she lived, her academic work progressed well, and her part-time job which had been marked by frequent arguments with her male superior was going more smoothly. She pondered this improvement, and said that the analysis must be contributory, but complained that, like her father, I was "too distant" to be a truly helpful, caring person. She still had episodes of binge eating, but these became less frequent and less "gross."

She then admitted for the first time that her father had always wanted her to be a boy. This attempt to have a boy, she believed, was an alternative explanation to her birth having been "an accident," coming as it did so long after the births of her sisters. With a gush of feelings, she recounted how badly she had wanted to be a boy. This, she said, had prevailed until her mid-teens when "I changed my bedroom and half of my clothes to pink," To her, in retrospect, this conversion was as inexplicable as it had been sudden since then she had undergone two or three other "quick changes" when she precipitously had felt either considerably more like a tomboy or more like a "frills and lace" girl. These shifts seemed to affect her wardrobe more than her behavior, but she did associate these changes with the much more frequent and current alterations between "dieting, being lean, and good with horses" and "pigging out, being soft, and not riding well." Even when she was in the latter phase, a man or "a good time with my horse" could make her feel more stable or confident about herself.

At about the beginning of the fourth month of treatment, she missed three sessions without warning or notice. When she returned she had a slight limp and said that while jumping, she had fallen off her horse and fractured three toes. The toes had been attended to medically, but then she had driven into the country to be by herself. She recalled that she had had a relatively bad fall as a senior in high school and following that had run away from home for five days. Falling was equated with rejection and abandonment. "It is like the breaking up of a love affair." More importantly, it was like being dismissed by her parents, a fear that haunted her all her life. It was at this time that she described the symbiotic feeling she experienced with the horse. "There is nothing closer than working one-to-one with a horse." She spoke of the "give and take" between rider and horse, the power surging beneath her, and the "flowing sense of oneness" during the jumps. Then, when she fell, she had the dismaying shock of recognition that the oneness was lost. Although some horses were more skillful than others, she believed that a fall was only rarely the horse's fault, but resulted from something the rider did wrong or from the horse being so finely attuned to the rider's mood that it sensed and reacted to the lack of confidence or control. She wondered if the horse sensed a change taking place in her.

My comments during this period were fashioned to help her explore the parallels between what she experienced with the horse and her feelings about her parents and expectations about the analysis and me. I pointed out linkages she had made but not seen: that she (like the sawhorse) always needed to be on the move to escape she knew not what; how important it was for her to control the horse as a substitute for herself, her parents, or her peers; and the fact that immersion in the horse world had proven to be not only an escape but also a detriment to her learning to face her feelings about herself and others.

At times she lashed out at me for either being too distant, trying to rule her life, or both, but she continued to come to her appointments and tried to unravel what was happening. She was considerably sobered for a while after the fall and more silent than usual, but her associations then suddenly turned to a man whom she had met at the stable. She described him as "fantastically" good and intuitive with horses, and said she realized that horses had much sexual meaning for her. She recalled having heard other girls talk about having sexual feelings while riding. She had never personally thought of them as sexual, but knew that being on top and in control of a large horse gave her a sense of power and excitement that was unique. During the next few weeks, she spoke of how sexually exciting she found the somewhat older male rider she was now beginning to date. He had the same first name as I do, was a talented and successful jumper in shows, and was eagerly trying to persuade her to join on the horse-show circuit, also as a jumper. He was described as a daredevil who "jumped with wild abandon" and who lived an independent life in which he wanted her to join him. Her awe of him caused her to discuss him with an excitement in her voice that I had not heard before. She began to debate out loud whether or not she should leave school, take a summer vacation, or take a whole year off so she could test and perfect her talents as a horsewoman and jumper. I raised the question what these actions would mean in regard to her wish to have a more stable life and whether they were a reaction to what she had been learning about herself. She admitted that she had been uncomfortable about the recent revelations that perhaps she received sexual gratification from grooming and riding. She had thought she was different from the "other girls." However, with her friendship and now burgeoning love affair, she felt less uncomfortable and more convinced that taking time off for the horse-show circuit was sensible.

At this point she had another fall. No bones were broken, but she suffered some "wicked" bruises. She missed two sessions and when she returned she was angrier and more determined than ever before. She now felt the fall was mainly the horse's fault, not her own. She then announced with the quality of a *fait accompli* that she had looked at "the nicest horse in the world." A "magnificent" show horse was up for sale. It was a skilled jumper, and her boyfriend was urging her to buy it; with such a horse she was bound to be a success on the circuit. The horse was expensive, but she had already spoken to her father, who was willing to look at the horse and speak with its present owner.

Once again it seemed as if she was going to use a horse to escape what had become an uncomfortable situation, and in the two weeks that she remained in treatment she acknowledged this intellectually. Emotionally, however, she felt a tremendous enthusiasm and "buoyancy" in anticipation "of being one" with such a perfect steed. While her parents at first counseled her to remain in school and analysis, her father rather quickly agreed to buy the horse and to support her for a year to see what she could do as a horsewoman.[1]

She left the analysis in the high spirits of someone who feels she has narrowly but successfully escaped a serious danger. In contrast to the time when she had been in kindergarten, her father did intervene to extricate her. Although able to admit intellectually that the analytic experience represented repetition rather than progress, she seemed quite genuine in thanking me for all my help.

DISCUSSION

While this young woman's psychopathology, her suitability for analysis, and the technical features of the treatment might be of interest, my discussion will focus on the ways that the horse became important for her. Some of the uses she made of horses are

---

[1] The suggestion of a trial of analysis had been made because, among other things, she had a history of trouble finishing things, had only few long-term relationships, and her basic lack of trust and fears of being poorly cared for suggested she might not tolerate the relatively abstemious character of the psychoanalytic situation.

identical to those of other girls and young women I have treated and may have some general applicability.

As would be expected of any abiding interest, the horse came to serve many functions. The horse is ideally suited for gratifying both pregenital and genital needs and for fulfilling aggressive fantasies. It can be an object of identification as well as represent self and object.

In addition to the narcissistic and sublimatory aspect, the horse may also serve defensive functions. Anna Freud (1965, p. 20) noted, "A little girl's *horse-craze* betrays either her primitive autoerotic desires (if her enjoyment is confined to the rhythmic movement on the horse); or her identification with the caretaking mother (if she enjoys above all looking after the horse, grooming it, etc.); or her penis envy (if she identifies with the big, powerful animal and treats it as an addition to her body); or her phallic sublimations (if it is her ambition to master the horse, to perform on it, etc.)." Freud (1926) listed object loss, loss of love, castration, and superego condemnation as four sources of anxiety. For this patient, the horse served as her protector from these anxieties.

Her intense separation anxieties, whatever their origin, were counteracted by her feeling at one with the horse, the sense of oneness at times representing a primitive fusion.

She believed her parents had never loved her and her peers did not like her. In working with and grooming the horse she felt loved and cared for. As seems true for many other "horse-crazy" girls and young women she enjoyed feeding the horse special treats. This trait to feed others is, of course, commonly seen in patients suffering from anorexia nervosa and/or bulimia. She could live out the first of her two early horse fantasies by being the cared-for baby. In this she not only identified with the horse, treating it as she wished to be treated, but also demonstrated how she should be cared for by her mother. She had felt that her very being was an aggressive demand on her parents, especially her mother, who admitted to not being up to the task of mothering. By being at the stable rather than at home, the patient consciously believed she spared her mother. Her obvious preference for the stable also, of course, served as a rebuke as well as a neutralization of her aggression.[2]

The horse became a love object par excellence. It would come when called, showed constancy of affection, and was the ticket of admission to a tightly knit and supportive group of aficionados. What has struck me with a number of horse-crazy girls is that although the horse consciously represents a male object, the female instructors and peer group provide important identification figures and a feminine sanction for the experience. This sanction modifies the amount of guilt the girl might otherwise feel for the libidinization of her feelings toward the animal. With this patient's dread of separation, having a regular routine for the horse's care was very stabilizing. It also kept her busy. She had long known that it was important for her to have "things" to do. She did not like free time and racing about indefatigably, like the sawhorse; doing stable-connected chores made her feel less alone. In the end, she bought the horse of her dreams, the surest way to keep a love object. It is reminiscent of Roheim's (1943) report that as an adult, Arpad, the Little Chanticleer of Ferenczi's paper, bought a poultry farm.

This young woman was brought up believing she should have been a man. She felt castrated and unable to please her father. Even as a young girl she always consciously thought of horses as male, and, in fact, the horses she rode were male. She believed she could acquire a certain amount of maleness through this identification. She feared her large father, but she also loved him. She projected and displaced these feelings onto the horse. She then educated and tamed that wild, powerful force into an obedient servant and at the same time felt more controlled herself. There was much anxiety also, especially because to a young girl the horse seemed so big. Ferenczi (1911) noted that girls' oedipal fears may be enhanced because of their awareness of the relative size of their father's penis in relation to their own small genitals. Therefore, riding well provided the exhilaration of controlling that large beast between her legs ("with just the pressure of my thighs") and of overcoming a great fear. For the patient this was

---

[2] The preoedipal, especially anal, wishes indulged in and associated with the stable and its sights, smells, and activities were only briefly discussed.

her second girlhood horse fantasy, to be in charge of the "king" horse. In this context it is significant here that the patient dated her riding to when other girls her age had reached menarche. Although her menarche was late physiologically, she realized that riding was linked with a sexual awakening. Indeed, I have known a number of such girls whose menarche was late. Greenacre (1948) emphasizes that horseback riding gives girls a heightened awareness of their genitals. For this girl, riding probably also acted as a substitute for conscious masturbation, which may have been the reason why she became so anxious when the other girls hinted at this meaning. Unfortunately for her, even when most successful astride a horse, she was still a female and never mastered her mixed feelings about her gender. Her ambivalence about being a woman also was expressed in her vacillations between a mannish and feminine wardrobe and between dieting and bingeing.

Just as she used the horse as a pregenital and a self-love object, it also played a role in her incestuous oedipal wishes and fears. At times she believed her interest in horses was a "secret" she shared with her father, and expected her mother to demand that she "cut back" or "stop" it. While on a defensive intellectual level she polarized the unemotional home from the "passionate" stables, the sanction given for her riding by parents and peers allowed her, for the most part, to feel comfortable about her preoccupation with horses. Indeed, the more she worked with the horse, the more in control she was and the less threatened she felt. That was why, following her falls and after the sexual aspects of her interest in horses began to be revealed in the analysis, she needed to "take a year off" and spend it exclusively to learn "how to obtain better control of the beast." Superego condemnation had come to the fore. The fantasy was if she could know and control a horse completely, she would be in control of herself and those around her. Joseph Wood Krutch (1956, p. 136) quotes Thoreau as noting that a hen that is allowed to wander about the house soon looks "too humanized to roast well." Familiarity, it was hoped by the patient, would deaggressivize and desexualize her feelings and protect her from the rising superego condemnation. It was in fact precisely when she revealed her sexual feelings that the analysis became too threatening. She saw me as an impediment to her continued successful use of the

horse, in large part because in the transference I was replacing
her father as a feared incestuous object. Her turning from me to
the horse repeated her earlier turn from father to horse.

She interpreted the falls as signifying rejection and abandonment. In the first she felt the horse sensed her rejection of it and
reacted accordingly. With the second fall, she blamed the horse
and felt it had turned against her. This time her response was to
replace the horse. It was at this point that she concluded that
either I or her life with horses, at least as she had known it, must
go. The choice was made quickly. It was not, unfortunately, that
which Adatto (1958) often found common in late adolescents
when the anxiety stirred up in the analysis allows the patient to
use the analyst as a bridge from parental to mature love objects.
The outcome was more reminiscent of Freud's warnings about
the "adhesiveness" of the libido (1916–1917, p. 348). As was the
case when she had left her parents for horses earlier, she left me
as she had felt left. In order to make the decision more understandable and acceptable, she enlisted the aid of her boyfriend
and father on the side of the horse. Her sudden and uncharacteristic burst of sexual passion for this young horseman was timed
perfectly to defuse the power of and the long-term sexual meanings associated with the horse and the paternal transference that
were coming to the fore in the analysis. The boyfriend served as
a horseman bridge. The father's agreement to buy her the "nicest
horse in the world" and to approve, at least tacitly, of her leaving
analysis and college further quelled feelings of guilt and anxiety.
Unlike the time when she was in kindergarten, he now supported
her wish to regress and not face the age-appropriate tasks con-
fronting her. The original and the peer male love objects joined
together in their support of her symbolic male love object. In
leaving treatment, she not only felt relieved, she felt triumphant.
She was going to be a horsewoman.

It would be an error to suggest that the meanings important
for this patient are the same for all girls and young women who
love horses. However, it is safe to say that in horseback riding, as
in all childhood passions, a greater or a lesser portion of the
intensity is due to the fact that it offers ways of fulfilling and
working through wishes and fears that are displaced from parents.
In this case a follow-up revealed that the patient jumped with her

horse for less than a year. She then had a bad fall which resulted in a serious injury, broken bones, hospitalization, and prolonged convalescence. She also had a diminished interest in horses, but this is not surprising since more than a year after the fall, she was jobless and still living with her parents. The circle was complete. Her horse had done its job. She finally had what she wanted initially—to be cared for by her parents.

REFERENCES

Adatto, C. P. (1958), Ego reintegration observed in analysis of late adolescents. *Internat. J. Psycho-Anal.*, 39:172–177.

Ferenczi, S. (1911), On obscene words. In: *Sex in Psychoanalysis.* New York: Basic Books, 1950, pp. 132–153.

—— (1913), A little chanticleer. In: *Contributions to Psycho-Analysis.* Boston: Richard G. Badger, 1916, pp. 204–213.

Freud, A. (1936), *The Ego and the Mechanisms of Defense.* New York: International Universities Press.

—— (1965), *Normality and Pathology in Childhood.* New York: International Universities Press.

Freud, S. (1909), Analysis of a Phobia in a Five-Year-Old Boy. *Standard Edition*, 10:1–147. London: Hogarth Press, 1955.

—— (1916–1917), Introductory Lectures on Psycho-Analysis. *Standard Edition*, 16. London: Hogarth Press, 1961.

—— (1926), Inhibitions, Symptoms and Anxiety. *Standard Edition*, 20:75–172. London: Hogarth Press, 1959.

Greenacre, P. (1948), Anatomical structure and superego development. In: *Trauma, Growth and Personality.* New York: W. W. Norton, 1952, pp. 149–164.

Krutch, J. W. (1956), *The Great Chain of Life.* Boston: Houghton Mifflin.

Kupferman, K. (1977), A latency boy's identity as a cat. *The Psychoanalytic Study of the Child*, 32:363–387. New Haven, CT: Yale University Press.

Mahon, E., & Simpson, D. (1977), The painted guinea pig. *The Psychoanalytic Study of the Child*, 32:283–307. New Haven, CT: Yale University Press.

Rappaport, E. A. (1968), Zoophily and zoerasty. *Psychoanal. Quart.*, 37:565–587.

Roheim, G. (1943), *The Origin and Function of Culture.* New York: Nervous & Mental Disease Monographs.

Schowalter, J. E. (1979), When dinosaurs return. *Children Today*, 8:2–5.
——— (1983), The use and abuse of pets. *J. Amer. Acad. Child Psychiatry*, 22:68–72.
Shaffer, P. (1973), *Equus*. Harmondsworth, U.K.: Penguin.
Sherick, I. (1981), The significance of pets for children. *The Psychoanalytic Study of the Child*, 36:193–215. New Haven, CT: Yale University Press.
Turner, E. S. (1964), *All Heaven in a Rage*. London: Michael Joseph.
Watson, J. B., & Raynor, R. (1920), Conditioned emotional reactions. *J. Experiment. Psychology*, 3:1–14.
Zeuner, F. E. (1963), *A History of Domesticated Animals*. New York: Harper & Row.

CHAPTER 4

The Wolf in the Consulting Rom

DWARAKANATH G. RAO, M.D.

> Then everything includes itself in power,
> Power into will, will into appetite;
> And appetite, a universal wolf,
> So doubly seconded with will and power,
> Must make perforce a universal prey,
> And last eat up himself [Shakespeare, *Troilus and Cressida*, Act I, scene 3, line 119].

The image of the wolf conjures up vaguely disturbing feelings, held in check only by a multitude of cultural charms and amulets, and uneasy individual defenses. The wolf is associated with unbridled cruelty, ferocity, ravenousness, treachery, speed, and lust but is also an animal held in high mystical esteem as self-sufficient and loyal to the pack. It is a revered animal of psychoanalysts, who from the time of Freud's description of his famous Russian patient, dubbed the Wolf Man, have elaborated on Freud's masterly exposition of a dream of wolves. Thus for the psychoanalyst, the wolf is a strangely instructive creature, a bedfellow from our training years, who stared at us impassively as we learned about primal scene, reconstruction, trauma, dream work, and indeed an entire model of the mind from topographic to structural to postmodern. These days we are newly reminded of the multiply determined vagaries of memory, and the need for wiser guidelines in understanding the truths conveyed in the languages of the couch: enactments, memories, body language, dreams, affects, and spoken language itself.

In this current ferment where might we situate the wolf as a symbolic respository of desire and conflict? Is the psychical wolf a close relative of the biological species? This chapter will examine these and related questions by a review of analytic thinking about the wolf, and by excursions into culture, myth, symbolism, children's stories, and tales of werewolves and feral children.

MYTHOLOGICAL AND CULTURAL PERSPECTIVES

Webster's Unabridged Dictionary (2nd edition) describes the wolf as "any of a large group of carnivorous, canine mammals of the genus *Canis,* the type of genus of the dog family, widely distributed throughout the Northern Hermisphere: the best-known species are the common gray wolf, *Canis lupus;* the American timber wolf, *Canis occidentalis;* and the prairie wolf, *Canis latrans.*" Several qualities are attributed to a wolf: cruelty, fierceness, or greed. Culturally familiar phrases include *lone wolf, crying wolf, to keep the wolf from the door, wolfing food down, wolf whistle, wolf in sheep's clothing, live with wolves, howl like a wolf. To see a wolf* means to lose one's voice. The word *wolf* connotes an aggressive philanderer, and in music refers to jarring, discordant, or untrue sounds.

Bartlett's Familiar Quotations (Kaplan, 1992) yields twenty-five references. A Biblical reference to the ideal of brotherhood and communality of living beings, and of the relationship of the meek to the mighty goes as follows (Isaiah 11):

> The wolf also shall dwell with the lamb, and the leopard shall lie down with the kid; and the calf and the young lion and the fatling together; and a little child shall lead them.
>
> And the cow and the bear shall feed; their young ones shall lie down together; and the lion shall eat straw like the ox.
>
> And the suckling child shall play on the hole of the asp, and the weaned child shall put his hand on the cockatrice' den.

There are warnings about wolf-nature: "Beware of false prophets, which come to you in sheep's clothing, but inwardly they are ravening wolves" (Matthew, 7:15, AV).

Homer's *Iliad*, on the other hand, makes a firm statement about the essential incompatibilities found in nature: "There are no compacts between lions and men, and wolves and lambs have no concord." Shakespeare is pragmatic here: "He's mad that trust in the tameness of a wolf, a horse's health, a boy's love, or a whore's oath" (*King Lear*, Act III, scene 6, line 20). Kipling articulates the wolf's peculiar code of survival in this way:

Now this is the Law of the Jungle—as old and as true of the sky; And the Wolf that shall keep it may prosper, but the Wolf that shall break it must die [Kipling, 1895, p. 29].

Bartlett's identifies the proverb "Live with wolves, howl like a wolf" as Russian in origin. See below for further meanings of the wolf in the Russian psychical landscape, in particular its relevance for representability in dreams and the Wolf Man's choice of animal for his dream.

In mainstream culture, the fascination with wolves is visible everywhere, from the movie *Wolf*, starring Jack Nicholson, *Second Nature*, a novel by Hoffman (1994), to interest in breeding and raising wolf-dogs. Hollywood in particular emphasizes the Jekyll and Hyde draw of the wolf as a rapacious but isolated creature.[1] In a recent Dear Abby column (April 7, 1996), a reader asks for advice on raising a wolf hybrid. Abby discourages the reader from owning these aggressive wolf-dogs, quoting *The Smithsonian* magazine (Hope, 1994, p. 36):

As all owners agree, the animals treat humans as other wolves. But, genetically programmed for the ongoing struggle with packmates for food and leadership, they have no compunction about challenging the dominant householder—usually the male—with warning growls and a flurry of bites (usually not deep bites) for his steak dinner or easy chair, or even for the attention of his spouse.

---

[1] In his feisty and insightful book on the myth of a human-beast from antiquity to the present, Douglas (1992) in a chapter entitled "Howling All the Way to the Bank" surveys the cinematic renditions of the werewolf myth from the 1935 *Werewolf in London* and the influential *Wolf Man* starring Lon Chaney (1941), to *An American Werewolf in London* (1981), and its relation to other transformation tales like *Dr. Jekyll and Mr. Hyde*. Douglas draws attention to storylines, costuming, and motivations in these movies that shaped (and were shaped by) popular sensibilities. He also notes that some movies seem to equate pubertal change with the transformation to a hirsute, impulse-ridden werewolf. He explores the tension between parody and tragedy in many of the more recent films, and its reflection of the anxiety that still pervades the relationship between man and wolf.

How to curb unwanted behavior is a subject of debate. When only swatted or yelled at, the wolves may not turn tail but growl and bite instead. Disciplined with a severe beating, they'll retreat—but, wolflike, will attempt the same challenge an hour or a day later—in an endless contest for dominance. . . .

Without food, confused, they may prowl the neighborhood attacking cats, rabbits, goats, dogs, even horses, all of which they see as prey. Their predatory instincts can also be triggered by humans, especially if those humans happen to be small or infirm, or if they flee or emit a frightened sound.

Since 1986, nine children in the United States, from toddlers to a 12-year-old, have been killed (and in one case, partially eaten) by wolf and wolf-dog pets. Many more people, both children and adults, have been maimed. While relatively few of these animals actually kill, most of the owners interviewed for this article report having been bitten.

Shipley (1984, pp. 444–445), in tracing the Indo-European word for *wolf* comes up with *ulkuo* meaning a flesh-tearing animal. He states that early names for *wolf* in Greek, Latin, and German were taboo, and the word for totem animals in certain American Indian tribes were unmentionable. Freud mentions in *Totem and Taboo* (Freud, 1913) the prohibition against speaking the names of the dead, and of the father-victims of tribal parricidal wishes in totemistic societies. In Greek myth, Lycaon, King of Arcadia, engages in human sacrifice (possibly his son) in honor of Zeus, who, in disgust, turns him and his family into wolves. Shipley also connects the Latin *lupus* with *Lupercalia,* an ancient festival celebrated at *Lupercal,* a grotto in Rome, where Pan is celebrated as *Lupercus.* A dog was sacrificed as part of this festival. Further evidence of the totemistic power of the wolf comes from the meaning of *lyceum,* a gymnasium where Aristotle taught, the name deriving from the nearby Temple to Apollo, *Lukheíos,* meaning wolf-slayer. Another derivation from the French *loup* for wolf (feminine, *louve*) is the "Louvre or the wolf field, where the palace of the French kings was built, now one of the world's greatest museums" (p. 445). A *loup* is also a half-mask worn by masqueraders, suggesting the wolf disguise is generically used.

From Wendy Doniger O'Flaherty (1988), an astute translator of Indic tales and myths, there is an echo of this striving for communion with the animal kingdom:

> The belief that all animals may be in some sense less other than they seem to be is the source of the ever-enchanting myth of a magic time or place or person that erases the boundary between humans and animals. The time of this animal paradise finds a close parallel in the myth that tells of the time when gods walked among people or people walked among gods. The place like the magic place in the Looking-Glass forest where things have no names, where Alice could walk with her arms around the neck of a fawn, is like the high mountain where people mingle with the gods. And the particular individual with these special powers finds a parallel in the myth of a particular person (often a shaman or a priest) who has the special ability to traffic with the gods [Doniger O'Flaherty, 1988, p. 94].

In her wide and somewhat irreverent scholarship, she includes among the mythical children raised by wild animals, such personalities as Davy Crockett, raised among mountain lions, and Pecos Bill, suckled by a puma. She also asks us to ponder the fact that King Arthur's education by Merlin the magician took place "among ants, geese, owls, and badgers, whose language Arthur understood." Doniger O'Flaherty joins Freud, Frazer the anthropologist, and academicians who have noted the ubiquity of the cultural equation between the fierceness of the totemic animal and the masculinity of men.

Frazer's (1922) encyclopedic classic *The Golden Bough* is prescient with psychoanalytic insights about ritual and belief, insights that Freud paid homage to in *Totem and Taboo*. Frazer is impartial, and although dated, spreads as wide a net as an anthropologist ever did. In discussing animals in ritual and myth, he tells us that in France, Germany, and Slavonic countries, a corn spirit was conceived as a wolf or dog. Thus, when the wind set cornfields in motion, peasants said, "The Wolf is going over, or through, the corn," or the "Wolf is in the corn," or the "big Dog sits in the corn" (p. 519). Note the substitution of the more domesticated dog for wolf. Frazer goes on to say children are warned about the oral predatoriness of the wolf: "The Rye-wolf will come and eat you up, children," or "the Rye-wolf will carry you off" (p. 520).

Here is a passage from Frazer that is of particular relevance to the symbolism of the wolf's tail in the Wolf Man's dream and his associations.

> [I]n the neighborhood of Feilenhof (East Prussia), when a wolf was seen running through a field, the peasants used to watch whether he carried his tail in the air or dragged it on the ground. If he dragged it on the ground, they went after him, and thanked him for bringing them a blessing, and even set tit-bits before him. But if he carried his tail high, they cursed him and tried to kill him. Here the wolf is the corn-spirit whose fertilizing power is in his tail [p. 520].

Frazer also notes the belief in a wolf actually sitting in the last sheaf of corn, which leads to fear of being the last one in the fields, as well as to an identification with the wolf by the last reaper. Sometimes the last sheaf of corn is shaped into a wolf form; in some places, "the sheaf called the Wolf is made up in human form and dressed in clothes. This indicates a confusion of ideas between the corn-spirit conceived in human and in animal form" (p. 521). In parts of France, a wether (a castrated ram) dubbed the "wolf of the field" was decorated with flowers and ears of corn and led in a parade with reapers marching behind it. The wether was then killed in the field, as if to ensure by a double castration, denial of the virility of the wolf-father.

Other examples of totemic beast-gods are the ram of Thebes, the goat of Mendes, the bull in Egypt, and the wolf of Lycopolis and certain American Indian tribes (Frazer, 1922; pp. 580–581). A common custom of wearing, or adorning an image with, the skin of the totem animal following a ritual sacrifice is also described by Frazer. Quoting a castaway who was imprisoned by the Indians of Nootka Sound, he writes:

> The Indian . . . chief "discharged a pistol close to his son's ear, who immediately fell down as if killed, upon which all the women of the house set up a most lamentable cry, tearing handfuls of hair from their heads, and exclaiming that the prince was dead; at the same time a great number of the inhabitants rushed into

the house armed with their daggers, muskets, etc., enquiring the cause of their outcry. These were immediately followed by two others dressed in wolf-skins, with masks over their faces representing the head of that animal. The latter came in on their hands and feet in the manner of a beast, and taking up the prince, carried him off upon their backs, retiring in the same manner they entered." In another place (the castaway) mentions that the young prince—a lad of about eleven years of age—wore a mask in imitation of a wolf's head. . . .

Every new member of (another) society (called the Tlokoala) must be initiated by the wolves. At night a pack of wolves, personated by Indians dressed in wolf-skins and wearing wolf-masks, make their appearance, seize their novice, and carry him into the woods. Next day the wolves bring back the novice dead, and the members of the society have to revive him. The wolves are supposed to have put a magic stone into his body, which must be removed before he can come to life. Till this is done the pretended corpse is left lying outside the house. Two wizards go in and remove the stone, which appears to be quartz, and then the novice is resuscitated [pp. 810–811].[2]

Frazer then elucidates the nature of the relationship of man to totem-beast, and more generally to clans and secret societies. He states that "the essence of the rite appears to be the killing of the novice in his character of a man and his restoration to life in the form of the animal which is thenceforward to be, if not his guardian spirit, at least linked to him in a peculiarly intimate relation: "[T]he Indians of British Columbia may imagine that their life depends on the life of some one of that species of creature to which they assimilate themselves by their costume" (p. 811). Frazer concludes that a common aim of initiation into a

---

[2] An example from another tribe: "Among the Niska Indians of British Columbia, who are divided into four principal clans with the raven, the wolf, the eagle, and the bear for their respective totems, the novice at initiation is always brought back by an artificial totem animal. Thus when a man was about to be initiated into a secret society called Olala, his friends drew their knives and pretended to kill him. In reality they let him slip away, while they cut off the head of a dummy which had been adroitly substituted for him. Then they laid the decapitated dummy down and covered it over, and the women began to mourn and wail. His relations gave a funeral banquet and solemnly burnt the effigy. In short, they held a regular funeral. For a whole year the novice remained absent and was seen by none but members of the secret society. But at the end of that time he came back alive, carried by an artificial animal which represented his totem [Frazer, 1922, pp. 810–811).

totem clan and a secret society is "the possibility of establishing a sympathetic relation with an animal, a spirit, or other mighty being, with whom a man deposits for safe-keeping his soul or some part of it, and from whom he receives in return a gift of magical powers" (p. 811).

FERAL CHILDREN: FACT AND FANTASY

Through myth and legend, and varying degrees of familiarity, feral children (children raised by wild animals, often wolves) populate our imagination and history books. Examples abound: Romulus and Remus, Tarzan, and Mowgli in legend and literature; in the annals of science, a listing covering the years 1344 to 1961, of over fifty recorded cases of children reared by wild animals or simply forced to live in isolation (Malson, 1972, pp. 80–82). In all of these cases, a vexing issue is not only authentication, but what feral upbringing means. Candland (1993) stresses the two-way passage of attributes, animal and human, when he notes that "feral" once meant going from domestic to wild, and over time has changed to mean going from "the wild into captivity a definition just the reverse of its earlier meaning" (p. 371). The change in meaning, even if apparent only to specialists Candland is familiar with, appears to reflect the readily observable commingling of wild and civilized attributes in animals and humans. This is particularly true of children of whom two kinds of observations exist, the child isolated in infancy, and the child "reared" by a wild animal. Of the isolated or imprisoned child, detailed accounts are available of the two best-known cases: Victor, the wild boy of Aveyron (Lane, 1977), and Kaspar Hauser, the wild boy abandoned by dastardly relatives from a princely family (Shengold, 1978).

    Victor was found in 1799 at age 11 in a wild state in France, and was presumed to have grown up in isolation; he was very likely retarded. A feral life is implied, but there is no evidence of his being raised by animals. He exhibited no behavior that could be construed as imitation of any species of animal. Of interest is the meticulous and psychologically astute observations of his benefactor and teacher, Jean Itard, the French physician (see

Malson, 1972). His classic efforts at rehabilitating Victor are regarded as the beginning of scientific attention directed at the abandoned, mentally ill, or retarded citizen. Itard, by his courageous example, is seen as the progenitor of what evolved into special education.

Kaspar Hauser was a boy of about 17 who appeared in Nurenberg, Bavaria, in 1827 and said that he had been kept in a dungeon from early childhood. The case illustrates child development under conditions of deprivation and exemplifies the crime of "soul murder" (formulated by A. von Feuerbach in his 1832 book on Hauser), according to Shengold (1978). Once out of captivity, Kaspar was rapidly able to socialize, speak, and converse, unlike Victor. Kaspar was assassinated as a young man by the same man who had imprisoned him, in a nefarious scheme to prevent his inheriting a noble family's legacy.

Authenticated cases do exist of children apparently brought up by wild animals who later exhibit animal behavior, and include surrogate upbringing by bears, gazelles, pigs, baboons, leopards, and wolves (Gesell, 1941; Singh and Zingg, 1942; Ogburn and Bose, 1959; Malson, 1972; Armen, 1974; Maclean, 1977). In terms of quality of proof, the cases vary from doubtful to authentic.

After a "European period" (Malson, 1972, p. 43)[3] of discovery of feral children, attention switched to South Asia. Between 1843 and 1895 there were fourteen cases in India, and at least three more since then. The reasons for this disproportionate reporting of feral children from India are thought to be greater chances of discovery because of the advent of British presence in India.[4]

---

[3] Linnaeus, the great classifier of nature and author of *Systema Naturae* (1758) gave feral man a Latinate name, *homo ferus*, listed seven cases, and described them as being quadruped (*tetrapus*), mute (*mutus*), and more imaginatively, hirsute (*hirsutus*). Subsequent literature confirms that all of the reported children are indeed mute, have an obligatory or preferential quadruped stance, but are not hirsute (quoted in Malson, 1972, p. 47).

[4] Major-General Sleeman was in the province of Oudh fighting "Thugs" during which time he reported seven cases (Malson, 1972, p. 44). Zingg (Singh and Zingg, 1942) and Malson (1972) consider the apparent closeness between men and animals in India, and the taboo against killing wolves in parts of the country. Zingg found that villagers would rather see a wolf carry off an infant than let a drop of the wolf's blood touch the ground for fear that the blood would render the land infertile. In 1871, it was estimated that at least 20,000 children died by either snakebite or falling victim to wild beasts. The majority of the latter group were killed or carried off by wolves (Singh and Zingg, 1942, p. 144).

Of the three most reliably documented cases in the literature, we have already briefly discussed two, Victor and Kaspar.
The third case is of Kamala, one of two wolf-girls of Midnapore,
India, captured when she was 7 and rescued by a missionary,
Reverend Singh, and his wife. Reverend Singh kept a diary which
forms the basis of further studies on Kamala. Early in the story,
having heard of a nearby man-ghost (*manush-bagha*), and having
identified a white-ant (termite) mount as its likely lair, the Reverend Singh and his party waited. Here is his entry for October
9, 1920.

> The same Saturday, October 9, 1920, evening, long before dusk,
> at about 4:30 or 5:00 P.M., we stealthily boarded the machan (a
> high platform from which one shoots wild animals) and anxiously
> waited for an hour or so. All of a sudden, a grown-up wolf came
> out from one of the holes, which was very smooth on account of
> their constant egress and ingress. This animal was followed by
> another one of the same size and kind. The second one was fol-
> lowed by a third, closely followed by two cubs one after the other.
> The holes did not permit two together.
>
> Close after the cubs came the ghost—a hideous-looking be-
> ing—hand, foot, and body like a human being; but the head was
> a big ball of something covering the shoulders and the upper
> portion of the bust, leaving only a sharp contour of the face visible,
> and it was human. Close at its heels there came another awful
> creature exactly like the first, but smaller in size. Their eyes were
> bright and piercing, unlike human eyes. I at once came to the
> conclusion that these were human beings [Singh and Zingg, 1942,
> p. 5].

Gesell (1941), a child psychiatrist at Yale, gives high marks
for this extraordinary diary, further authenticating the researches
of Professor Zingg of the University of Denver who traveled to
India to study Kamala's case as well as numerous others. Kamala
when first found, could only run on all fours, or crept on hands
and knees, although she was estimated to be about 8 years old.
She cried like a wolf at specific times in the night, had no human
articulation, lapped liquids and food, and ate carrion. She was
completely unafraid of the dark, and showed teeth and made
harsh noises when approached. Through the ministrations of

Mrs. Singh (often by regular massaging of Kamala's limbs) and the other children at the orphanage, Kamala shed her wolf life in a slow and agonizing process. Two years after reestablishing human contact, she began to eat from a plate. A few months later she said "ma" for Mrs. Singh and could articulate the sound meaning "hungry." In 1923, at age 11, she stood alone on her two feet without support. Four years after her capture, she began to be afraid of the dark. By age 14, she had a vocabulary of thirty words, and was able to show displeasure whenever Mrs. Singh had to leave the orphanage. In the next two years, she was able to learn more human activities: she ran errands, knew children's names, became bashful, and would not leave her dormitory without her dress. She began to mind the babies, and her vocabulary was a full forty-five words and growing. Kamala died in 1929 at age 17 of an illness described as uremia. Gesell (1941) estimates that had she lived, Kamala would have continued to develop language and social skills consistent with the adults in her community.

Kamala's story is haunting and poignant, but is it convincing as a factual account? The evidence marshaled by Zingg, and the internal consistency of the diary entries by Singh, including photographs, meet criteria for full authenticity, according to Gesell (1941), Malson (1972), Candland (1993), and Maclean (1977). They all agree, however, that hoaxes at one time were all too common, and that each case must be sifted carefully by dispassionate scholars. They believe that the case of Kamala and several others are factual.

From the available literature, it is clear that the feral child fantasy is laced with a good deal of fact. See, however, Favazza (1977) who concludes there is scant scientific evidence for animals rearing humans, and feels "feral" children are in fact severely deprived, abandoned children. In its heyday, the discovery of feral children raised hotly debated questions about nature and nurture. An abiding result was the understanding of the importance of childhood for the acquisition of human traits, such as language, upright posture, and food preferences, which at the time were often considered innate and a human birthright. The recognition of parenting as a mammalian longing that could bond species sparked the imagination of many, including Rudyard Kipling, whose *Jungle Books* (1895) told the tale of a feral boy, Mowgli. The tale of Mowgli and his circle of solicitous animal friends has enchanted children worldwide. Kipling, however, is now known to have been abandoned and mistreated by his parents as a child, and left in India at age 6. Shengold (1975) regards Kipling's experience as "soul murder" and describes the resolution of his trauma and emergence as a writer. Mowgli, the beloved child of the animals, without doubt is the abandoned Kipling transforming harsh neglect and privation into wondrous satisfaction.

If nineteenth-century events seem dimmed by time, a rash of killings of children by wolves in Uttar Pradesh, India, in August 1996 propelled the nightmare into modern India. Mothers were reported to be keeping children from the fields, rumors were abuzz that the killings were the work of werewolves, or Pakistani infiltrators dressed up as wolves. As the hysteria spread, a 10-year-old girl was reported describing the wolf coming across the grass on all fours before pouncing on her 4-year-old brother and killing him. She then said, "Then it (the wolf) threw him over its shoulder. It was wearing a black coat, and a helmet and goggles."[5] *The New York Times* also reported the spread of fear through "Indian versions of 'Little Red Riding Hood'—in which wolves, and werewolves, are represented as among the most cunning and dangerous of all creatures."[6]

---

[5] The *New York Times* (September 1, 1996) reported a front page story headlined "In India, Attacks by Wolves Spark Old Fears and Hatreds." The *Times* reported that in a five-month period, thirty-three children had been carried off and killed by wolves and twenty more seriously mauled. Not for a hundred years were wolf killings a problem of this magnitude. In 1878, however, the *Times* report indicated that British officials recorded 624 human killings by wolves in this area. Bounties were offered then as now for bringing in dead wolves. It took nine months and the slaying of 2600 wolves before the 1878 wolf killings stopped. The reason for wolves turning man-eaters this time is reckoned to be overpopulation by wolves through conservation measures.

[6] Indian folk tales refer most often to the jackal, a smaller animal than the European wolf, usually portrayed as cunning, sly, or wise. The *Panchatantra*, which is a five-part collection of Indian fables in the manner of Aesop and the Arabian Nights, is populated and narrated by animals. It contains the story of a baby jackal raised by a sympathetic lioness, a tale of "feralization" in the animal world. When the jackal and his lion siblings grow up, and try to attack an elephant, the jackal turns tail and heads home. The lioness mother then reveals to the jackal his true nature, and warning him about his dangerous lion siblings, sends him away to live with his own kind (Ryder, 1956).

We come full circle to the psychological currents that render the man-nourishing wolf to the man-eating wolf to a wolf-man, a werewolf, and this brings us to the subject of lycanthropy.

THE SYNDROME OF LYCANTHROPY

Lycanthropy as a psychiatric syndrome is defined as the rare delusion of being a wolflike creature with the cravings attributed to the wolf. Symptoms include (1) altered states of consciousness that involve assuming the voice and posture of a wolf; (2) alienation from self and society that lead to the frequenting of cemeteries and woods; (3) bestial compulsions marked by an appetite for raw meat or wolfish sexual activity; (4) obsession with the evil eye, invasion of the body, and other persecutory ideas; and (5) acute accompanying anxiety. Lycanthropy is thus a symptom complex (Rosenstock and Vincent, 1977; Surawicz and Banta, 1975) for which a differential diagnosis would include schizophrenia, organic brain syndrome, psychotic depressive state, dissociative disorder, manic-depressive disorder, psychomotor epilepsy, and hallucinogen use. While rare, lycanthropy is still seen in both industrialized and nonindustrailized societies.

Coll, O'Sullivan, and Browne (1985), for example, report on a 66-year-old woman who presented with full-fledged symptoms of lycanthropy. A severe depression was treated with ECT and the symptoms disappeared. The authors regard lycanthropy as a severe form of depersonalization that could characterize any of several psychotic disorders, including Cotard's syndrome consisting of severe depression, depersonalization, and nihilistic delusions. Lange's (1970) case involved an inebriated man who barked like a dog, and ran around on all fours. He was part of a folie à trois—he shared a bedroom with his mother and a grandmother, and felt he led a "dog's" life.

Offering a more sophisticated account, Rosenstock and Vincent (1977) report on a schizophrenic woman who believed she was a wolf, feeling like an animal with claws. The authors believe that the delusional metamorphosis provided temporary relief from a consuming sexual conflict that would otherwise have led to suicide. Mitchell and Wright (1975) in their study of the character of Duke Ferdinand in *The Duchess of Malfi* by the seventeenth-century dramatist John Webster, conclude that the Duke's descent into madness involving lycanthropy and necrophilia was an unconscious strategy for disguising an incestuous attraction to his sister.

Raspaolo (1988) suggests that in today's rare cases of lycanthropy, the patients, under threat of psychic disintegration, attribute their imagined change in body image to sinful yielding to animal instincts. For a review of multiple etiologies see Kulick, Pope, and Keck (1990); "serial" lycanthropy (Dening and West, 1989) in which a female patient successively felt she was a cat, dog, wolf, and a horse; and ritual, symbolic lycanthropy among Navajo Indians (Merkur, 1981).

Psychodynamically, the lupine temperament, reputation, and legend is as sought after as it is felt to be repellent, whether for totemistic, counterphobic, or other identificatory purposes. The wolf is a cachet, an identity, a trademark of diverse trends in the mind. This feared longing, when realized in fantasy, results in lycanthropy. Long the stuff of myth and legend from ancient times, lycanthropy has been the subject of mystical cults and lurid slasher movies, over fifty of which were produced. Like stories of vampires, Frankenstein, and Jekyll and Hyde, lycanthropy was associated with pseudoscience and fictional sensationalism against the backdrop of the evil, demonic, human emerging as a grotesque beast. For an excellent review that combines case reports, early expositions of myths like Ovid's *Metamorphoses*, religious symbolism, cases of werewolves put on trial, and a critical look at werewolf fiction, see Otten (1986).

A werewolf search on the World Wide Web yielded a plethora of web pages devoted to the subject. Several were cultlike and phantasmagoric; others attempted to provide historical information and assist anyone who wished to become a werewolf. The authors seem to play fast and loose with reality, claiming at times no more than a scholarly interest, yet needing the belief that lycanthropic transformation was possible. Lycanthropy, in conclusion, represents archaic wishes to dispossess oneself of unbearably conflicted instinctual urges. When at the same time the person is able to use neither symbol nor totem, ritual nor fantasy, regressive and delusional efforts to recapture primitive states ensue, with accompanying experiences of merging with the powerful bestial figure.

PSYCHOANALYSIS, TOTEMISM, AND THE WOLF

Writing in the 1890s, Frazer asks, "why do men desire to deposit their life outside their bodies?" (p. 812). He answers that in times of danger, as during puberty, totemism serves to preserve the endangered soul from the perils of sexuality, the origins of which he finds obscure. Freud (1913), pursuing the origins of sexual fears, offers the following definition of *totem*:

> It is as a rule an animal (whether edible and harmless or dangerous and feared) and more rarely a plant or a natural phenomenon (such as rain or water), which stands in a peculiar relation to the whole clan. In the first place, the totem is the common ancestor of the clan; at the same time it is their guardian spirit and helper, which sends them oracles and, if dangerous to others, recognizes and spares its own children. Conversely, the clansmen are under a sacred obligation (subject to automatic sanctions) not to kill or destroy their totem and to avoid eating its flesh (or deriving benefit from it in other ways). The totemic character is inherent, not in some individual animal or entity, but in all the individuals of a given class. From time to time festivals are celebrated at which the clansmen represent or imitate the motions and attributes of their totem in ceremonial dances [pp. 2–3].

Freud then goes on to explicate his views on the near ubiquitous presence of exogamy wherever totemism was practiced. He traces its relation to the horror of incest, development of the Oedipus complex, and the infantile origins of taboo and superstition. Freud mentions in a footnote (p. 104) the she-wolf in her cage beside the steps leading up to the Capitol in Rome, as a vestige of the proclivity of clans to rear a totem animal in captivity.

Freud in *Totem and Taboo* relates two instances of phobic identification with animals in children: that of Little Hans's phobia of horses which was accompanied by feelings of admiration and interest in the creature. Little Hans jumped about "like a horse and in his turn bit his father" (Freud, 1913, p. 129), and identified his parents with other large animals. Freud then describes Ferenczi's patient, Arpád, a 2½-year-old boy who had tried to urinate in a chicken house and a chicken had pecked at his penis. Freud summarizes:

> A year later, when he was back in the same place, he himself turned into a fowl; his one interest was in the fowl-house and in what went on there and he abandoned human speech in favour of cackling and crowing. . . . he had recovered his speech, but his interests and his talk were entirely concerned with chickens and other kinds of poultry. They were his only toys and he only sang songs that had some mention of fowls in them. His attitude towards his totem animal was superlatively ambivalent: he showed both hatred and love to an extravagant degree. His favourite game was playing slaughtering fowls. . . . But afterwards he would kiss and stroke the slaughtered animal or would clean and caress the toy fowls that he had himself ill-treated.
>
> Little Arpád himself saw to it that the meaning of his strange behaviour should not remain hidden. From time to time he translated his wishes from the totemic language into that of everyday life. "My father's the cock," he said on one occasion, and another time: "Now I'm small, now I'm a chicken. When I get bigger I'll be a fowl. When I'm bigger still I'll be a cock." . . . He was very generous in threatening other people with castration, just as he himself had been threatened with it for his masturbatory activities. . . .
>
> He [Arpád] showed that he had formed his own choice of sexual objects on the model of life in the hen-run, for he said one day to the neighbour's wife: I'll marry you and your sister and my three cousins and the cook; no, not the cook, I'll marry my mother instead" [pp. 130–131].

Edmunds (1985), whose work addresses the analogs of the Oedipus legend across diverse cultures and traditions, mentions the occurrence of feral nursing or foundling status of the oedipal protagonist, often implying divine protection against death by parental abandonment (pp. 26–29, story HU2, p. 102). He also collates Oedipus stories by geographic region. The Finnish group of folktales contain a forewarning or prophecy to the parents about the parricidal and incestuous son about to be born. This forewarning by wizards, sorcerers, or holy men, concerns the simultaneous birth of a lamb which they prophesy is doomed to be eaten by a wolf (pp. 119–151). The parents, who are also told that their newborn son will kill father and marry mother, frantically try to stave off the unthinkable by first trying to protect the lamb or its cooked meat from wolves. Inevitably they fail, the wolf grabs the meat while it is cooling near the window and makes off with it. It is then that the parents, in an effort to prevent incest, seriously injure their newborn son, but stop short of killing him. They then abandon him to the mercy of fate, the seas, the forest, where they hope he will die. The baby is picked up by someone who nurses him back to health. The son returns, and unknowingly, often at the provocation of the father, kills father and marries the mother.

The Finnish oedipal stories are striking for their use of the wolf portending a particular kind of danger, the wolf representing ravenous, unstoppable appetites, an oral premonition of oedipal strivings. At the same time, the stories, by timing the birth of the oedipal son with the birth of a lamb, suggest the identification by the threatened father with the wolf—the father desires to destroy, eat up his newborn son.

It is known that the wolf was very much part of the Wolf Man's cultural and personal experience. As a child in Russia, he was exposed to farm animals being killed by predators, wolf hunts (Wolf-man, 1971, p. 12), and was familiar with fairy tales with wolves, *Little Red Riding Hood*, and *The Seven Little Goats* (Freud, 1918, p. 176). The Wolf Man in his autobiography (1971) reports that his sister once frightened him with a picture of a girl (Little Red Riding Hood) about to be swallowed up by a wolf standing up on his hind feet, jaws wide open (p. 7). The Wolf Man's famous painting of his dream reflects the wintry, snow-laden backdrop of his homeland, and no doubt anchors the dream in a cultural as well as personal landscape. The dream:

> I dreamt that it was night and that I was lying in my bed. My bed stood with its foot towards the window; in front of the window there was a row of old walnut trees. I know it was winter when I had the dream, and night-time. Suddenly the window opened of

its own accord, and I was terrified to see that some white wolves were sitting on the big walnut tree in front of the window. There were six or seven of them. The wolves were quite white, and looked more like foxes or sheep-dogs, for they had big tails like foxes and they had their ears pricked like dogs when they pay attention to something. In great terror, evidently of being eaten up by the wolves, I screamed *and woke up* [Freud 1918, p. 29; emphasis in original].

Many analytic interpretations have been offered over time about this dream, besides Freud's own exhaustive exposition (Blum, 1974; Meissner, 1979; Mahony, 1984, to mention a few). Freud spoke resoundingly and reassuringly of several pillars of analytic thought he felt were reinforced by the Wolf Man case: the infantile neurosis, the primal scene as fact and fantasy, negative oedipal strivings, and erotism, castration, and perhaps most tellingly, the centrality of the dreamscape for recovery of memories and their day-residue antecedents.

Less well studied is the wolf as a symbol with a host of lexical, cultural, and personally idiosyncratic meanings (Mahony [1984] is an exception). Psychoanalysts have followed Freud in the main by emphasizing his zoological vision of animals as father-surrogates in children's phobias, and as totems in the larger vision of oedipal development (Genosko, 1993). Addressing the problem of incompatible theories that appear compatible, Bernardi (1989) asserts that there are significant, and in his view insurmountable differences among post-Freudian theorists when they attempt to look at the Wolf Man. He feels different paradigmatic determinants result in different psychoanalytic interpretations, leading to at least three kinds of wolves: Freudian, Kleinian, and Lacanian. This opens up the study of personal as well as theoretical models of a mental wolf, and lets us ponder at least the caricatures of a Freudian wolf who is all intrapsychic drive and defense, or a Kleinian wolf who is all wolf cub filled with schematic fantasy, or a Lacanian wolf who is all language and symbol. For a rebuttal, see Mezan (1990) who asserts that contemporary theories are not paradigmatically divergent, and that all take Freud to be a common referent. Jacobs (1994) emphasizes the wolf-dog connection elaborated in fable and myth, and believes that Freud, by not seeing the importance of dogs in his own life, missed important transference material in the Wolf Man case.

Drawing on the larger symbolism and cultural connotations this study of the wolf dream has yielded, I offer the following thoughts on three aspects of the dream:

1. The accompanying drawing by the Wolf Man of the dream depicted a large walnut tree with several limbs upon which the six or seven wolves sat. Freud mentions the connection to a Christmas tree, and to the notion of a large tree offering a scoptophilic opportunity to see everything, without the observer being seen (Freud, 1918, p. 43). Of note is the peculiarity of the tree itself: the trunk appears to be broken off at some height from the ground, leaving the impression that the tree is dead or decapitated. Thus the drawing depicts a bleak picture of a dead tree, massive though it appears, condensing deadness, nonnurturance, and castration. See Lubin (1967) for an interpretation of the tree as a cross, with the white wolves representing lambs, five in number, the number of wounds on Christ.

2. *"[L]ooked more like foxes or sheep-dogs, for they had big tails like foxes and they had their ears pricked like dogs when they pay attention to something."* From the evidence in folklore suggesting the psychic interchangeability of dog with wolf, and the interest in owning and raising wolf-dogs alluded to earlier in this chapter, it should not surprise us that the Wolf Man too struggles in his dreamwork between depicting his symbolic animal as feral and as domesticated. The wolf represents the Wolf Man's personal experiences with animals on the farm where he was raised (Freud, 1918, p. 25), the projection of his instinctual wishes, and the taming of such wishes by mental domestication. The dog in the dream attains the status of "man's best friend" through the convergence of feral and domestic attributes, both biologically and psychically. In the Grimms' version of *The Wolf and the Seven Young Kids* (Zipes, 1987), the wolf disguises himself as goat mother by imitating her voice, and coloring his paw white with flour, before he is let in by the hapless goat children. For practical purposes, then, the wolf has been in dog's (or goat's) clothing for some considerable biological time, providing man with an exemplary pet genetically tamed by nature and nurture, and a hybrid psychical creature that fulfills totemistic wishes.

3. *In great terror, evidently of being eaten up by the wolves, I screamed. . . .*" Freud notes that this fear was rooted in the fairy tale (*The Seven Little Goats*), in which six of the goat-children are eaten up by the wolf-father, and adds that this could represent a memory of the Wolf Man's father making threats in jest (Freud, 1918, p. 44). Edmunds' survey of the Finnish oedipal tales suggests that the wolf in certain cultures reaches totemistic ascendancy and often contains the subtext, indeed a tragic chorus, of a wolf devouring a newborn lamb. It may rightly be asked why Finnish tales, and not other ethnic versions, contain the submotif of the orally incorporative wolf. Whether the devouring oedipal wolf was part of the Wolf Man's folklore legacy is beyond the scope of this chapter, but deserves further research.

Thomas (1992) argues that Freud's analysis of the Wolf Man contained many elements associated with self psychology, such as unmet narcissistic needs of the Wolf Man for mirroring by his father. Another self-psychological view (Magid, 1992) stresses that the Wolf Man masochistically acquiesced to Freud's primal scene interpretation in order to sustain vital self-object ties with his analyst. From self-psychological as well as classical analysis, the wolf-analyst then serves a mirroring function, shoring up object ties in the patient to preserve psychic equilibrium. A Russian tale supports the idea of the wolf as a powerful and magical savior, rather than as the feared castrating father. In *Prince Ivan and the Firebird* (Gal, 1991), a csar's son searches for the Firebird that stole golden apples from the csar's garden. Helped by a magical wolf, Prince Ivan is returning with the Firebird, a beautiful princess, and a horse with a golden mane when he is murdered by his two jealous brothers. Restored to life by the wolf, Ivan marries the princess. The Wolf Man, it might be said, from a modern structural perspective, chose to conjure up the wolf repeatedly, not only to convey and master trauma, but to reassure himself that his trusty wolf would always be with him.

In recent years, the wolf-dream has been mined for evidence of narrative and historical truth (Wink, 1990). May (1990) compares Schafer, Kohut, and Freud to understand psychoanalytic attempts to establish veridical history, and credits Freud with establishing psychoanalytic willingness to remain steadfastly in the ambiguous area between fact and fiction. Within the larger analytic enterprise, veridical truth and psychical or motivationally altered "truth," have been subjects of new debate (Brenneis, 1996; Good, 1996). Blum (1996) stresses the multiply layered effects of seduction trauma, both immediate and phase specific. He notes the "extraordinary developmental significance" (p. 1154) Freud attached to the Wolf Man's dream, during which momentous regressive and progressive developmental events unfolded. The Wolf Man, Freud asserts, "had reached a new phase in his sexual organization. . . . The activation of the primal scene in the dream now brought him back to the genital organization. He discovered the vagina and the biological significance of masculine and feminine" (Freud, 1918, pp. 46–47). Blum further summarizes the interplay of present and past in the dream, and the nature of trauma and deferred action (*Nachträglichkeit, aprés coup*):

> Freud inferred that the single, actual parental primal scene experience and associated sexual seduction by his sister and nursemaid shattered the Wolf Man's psychosexual development via deferred action. Freud proposed that this primal scene at 18 months was not traumatic then, not traumatic until a developmental reorganization at age 4. An earlier memory ostensibly became a "retrospective trauma" under present conditions. . . . What is more remarkable is that this altered representation and understanding which resulted in traumatic experience, occurred during a dream on the Wolf Man's fourth birthday—a dream which activated and altered the Wolf Man's presumed primal scene experience at the age of 18 months. . . . The dream (a nightmare) became a "fresh trauma" which, on analysis, led to the classic exposition of primal scene oedipal trauma. It is doubtless the cardinal example of deferred action, and is also relevant to important, contemporary issues concerning, for example, psychic reality and external reality; memory and myth; and developmental arrest and progression [1996, pp. 1153–1154].

Blum feels the idea of deferred action tends to artificially force pathogenesis into a strictly oedipal configuration. He prefers the idea of developmental transformation: in the formulation, for example, that the Wolf Man's "preoedipal fears of separation and object loss were revived and were reexperienced as threats of castration and death at the time of his fourth birthday nightmare" (p. 1155). Glenn (1993), using the Isakower phenomenon as an example, lists the theoretically and developmentally salient meaning of this dreamlike phenomenon: "as a symptom, a transitional phenomenon, a compromise formation, a defensive regressive expression, a screen memory, or a manifestation of a memory trace" (p. 1125). One could add more (and overlapping) dimensions such as trauma, enactment, transference urgencies, and somatic compliance. As Glenn ably illustrates, it is clinical exigency that held sway in his interpretive moments rather than the theoretical stances the list can evoke.

Here we are forced to ask what clinical exigency is. Why is the wolf important in the wolf dream, and when in the course of treatment, and for whom? The wolf in the wolf dream is a central, dramatic, repetitive, figure. The frightening and historically rich evocativeness is unmistakable. Abraham and Torok (1976), in their otherwise controversial study of language use in the Wolf Man's analysis, make "the startling revelation that witnessing and dreaming in Russian are essentially the same word" (quoted in Mahony, 1984, p. 114). As the manifest content of a dream, the wolf presages modern studies that look upon manifest content as a rich lode of understanding (Pulver, 1987). The wolf thus is representative of highly condensed conflicts. It also scores high on the representability index by virtue of multiple enduring meanings in myth, legend, childhood, and folktales, for both Freud and the Wolf Man. The terror and relief are uniquely shared by analyst and analysand, paving the way for mutually agreed upon introspection.[7] The result is a sustained discourse on topics central to psychoanalysis, to Freud, and to the Wolf Man. Clinical exigency for Freud consists of positivistic, historical,

---

[7] For a comprehensive account of Freud's psychological connection with his Russian ancestors, and its effect on his treatment of the Wolf Man, see Rice (1993). There is evidence that Freud spoke in earnest and sometimes in jest, of a typology of the Russian character, describing it as "ambivalent" (p. 116). Rice also mentions Freud's familiarity with Dostoevsky, especially Raskolnikov, the hero of *Crime and Punishment*. Rice draws a parallel between Dostoevsky's autobiographical *Peasant Marie* in which "the boy hero hysterically flees from a hallucinated cry of 'Wolf!' to the comforting caresses of a 'motherly' peasant ploughman. One senses that this famous story could be the paradigm of the Wolf Man" (p. 114).

symbol-as-code experiences in which affect, theory, and transference came together in an arcing moment. Furthermore, analysis was conducted in an atmosphere in which assumptions about the world and causality were either shared or came to be mutually agreed upon. By contrast, the semiotic, intersubjectivist, social constructivist, bipersonal field of experience, some would argue, took a beating in Freud's day with the wolf. Freud's theory-building proclivity they would say was ever present in the Wolf Man case, leading to a kind of clinical exigency marked by prestructural technique and topographic dominance.

Today, however, the question is where in our universe of technique would we situate Freud's analysis with the Wolf Man? In order to answer this question, I would first say that in the Wolf Man case, Freud demonstrates not technique but a theory of why certain elements in the case, the wolf dream, for example, were important to him. Recurring and fearsome as the dream was for the Wolf Man, and for Freud, an exemplar of the primal scene that he could present for the edification of Jung and Adler, it seems to me first and foremost, that it was Freud as adroit writer (Mahony, 1987) who calls attention to the wolf theme. Perhaps the writer in Freud strove to bring together points of analytic urgency and thus become a creator of meaning. It is probably no accident that the Wolf Man recreated the dream in his famous painting, and achieved some artistic success with it. The dream with the lupine motif became iconic, further suggesting the depth of unconscious artistry by the dreamer as well as the literary masterliness of Freud (see Edelheit [1971] for an account of the mythopoetic process in primal scene experiences). The dream is phantasmagoric, hallucinatory, compelling; a screenplay of the mind to which the Wolf Man, Freud, and his readers immediately react. The stillness of the wolves is high drama; the plot is also slyly beckoning, mystifying, like an absurdist play that froze in Act I. Primal scene is now firmly theater, albeit an analytic one (Perez, 1988). The reader and viewer are helplessly caught in this surreal dreamer's moment, desperate for enlightenment. Defying common logic, Freud in his genius then calls on the uncommon logic of psychoanalysis. Neither reader nor patient can resist. Meaning is created, sometimes foisted, with ensuing relief and insight. The wolf in the dream becomes the wolf of the mind. An animal from the pages of a child's book springs into preternatural action, fathers and mothers become disguised demons, wolf goes from lexical to somatic meaning. The Wolf Man cannot feel a wolf; he feels terror, he cannot even cry Wolf! Something wolflike has now joined the cast, and the stage is forever changed. The wolf is now clearly in the consulting room, and by resonating as myth, fantasy, and reality in the minds of the occupants, is now a clinical exigency.

Clinical exigency of the kind described above leads to interpretive activity. Coen (1996) for one, citing Erikson's interpretation of the Irma dream, sees bold, playful creativity as crucial in the interpretive work with dreams. Friedman (1995), in a finely wrought commentary on Lichtenberg's motivational theory, discusses the emergence of a "main meaning" during the course of therapy. He yokes points of urgency in the patient (as well as in the analyst) to "source motives" (p. 458):

> [It is a clinical situation in which] we are not free to make up any old narrative we wish that something particular is at stake. We may be able to tell the story in many ways, but we feel that the limits are narrow. On the other hand, these are times in treatment when, though we assume that the patient is "up to something" the assignment of a single banner to his campaign feels quite arbitrary and reflects the therapist's convenience as much as the patient's reality [p. 458].

What anchors the analytic activity in my view, are individual and sociocultural dynamics and conflicts that are extended relics of imagined or real history. Anamnesis, fantasy, affects, and their creative merger in dreams, shaped by the psychoanalytic laws of the mind, excel as conceptual tools with considerable curative power, and define the domain of clinical psychoanalysis quite well. But are these anchors feeling too safe? Is there in our newer sensibilities the beginnings of a postmodern wolf—a wolf representing cultural hegemony and relativism by its very use as a symbol, and in truth being another unconscious exercise in self-deception? For those who believe that psychoanalysis should rightly address cultural issues selectively and only in analytic context, postmodern concerns seem to veer toward the truly existential, beyond the purview of clinical psychoanalysis. For others, postmodernism (leaving out the multitude of nonanalytic battles fought under its flag), promises the lifting of a new kind of repression and an uneasy freedom from history, if not from the imperatives of language itself.

CONCLUDING REMARKS

The psychoanalytic wolf is a diverse discourse, touching on phenomenology, symbol, myth, metaphor, symptom, development, fantasy, and identification, and subject to subtle sociocultural influence. Such an emerging gestalt is common when the wide-angle lens of psychoanalysis is trained on a topic. When the wolf enters our consulting rooms, we narrow considerably the focal length of our discourse to understand the individual analysand. We seek the bedrock essence of human experience, questing for a body epistemology that can elevate symbol to sensation. Technical innovation in our consulting rooms involves shared creation and discovery by analyst and analysand—of a veritable wolfscape. Our success will depend on the recognition of multiple and complementary levels of discourse on a subject such as the wolf. This chapter, it is hoped, has shown that there is no escape from the positivist terrors of the big bad wolf, or from the modernist, Little Red Riding Hood legacy of our ancient bond with this animal. When the wolf huffs and puffs, our conceptual house, whether postmodern or not, had better be built from experiential brick. As Kipling's Mowgli says, "It is true that I am a Man, but it is in my stomach that this night I have said I am a wolf."

REFERENCES

Abraham, N., & Torok, M. (1976), *The Wolf Man's Magic World: A Cryptonymy.* Minneapolis: University of Minneapolis Press.

Armen, J-C. (1974), *Gazelle Boy.* London: Bodley Head.

Bergerman, S. [Producer], & Walker, S. [Director] (1935), *The Werewolf of London* [Film]. Universal [Distributor].

Bernardi, R. (1989), El poder de las teorias: El papel de los determinantes paradigmaticos en la comprension psicoanalitica. *Revista de Psicanalisis,* 46(6):904–929.

Blum, H. P. (1974), The borderline childhood of the Wolf Man. *J. Amer. Psychoanal. Assn.*, 22:721–742.

—— (1996), Seduction trauma: Representation, deferred action, and pathogenic development. *J. Amer. Psychoanal. Assn.*, 44:1147–1164.

Brenneis, C. B. (1996), Memory systems and the psychoanalytic retrieval of memories of trauma. *J. Amer. Psychoanal. Assn.*, 44:1165–1187.

Burns, J. F. (1996), In India, attacks by wolves spark old fears and hatreds. *NY Times*, September 1, 1, p. 1.

Candland, D. K. (1993), *Feral Children and Clever Animals.* New York: Oxford University Press.

Coen, S. J. (1996), The passions and perils of interpretation (of dreams and texts): An appreciation of Erik Erikson's Dream Specimen Paper. *Internat. J. Psycho-Anal.*, 77:537–548.

Coll, P. G., O'Sullivan, G., & Browne, P. J. (1985), Lycanthropy lives on. *Brit. J. Psychiatry*, 147:201–202.

Dening, T. R., & West, A. (1989), Multiple serial lycanthropy: A case report. *Psychopathology*, 22(6):344–347.

Doniger O'Flaherty, W. D. (1988), *Other Peoples' Myths.* New York: Macmillan.

Douglas, A. (1992), *The Beast Within.* London: Chapmans.

Edelheit, H. (1971), Mythopoiesis and the primal scene. *The Psychoanalytic Study of the Child*, 5:212–233. New York: International Universities Press.

Edmunds, L. (1985), *Oedipus: The Ancient Legend and Its Later Analogues.* Baltimore, MD: Johns Hopkins University Press.

Favazza, A. R. (1977), Feral and isolated children. *Brit. J. Med. Psychol.*, 50(1):105–111.

Feuerbach, P. J. A., Ritter von (1832), *Last Prince: The Unsolved Mystery of Kasper Hauser*, tr. J. M. Masson. New York: Free Press.

Folsey, G., Jr. [Producer], & Landis, J. [Director] (1981), *An American Werewolf in London* [Film]. Lycanthrope Films/Universal [Distributor].

Frazer, J. G. (1922), *The Golden Bough.* New York: Macmillan, 1979.

Freud, S. (1913), Totem and Taboo. *Standard Edition*, 13:1–161. London: Hogarth Press, 1955.

—— (1918), From the History of an Infantile Neurosis. *Standard Edition*, 17:3–122. London: Hogarth Press, 1955.

Friedman, L. (1995), Main meaning and motivation. *Psychoanal. Inqu.*, 15:437–460.

Gal, L. (1991), *Prince Ivan and the Firebird. A Russian Folk Tale.* Toronto: McClelland & Stewart.

Genosko, G. (1993), Freud's bestiary: How does psychoanalysis treat animals? *Psychoanal. Rev.*, 80:603–632.

Gesell, A. (1941), *Wolf Child and Human Child. Being a Narrative Interpretation of the Life History of Kamala, the Wolf Girl.* New York: Harper & Brothers.

Glenn, J. (1993), Developmental transformations: The Isakower pohenomenon as an example. *J. Amer. Psychoanal. Assn.*, 41:1113–1134.

Good, M. I. (1996), Suggestion and veridicality in the reconstruction of sexual trauma, or can a bait of suggestion catch a carp of falsehood? *J. Amer. Psychoanal. Assn.*, 44:1189–1224.

Hoffman, A. (1994), *Second Nature.* New York: Berkley Books.

Jacobs, A. (1994), Freud and the interpretation of the Wolf-Man dream: A dog story? *Contemp. Psychoanal.*, 30(4):845–854.

Kaplan, J., Ed. (1992), *Bartlett's Familiar Quotations*, 16th ed. Boston: Little, Brown.

Kipling, R. (1895), *The Jungle Books.* Harmondsworth, U.K.: Puffin, 1987.

Kulick, A. R., Pope, H. G., & Keck, P. E. (1990), Lycanthropy and self-identification. *J. Nerv. & Ment. Dis.*, 178(2):134–137.

Lane, H. (1977), *The Wild Boy of Aveyron.* New York: Allen & Unwin.

Lange, E. (1970), A dog's life: Lycanthropic behavior during alcoholic intoxication. *Psychiatrie, Neurologie und Medizinische Psychologie*, 22:6–10.

Lubin, A. (1967), The influence of the Russian Orthodox Church on Freud's Wolf Man: A hypothesis. *Psychoanal. Forum*, 2:145–162.

Maclean, C. (1977), *The Wolf Children.* New York: Hill & Wang.

Magid, B. (1992), Self-psychology meets the Wolf Man. *Psychoanal. & Psychother.*, 10(2):178–198.

Mahony, P. (1984), *Cries of the Wolf Man.* New York: International Universities Press.

—— (1987), *Freud as a Writer*, rev. ed. New Haven, CT: Yale University Press.

Malson, L. (1972), *Wolf Children and the Problem of Human Nature.* New York: Monthly Review Press.

May, R. (1990), The idea of history in psychoanalysis: Freud and the "Wolf Man." *Psychoanal. Psychology*, 7(2):163–183.

Meissner, W. W. (1979), The Wolf Man and the paranoid process. *Psychoanal. Rev.*, 66:155–172.

Merkur, D. (1981), The psychodynamics of the Navajo Coyoteway ceremonial. *J. Mind & Behav.*, 2(3):241–257.

Mezan, R. (1990), Existem paradigmas na psicanalise? Sobre um artigo de R. Bernardi. Percurse. *Revista de Psicanalise*, 2(4)[1]:43–52.

Mitchell, G., & Wright E. (1975), Duke Ferdinand's lycanthropy as a disguise motive in Webster's *The Duchess of Malfi. Lit. & Psychol.*, 25:117–123.

Ogburn, W. F., & Bose, N. K. (1959), On the Trail of the Wolf Children. *Genetic Psychology Monograph*, 60:117–193.

Otten, C., Ed. (1986), *A Lycanthropy Reader: Werewolves in Western Culture*. Syracuse, NY: Syracuse University Press.

Perez, C. D. (1988), Del Hombre los Lobos, la Niña de los Vestidos y l tragedia griega (The Wolf Man, the Dress Girl, and Greek tragedy). *Revista de Psicoanalisis*, 45(1):107–115.

Pulver, S. E. (1987), The manifest dream in psychoanalysis: A clarification. *J. Amer. Psychoanal. Assn.*, 35:99–118.

Raspaolo, D. (1988), Su una possibile interpretazione della leggenda del lupo mannaro (A possible interpretation of the story of the Wolf Man). *Giornale Storico di Psicologia Dinamica*, 12(23):62–76.

Rice, J. L. (1993), *Freud's Russia. National Identity in the Evolution of Psychoanalysis*. New Brunswick, NJ: Transaction.

Rosenstock, H. A., & Vincent, K. R. (1977), A case of lycanthropy. *Amer. J. Psychiatry*, 134(10):1147–1149.

Ryder, A. W., Tr. (1956), *The Panchatantra*. Chicago: University of Chicago Press/Phoenix Books.

Shakespeare, W. (1925), Troilus and Cressida. In: *The Complete Works of William Shakespeare*, ed. W. J. Craig. New York: Oxford University Press.

Shengold, L. (1975), An attempt at soul murder: Rudyard Kipling's early life and work. *The Psychoanalytic Study of the Child*, 30:683–724. New Haven, CT: Yale University Press.

——— (1978), Kaspar Hauser and soul murder: A study of deprivation. *Internat. J. Psycho-Anal.*, 5(4):457–476.

Shipley, J. T. (1984), *The Origins of English Words: A Discursive Dictionary of Indo-European Roots*. Baltimore, MD: Johns Hopkins University Press.

Singh, J. A. L., & Zingg, R. M. (1942), *Wolf-Children and Feral Man*. New York: Harper.

Surawicz, F. G., & Banta, R. (1975), Lycanthropy revisited. *J. Can. Psychiat. Assn.*, 20(7):537–542.

Thomas, K. R. (1992), The Wolf-Man case: Classical and self-psychological perspectives. *Amer. J. Psychoanal.*, 52(3):213–225.

Waggner, G. [Producer & Director] (1941), *The Wolf Man* [Film]. Universal [Distributor].

Webster, J. *The Duchess of Malfi*. Mineola, NY: Dover, 1999.

Wink, P. (1990), Freud, truth and the Wolf Man. *Psychoanal. & Contemp. Thought*, 13(3):365–416.

Wolf-Man (Pankejeff, S.) (1971), *The Wolf-Man by the Wolf-Man*. New York: Basic Books.

Zipes, J., Tr. (1987), *The Complete Fairy Tales of the Brothers Grimm*. New York: Bantam Books.

Part III
Other Animals

CHAPTER 5

Man's Best Friend

PHILIP J. ESCOLL, M.D.

> Affectionate without ambivalence, the simplicity
> of a life free from the almost unbearable con-
> flicts of civilization, the beauty of existence com-
> plete in itself and yet, despite all divergences in
> organic development [there is] that feeling of
> intimate affinity of an undisputed solidari-
> ty ... a bond of friendship unites us both ..."
> [Freud, about his beloved chow, Jo-Fi, 1936].

Dogs have played a part in the life of humans for about 12,000 years. Dogs, "man's best friend," as the old saying goes, have become a significant part of human experience and culture. In ancient Egypt, for example, they were used as icons, totems, and even gods (Halpert, 1980). Dogs have also assumed a role since ancient days as pets as well as workers. In recent times they have served in settings such as psychiatric hospitals and nursing homes as therapy dogs. Dogs have served as guides and helpmates to the blind and, more recently, to the hearing impaired. They have participated in the military as "canine corps," and they have worked with law enforcement to trick criminals and also to sniff for drugs. They are used as sled dogs, to herd sheep, work with hunters, and as watch dogs. They are also widely used as subjects

Acknowledgments. The author wishes to thank Dr. Salman Akhtar for his valuable suggestions, Ellen Young for her expert secretarial assistance, and Toni Yancey, librarian, for her generous help.

127

for research (Pavlov, 1927). They have customarily been used to find survivors in disasters, such as the Oklahoma City bombing. Dogs have also been used to intimidate or attack: in Nazi Germany, dogs were used to herd victims in the concentration camps.

In the wild, as well as when unattended even in city areas, dogs form packs and act to defend the group, and as such, can be dangerous and destructive. Dogs form positive relationships with their human associates, barking at the door to defend the home, for example. While having a dog, being seen with a dog, often promotes an image of security and friendship with others, and is a way of widening one's social circle, it can also lead to difficulty and antagonism between neighbors. I know, for example, of a situation in which a neighbor had a dog who got into serious fights with other dogs. She then accused a neighboring family of having a dog that led her own dog astray! It is commonly observed that dogs seem to take on traits of the owner.

Dogs are closely associated with children, as they become their companions and virtual siblings. They participate with children in all kinds of endeavors, as idealized in Norman Rockwell's paintings. For children, dogs are objects of security and can serve as transitional objects.

Dogs regularly tend to be anthropomorphized. A dog's expression and behavior may be used to attribute to it such human qualities as sympathy, kindness, and love, or, less commonly, neglect, selfishness, and hostility. This is beautifully illustrated in the comedy *Sylvia*, by Albert Gurney. An actress assumes the role and behavior of a dog. Conflicts develop with a couple, and the husband, a Manhattan investment banker, becomes more and more attached to his dog, eventually falling in love with it. The man begins to favor the dog over his wife, and he assumes aspects of the dog. Later on, his wife, to a lesser degree, begins to do this also. In this situation the humans take on the traits of the dogs. The dog, in turn, begins to assume some human qualities. Through projection, dogs can represent for humans aspects of the unconscious that are warded off, such as aggressivity, hostility, and sexuality. Dogs may also be seen as totally loving, understanding, and always helpful, as the husband in the play feels about his dog. Of course, dogs may actually have some of these qualities. Total loyalty and their often successful attempts at protection and even rescue certainly occur, but one has to always consider the projection for which individuals use dogs.

Dogs have their own personality difficulties which can create problems for the owner and family. Dogs who bite, dogs who become psychotic, dogs who frequently become ill, clearly are problematic. Of course, dogs have different temperaments which influences the interplay with their owners. Dogs may be reared to heighten their aggressivity. An extreme example of this is seen with some owners of pitbulls who train their dogs to fight and kill to earn money in betting on competitions with rival dogs. Dog owners may express their sadism in their cruelty to their dogs. Sexuality is also an important issue, with children observing mounting, which can be confusing and disturbing, with primal scene implications. One patient reported his childhood curiosity about his dog's body and his attempts to penetrate her. Another patient described that as a boy, in his preteen years, he became very interested in his dog's body, and when this elderly dog began to fail, he managed to kill it and then dissect it. In associating to this, he revealed his degree of hostility to the dog, who was a sibling rival, as well as an object of great curiosity. He experienced both a sense of pride as well as guilt about what he did with this dog.

Dogs are often seen as siblings, inviting closeness as well as rivalry. Of course, dogs, on their own part, show rivalrous behavior when there is a new child in the family taking attention away from them. An additional point relates to the pet dog who becomes very ill. This raises conflicts in the family about the extent to which medical treatment, even surgery, is considered. These issues may divide families. When a dog begins to seriously deteriorate, and more and more heroic measures are needed to save it, the question then is raised about "putting the dog to sleep." This euphemism is obviously designed to reduce the fear and guilt related to killing the animal. With many families, once the deed is done, there is comfort in knowing the dog is out of pain, but at the same time there is guilt, often also anger on the part of children, feeling their parents have not done all they could for the dog. The related feeling is, therefore, that their parents might not do all they could for them, and they could, in some fashion, get rid of them also.

There is a commonality between dogs and man, including the idea that both, in a sense, are immigrants. This is not the same as immigrating to a new country (Akhtar, 1995), but, human beings, one might say, have emigrated from the animal kingdom, although animals remain an important part of their lives. Dogs have also emigrated from the world of pack animals, perhaps jaguars, to being domesticated animals (Lorenz, 1952). An early archaeological find, indicative of the human-animal bond, was discovered in 1976 by Simon Davis of Hebrew University. He excavated a human skeleton in a tomb in northern Israel, estimated to be approximately 12,000 years old. Clutched tightly in the hands of the skeleton were the remains of a puppy (Cusack, 1988, p. 1). Another indication of the degree to which dogs have been an integral part of human society and the human mind are the many terms in everyday use related to dogs.[1]

In Egypt, a dog, or jackal-headed god, Anubis, reigned over the dead; Anubis was also seen as a good mother, a bad mother being Ammit (Halpert, 1980). On the other hand, dogs were seen as malevolent by Egyptians who feared being eaten by dogs after death. Dogs have often been associated with death; the image of dogs in dreams often relates to this (Halpert, 1980). Dogs are important in the legends of many cultures. In the Muslim tradition, according to the Prophet Mohammed, animals have souls, and to make an animal happy is to live by the principle of Islam. There is the legend that once, long ago, in the East, a woman of the night wandered into the desert; she was dying from thirst, and then climbed into a deep hole in the earth and found water. When she climbed back on the parched desert surface the woman saw a dying and withered mongrel whereupon she returned to the well, then filled her shoe with water and saved the dog's life. According to the teachings of the Prophet Mohammed, at that instant the woman was assured a place in the garden of heaven.

DOGS IN PSYCHIATRIC SYMPTOMATOLOGY

Dogs, as is the case with other animals, are involved in a variety of ways in patients' symptoms and conflicts. In delusional manifestations, for example, a dog may be experienced as a ferocious

---

[1] Examples are *doggone, dog day, doggedly, bitch, son of a bitch, she looks like a dog, yellow dog, having the black dog* (Storr, 1988), *dog tired,* and, of course, *a dog is man's best friend.*

beast out to destroy the individual, or in a wide variety of other roles. In the notorious case of "Son of Sam," Sam, the neighbor's dog, became the delusional father of the murderer. Hallucinations also involve dogs who are seen in many different images, such as evil, satanic creatures, or occasionally, benevolent protectors or saviors. Dogs are also used for sexual experimentation, as well as sexual perversions.

Phobias of animals have been described in the analytic literature for a long time, beginning with Freud's paper about Little Hans (Freud, 1909). In the more recent literature, Tyson (1978) wrote about a 5-year-old boy who had a fear of dogs established before age 3. He had multiple fears of a dog which seemed to sequentially follow the birth of his brother when the patient was 2 years, 9 months. E. Sterba (1935) also wrote about the analysis of a child with a dog phobia. She states that nearly all children show a transitory fear of one animal or another. She quotes Freud's views in *Totem and Taboo* (1913) about these early years and then goes on to say that the animal becomes a substitute for the feared person, with libidinal and aggressive strivings being displaced. Fraiberg (1951) and Harley (1967) make similar points, with Fraiberg emphasizing the mother represented as the dangerous animal. E. Sterba goes on to indicate the many ambivalent relationships with the animal. Her patient was a $7^1/_2$-year-old girl who received many enemas. She developed what was called the "tube game" involving enemas and penis symbols with an identification with the aggressor-dog. Sperling (1952) wrote about a 2-year-old girl who had fears of a dog (also fears of "Kitty" and "fish"). This began following the birth of her brother when she was 26 months old. She would wake up nightly with fears of being bitten and projected her own oral-sadistic impulses onto the dog. She experienced anorexia and sleep disturbances with aggression related to the phobia.

Alper (1933) wrote, "It is stated that pets play a critical role in providing self-object functions in the young developing child, particularly in an otherwise impoverished or exploitative self-object environment" (p. 257). Alper, continuing in a self-psychology framework, stresses the importance of the dog to the patient noting, mirroring, recognizing, confirming uniqueness and greatness. The author discusses Hilary, age 28, who presented with complaints of unhappiness, difficulties with self-esteem, and drug dependency. Subsequently, she received a dog to whom she read poetry, and she asked the dog, "Do you like it?" The dog responded by wagging its tail, jumping up and down, and licking Hilary (p. 262). The dog provided affirmation that the parents were unable to provide. The dog also helped her with her creativity. Alper feels that an owner's capacity for empathy is aided by putting the self in the dog's shoes. It may become a problem if a pet dog becomes the primary object and the central affective tie is with the dog.

Heiman (1956, p. 268) quotes Francis Galton (1883): "The animal which above all others is a companion is the dog, and we observe how readily their (man's and dog's) proceedings are intelligible to each other." Heiman also cites Jelliffe and Brink (1917). They point to the significant role played by animals in symptoms as well as dreams. Heiman also focuses on Marie Bonaparte's relationship with her dog, Topsy, who helped her survive a serious illness. Bonaparte (1940) wrote about Topsy who had herself been ill with cancer and was saved through radiation treatment. Bonaparte wrote, "And as in bygone times from Mimau [her nurse who had died], a power seemed to emanate from Topsy, as from a talisman of life" (pp. 78–79). Topsy conquered cancer and, therefore, due to Bonaparte's efforts, Topsy was a talisman that "conjures away death" (p. 79). Bonaparte added, "A simple dog, lying there by me, just like Mimau by the child that I was, she guards me, and by her presence alone must bar the entrance of my room to a worse ill, and even to death" (p. 79).

BOOKS AND FILMS

There are many interesting works regarding behavior of dogs, as well as accounts about animal behavior as correlated with humans. Masson and McCarthy (1995) have written about their view that animals have emotions in their book, *When Animals Weep*. Elizabeth Thomas (1993) in her book, *The Hidden Life of Dogs*, has written about the anthropomorphism attributed to dogs, such as seeing a dog "smile." She describes this as a mannerism of the face of the dog and the movement of muscles which is not a smile. Thomas studied at length the habits of a number of dogs whom she allowed to run freely; she describes the culture of the dogs and the way in which they helped and responded to each other. She depicts a civilization or society of dogs, the dogs traveling freely, running for miles together, and how they collaborated with each other and how they related to their owners. There is clearly much anthropomorphization in her view of these dogs as well.

Dogs have been the major fictional characters in books, notably those by Albert Payson Terhune and Jack London. Examples of Terhune's work for children are *Highland Collie* (1927) and *Lad, a Dog* (1966—seventy-sixth printing!). London is also known for a number of books about dogs such as *The Call of the Wild* (1963) and *White Fang* (1933). Eric Knight introduced a famous animal in *Lassie Come Home* (1940). Dogs are also portrayed in short stories, films, television, comic strips, and paintings. Lassie and Rin Tin Tin starred in movies, and Toto and Snoopy are household names. Lassie was, and remains in T.V. reruns, a very heroic animal. She is always beautifully groomed, kind, responsive, smart, faithful, and truly heroic. She periodically rescues someone, tracks a criminal who is brought to justice, and, through her posture and barks, she identifies dangerous places and people. A significant relationship is with a young boy who is her master and yet, in many ways, Lassie is depicted as the one taking the lead. Important aspects of childhood development are present in these scenes, a similar experience reminiscent of real-life experiences, as the child forms a close, reciprocal bond with Lassie.

In the movie *My Life as a Dog*, again, a little boy is involved. In this poignant film, he is attached to his mother who is ill, possibly with tuberculosis, and he is also very attached to his dog. He is sent to relatives where he seems to be happy, but he later fights with a girl over who shows "what to whom." In a later fight with her, he then pretends to be a dog and barks, pushes two hands in front of him as a dog would with its paws, assuming the role of his dog. His mother dies and he desperately wants the dog that has been left at home. He has a fantasy of living in a small building with the dog, and is shocked when told the dog has died.

In the movie *Umberto D*, a film by DiSica, a poverty-stricken man, Umberto, has his dog, Flag, as his only companion. Flag is devoted and absolutely loyal to his owner. Flag even begs on his behalf with a hat. Later Umberto tries to give Flag away because he is penniless and cannot take care of Flag. First, he goes to a heartless couple who exploit dogs, then to a little girl whose parents will not accept Flag. In his desperation, in the last scene of the movie, Umberto attempts suicide by a train. Flag, who has been tied up by Umberto, manages to free himself, and runs away from Umberto because he is now disapproving and mistrustful of him because of Umberto's desertion. Umberto turns away from the train to get Flag, attempting to coax him back with a game which involves throwing a pine cone; finally, he succeeds in enticing Flag to play. Umberto is ecstatic, calls to Flag steadily, praises him, and, as the film ends, they continue to joyfully run and play in their reunion. In essence, Umberto saves the dog's life and the dog saves Umberto's life. Each one cannot live without the other and each has ultimate loyalty to the other. In the game at the end, Umberto has to demonstrate clearly that he is the old Umberto, trustworthy, and not threatening Flag with abandonment. In turn, Umberto is not abandoned by Flag.

In Conan Doyle's *The Hound of the Baskervilles* (1902), Sherlock Holmes is depicted as dealing with "an enormous coal-black hound, but not such a hound as the mortal eyes have ever seen. Fire bursts from its open mouth, its eyes glowed with a smoldering glare, its muzzle and hackles and dew laps were outlined in flickering flame. Never in the delirious dream of a disordered brain could anything more savage, more appalling, more hellish, be conceived than that dark form and savage face which broke upon us out of the wall of fog" (p. 887). The dog is frightening, dangerous, an apparition, and finally has to be shot by Holmes. Here we have a depiction of absolute evil, just the opposite of Lassie. In the story, the bad dogs are portrayed as big and black and howling and barking and the good dogs are portrayed in just the opposite fashion. The extremes of good and bad objects are displayed. Mark Twain had an opinion along these lines. He viewed man as more dangerous than dogs. He said, "if you pick up a starving dog and make him prosperous he will not bite you; that is the principal difference between a dog and a man."

In *Deep in the Green* (1995), Ann Raver discusses her dog, Molly. She says that Molly is the self-appointed guardian of her affections; Molly always places her body protectively between Raver and a new friend, on the couch. She describes Molly as something of a barometer. If people in the room speak in nasty tones of voice, "Molly begins to blink . . . her lips flatten out, making her look more platypus than dog" (p. 148). Raver states, "It's easy to love a dog, because a dog doesn't talk back. There are no arguments about which movie to see, or where to live . . . a dog just loves you back, even if you're fat" (pp. 148–149). Molly doesn't criticize Raver for eating potato chips, and the author goes on to say, "When she holds her tongue, what I could learn from her: that a little more unconditional love might strengthen my human relationships" (p. 149). She goes on to talk about Molly's flaws and says that with Molly she just shrugs but, "Somehow it's harder to accept imperfect people. But at least they live longer than dogs. The painful deal with animals is this: they love us no questions asked, but we have to go on without them" (p. 149).

In the Mind of the Dog, by F. J. J. Buytendijk (1935), the author points out that dog and man live in a unique relationship and between them there is a unique bond of sympathy. He attributes this to the idea that both are exiles from the simple straightforward life of nature. While the dogs have left the wolfpack and cling to man, man becomes more of a master than the leader of the wolfpack was. He describes the dog as forming an attachment to man not just because of food and comfort but, having lost the security of the herd and the pack, there is a dependency on a human master as a substitute. He sees man also as having developed his morality from the situations of life in a primal hoard and he sees this as part of a peculiar kind of bond including moral sympathy with man playing the role of superego. He describes the dog as displaying striking similarities to man in the sexual arena. He sees the dog as having polymorphic perversity as though it's a virtual caricature of human sexuality.

Frans de Waal (1996), in his book *Good Natured, The Origins of Right and Wrong in Humans and Animals,* makes the point that morality is not limited to humans and that animals can express or feel guilt or shame over some violations of rules. He speaks of monkeys in this regard, but I think this is certainly seen in dogs as well. The author feels that this is part of the evolutionary continuum linking humans and other animals. He states that animals do not have a concept of right and wrong in the way that humans do, but rather there are aspects of behavior of some animals that served as the evolutionary stimulus for morality in humans. In the book *Last Days of the Dog-Man* (1996), Brad Watson writes a number of imaginative short stories. Dogs play a vital part in each of the stories as the intricate relationships of men and women are enacted with and around them.

Willie Morris (1995) wrote a very charming and poignant book entitled *My Dog Skip*. Morris's narrative is so descriptive and vivid that I am quoting from it at length. The author describes his life with his dog, Skip, from the age of 9 until the time when he went to Oxford years later. He states that he and the family had a whole string of dogs before Skip but that "none of these other dogs ever came up to this one. You could talk to him as well as you could to many human beings and much better than you could some" (p. 5). Morris states that Skip was special from the start in that his father had ordered him from a dog breeder in another state. His first meeting with Skip is depicted in this way: "He jumped into my lap and began nuzzling my hand with his nose. When I leaned toward him, he gave me a moist lick on my chin. Then he hugged me . . . he went to sleep in my arms. I was an only child and he was an only dog" (p. 4).

Morris describes his boyhood exploits and how Skip was so much involved with them. Just by talking to Skip about going for a swim or playing baseball or football, Skip would eagerly get up to participate in these activities. He would curl up at night and sleep in a bend of Morris's legs; in the morning they would go for a run together and then, "We both had a breakfast of raisin bran and milk and he would walk with me towards school" (p. 18). The author describes adventures with Skip, in the woods, fishing, and an encounter with a skunk. In World War II, for two and a half years, "Skip was a war dog because I was a war boy" (p. 35). When Hitler would be on the radio Skip did very strange things; his ears would twitch in pain, then he would begin "strutting about the room, emitting deranged little howls, his snout lifted mightily upward much as he had done in the cemetery when we accosted the man making the shortcut" (p. 38). When a kitten, who seemed to be homeless and starving, three months old or so, showed up on the back steps, Skip was transformed. He licked the kitten's face, he laid down next to her and "he felt sorry for her I suppose, but he was also smitten by her and his response to her struck something in me, too. The little kitten tugged at my heart" (p. 51). When the kitten died, "Skip acted sad and strange" (p. 53).

When Morris went to England, he says he knew he would never see Skip again. On leaving, Skip nuzzled him with his nose "as he had done the first time I had seen him as a puppy" (p. 121). Morris says he told him that "I had to go and that I would miss him. He looked at me again, and licked my cheek" (p. 121). As his car pulled away from the house, he looked back and saw Skip walking along the front lawn and then sitting down and gazing at him. A month later he received a call at Oxford from his father and was told that Skip had died. Later Morris says he "wandered alone among landmarks in a medieval town" (p. 121). He concludes his book saying, "Walking alone in the teasing rain, I remembered our days together on this earth. The dog of your boyhood teaches you a great deal about friendship, and love, and death; Old Skip was my brother. They had buried him under our elm tree, they said—yet this was not totally true for he really lay buried in my heart" (p. 122).

This account reveals much more than anthropomorphism, although there is much of this, of course. It brings home the integral part that the dog played in Morris's life and mind as an only child, through his boyhood, adolescence, and even in young adulthood. The dog was his constant companion and, as he concludes in his last sentence, Skip played the part of a sibling, a sibling with whom there was no rivalry except in fun and games. This was a sibling whom he could intrapsychically view as he wished, a sibling who, in his behavior, was experienced as fulfilling the role of steady companion with unconditional interest and love. Morris identified with Skip in his exuberance and loyalty. There was an individuality to the dog, this companion, and, as the author says early on, he was different from the other dogs that he and the family had. This was recognized from the start and, while clearly special attributes were given to him by Morris, he was unique and assumed a unique position in the author's life.

PET-FACILITATED THERAPY

There is much in the literature, predominantly by psychologists, about animals, especially dogs, in a wide variety of therapeutic roles. Dogs have been used in psychiatric hospitals, especially as companions to schizophrenics, on adolescent units, and in prisons. They have also been involved with autistic children and with geriatric patients in a number of settings. Dogs also play an important role in helping individuals with conditions such as muscular dystrophy, multiple sclerosis, and other brain or spinal cord injuries. Dogs are taught to perform everyday tasks such as turning lights on and off, opening refrigerator doors, and helping to pull clothes on and off their masters.

Although the use of animals in institutional settings goes back to the York Retreat in England in 1792 (Cusack, 1988, p. 2), it was not until 1953 that dogs began to be used as adjuncts in the milieu of psychotherapy. Boris Levinson was a pioneer in that area; he accidentally used his dog, Jingles, as an intermediary between himself and a child patient, and found this to be very helpful in the youngster's development of trust. As Cusack (1988) states, with Levinson's publication of an article about this experience, entitled "The Dog as Co-Therapist" (1962), pet therapy formally began. Levinson later enlarged on these themes in his book, *Pet-oriented Child Psychotherapy* (1969). Other individuals are recognized as pioneers because of their use of dogs with hospitalized adolescent patients and in nursing homes. Their studies on this work demonstrated very significant patient improvement in many aspects.

Aaron Katcher, a psychiatrist, along with Alan Beck, edited a very significant book (1983) which provides a wide array of studies related to animals, particularly dogs, and their interaction in a great variety of situations with individuals and families. An example is a study by Stewart (1983, pp. 390–407) of bereavement, how children and adults react to the death of a pet as compared to reactions to the death of a human. Another example is an interesting article by Serpell (1983, pp. 57–63) who addressed the issue of the personality of the dog and how this influences the "pet-owner bond."

Another volume of importance was written by Odean Cusack (1988). Many studies are described, along with Cusack's introduction about the development of "pet-facilitated therapy," and his chapters on the "human-animal bond," and one entitled, "Why we love our pets: a naturalistic/psychoanalytic approach." There are several chapters in Cusack's book about pet therapy and the role of pets in a variety of settings. He describes the psychological benefits involved in pet-facilitated therapy, and offers an idealized view of what pets offer. "Pets provide an unlimited source of love, affection, and companionship. . . . The pet is always there, always loving, and always ready both to give and accept affection. Unconditional and nonjudgmental love and affection are the most frequently cited benefits of pet association" (p. 11). Touching dogs seems to be very important, he notes, especially as this is appropriate with dogs "rather than with veterinarians or therapists" (p. 13).

Animals and children are very much interrelated, and animals, especially dogs, play a significant part in child and adolescent development. Freud (1913) wrote about the relationship of children to animals. "Children have no scruples over allowing animals to rank as their full equals. Uninhibited as they are in the avowal of their bodily need, they no doubt feel themselves more akin to animals than to their elders, who may well be a puzzle to them" (1913, p. 127).[2] Bettelheim (1977) suggested that children identify with the animals they find in fairy tales and in this way work out many of the psychological problems related to development and maturation. In a study analyzing dreams by

---

[2] Freud was very much involved with his dogs. It is interesting to note that while Freud was indifferent to music, he would hum when he played with Jo-Fi. His chows were frequently present in his office while he was seeing patients. Dogs also played an important role in the life of Anna Freud. She was delighted when, in 1925, her father gave her a black Alsatian dog, named Wolf. "She and her father treated the dog like a child . . ." (Young-Bruehl, 1988, p. 99). For Freud's birthday Anna gave him a picture of Wolf and wrote to Lou Andreas-Salomé, "I brought only a picture of Wolf that I had made as a joke, because I always assert that he transferred his whole interest in me onto Wolf." Later, after the death of her devoted friend and companion, Dorothy Burlingham, her greatest joy came in the form of a chow puppy, Jo-Fi, named after a chow Burlingham had given to her father (Young-Bruehl, 1988, p. 444).

Van de Castle (1983), the dreams of four hundred and fifty-seven children were studied and it was found that more than 60 percent of the dreams of 4-year-olds involved animals. By the age of 15 or 16 only 9 percent of the dreams involved animals. The most common dream animals were dogs and horses. Aggression was particularly noted in these dreams, the dreamer often being the victim of the aggressive act. There seemed to be fear or apprehension in these animal dreams with the animal figures symbolizing unacceptable unconscious impulses that stirred anxiety about their breaking through into expression or consciousness. The author felt that the animal figures in dreams seemed to represent the primitive "animal" aspect of the human personality.

Cusack (1988, p. 31) discusses pets as surrogates. They take the place of people and are endowed with human characteristics. Veevers (1985) said that most interactions with animals involve a certain amount of anthropomorphism and, therefore, can be seen as surrogates for relationships with human beings. Pets can certainly be a displacement for love experience or hate experience for a child or a spouse. The popularity of toy breeds goes along with this, according to Cusack (1988, p. 32), with many pet owners referring to their charges as "my child" or "my baby." There are other dimensions that Cusack points out (pp. 32–33). It is socially permissible to lavish physical affection on a pet, something that we cannot do with human strangers. There is a quest for variety in sensuality to be sublimated through the human-animal bond. Kindness and affection toward animals is considered a higher cultural achievement than indiscriminate promiscuity. And animals serve as social lubricants. With animals as human surrogates, especially with children and adolescents, there is no risk of betrayal or ridicule by exposing thoughts and action to the dog. They can function as a surrogate mate and can also prolong parenthood for middle-aged and elderly parents. In role reversal, they can play the part of the parent for the child whose parents are in the process of divorce or separation. Pets may be idealized as "a perfect entity that seems to react correctly to every situation, to respond to every mood" (Cusack, 1988, p. 33). The author points out that "pets seem to bring out the best in us, our capacities for affection and compassion for empathy may be overlooked by our human fellow but a pet has an uncanny ability to ferret it out" (p. 33). In pet therapy, as has been noted by a number of authors, we see the reversal of the process of domestication. With someone who is mentally ill, for example, a pet animal can become the vehicle by which socialization occurs, that is, it is the animal who domesticates the man rather than the reverse (Savishinsky, 1983).

Cusack (1988) presents significant studies indicating the importance of pets, such as dogs, in helping someone who is depressed; the experiences and feelings of loss, desperation, and suicidal ideas are helped by the presence of a pet such as a dog. This includes the necessary activity and responsibility of taking care of a dog. Pet therapy with cancer patients is noted. The author also describes a "cotherapist," a dog named Tiffany who participated with a psychologist, Carroll L. Meek (1982), in a university student health center, as well as in her private practice. She found it very useful in her work with several individual students, especially helping them with feelings of self-consciousness. She also states that it helped the atmosphere when students met in groups, such as in the waiting room.

CLINICAL EXAMPLES

Dogman

Volkan (1995) describes a male patient in his late thirties who had facial tics and recurring facial grimaces. This contributed to making him look like a snarling dog. He would sniff the air in an involuntary fashion, looking like a dog trying to catch a passing scent. He was unhappily married, he lost his temper, and at times would strike at his wife. He was afraid that he might maim her or even kill her and these fears exacerbated his tics, about which he had a great deal of self-consciousness. He was a college-educated man and reasonably successful plant manager with a local company. The company's logo depicted a funny-looking dog. The patient volunteered to represent the company at their public relations events. He wore a dog costume and became the company's official clown. While he reveled in the costume, doing clownish antics around the staff of the company and friends, and thought of himself as a comedian, he used his wit to both hide and express his anger. Volkan states that "before official appearances he would frolic about the plant in his dog costume, snarling and hiking up his leg, pretending to urinate on the amused employees" (p. 176).

From the beginning of his five-year treatment by Greer, with Volkan as supervisor, there were indications in his tics and sniffing behavior that he may have unconsciously identified with a dog and that he voluntarily accepted "becoming" a dog in serving his company. He also often lied about himself and his background, and he made up stories about his past exploits to encourage his son to be proud of him. He often daydreamed of himself as a supermanlike hero. It was felt that dogman had an infantile psychotic self, which was substantially helped during the course of his treatment, even though a mutually agreed upon therapeutic termination did not take place. The therapy was long and difficult.

The patient had few conscious memories of his early childhood and it was impossible to know whether or not there had been a real dog in his early environment. He did, however, have a dog when his treatment began, and at times he identified with it. When his wife was harsh with the dog he felt pain. His mother had a number of hospitalizations and died when he was 6 years of age. His sister and grandmother used to dress him up in clothing of a girl and parade him around the neighborhood. Although humiliated, he rarely complained of these practices. He experienced sexual abuse at the hands of a man who offered him rides and he in turn abused his 3-year-old son. In treatment, he presented himself as if he were two "entirely different men" (p. 182). One side was the competent plant manager who was respected by his associates, especially when he did not act like a clown. The other side was a helpless, bewildered, suspicious infant-child. He was very dependent on his wife. For example, she drove him to the therapist's office and after shopping returned to fetch him when the session was over. Pedophilic activities occurred during the course of his therapy.

The author states that "As a dog/clown he wished to change the horrible affects that saturated the fused child-mother representation in his infantile psychotic self. Beneath the pleasure-giving dog/clown there was a dog, a sense of self as being less

than a human infant. When saturated with 'bad' affects the dog
would be vicious" (p. 192). The experience he had of being
dressed as a girl, and his recollections of how a nun made him
wear large baggy trousers, may have played a role in his "unconscious choice of a dog symbol to represent his fragile core's psychic tissue. As a dog, he invited love and nurturing but also
expressed snarling aggression. Through his humorous antics and
acerbic wit he could express his enormous aggression yet maintain object ties. Furthermore, by being a dog/clown he could . . .
try to establish a relationship with the representation of his father" (p. 193). His father had used the patient to entertain
friends in a bar and in this way he received his drunken father's
approval while still hating him. "This understanding of different
meanings of the dog symbol was interpreted at appropriate
times" (p. 193). The author goes on to say that after the "dog"
was unmasked, the patient came to his sessions anxiously searching for his therapist's car. As his transference became more and
more intense, he improved in the external world and his relationships improved. "As time went on he recalled and re-examined
his pedophilic experience with his son, and his wish and dream
of performing fellatio on his therapist. He then thought of ferocious dogs and the pleasure he derived from needling the women
at work" (p. 196). The ferocious dogs represented his oral sadism.
He had subsequent psychoticlike episodes but was able to keep
working in the therapy and understanding more about his experiences. He left treatment before he was fully able to integrate the
good and bad object representations but he certainly made very
significant headway and important modifications in his infantile
psychotic self.

The information, including quotations, in the following clinical examples is disguised, altered and paraphrased to protect confidentiality.

Sally and Rough

Sally was 19 years old, a sophomore at a local university. She
originally consulted the student health service and then was referred to me. She complained of depression, compulsive eating,

and the feeling that her life was becoming more and more disorganized, which she attributed to the rigid demands of her parents and her reactions to this. She was attending classes erratically and the university was considering suspending her for not only missing classes, but also skipping her final examinations. Sally described herself as becoming more and more depressed. She hinted at suicidal ideas and expressed morbid thoughts in her writing. She clashed with her parents when they insisted she leave the apartment where she was staying with some boys, and return home. When she refused, her parents called the police, and under this threat she returned home. She later returned to her apartment but was fearful of leaving it for classes and for coming to her appointments with me.

She said, and her mother concurred, that she was a "normal baby who was a wanted child." However, she had a "feeding problem from the start" until she was age 5, when her sister was born. She described herself as an extremely precocious child with a labile temperament who cried frequently. Developmental milestones were achieved at early ages.

When she was 11, she became extremely fond of animals. She asked again and again for a dog, and finally her parents complied. She seemed very attached to the dog and spent much time with it, but, according to the parents, she refused, and, according to her, she neglected to house train the dog. This led to many arguments at home which revolved around this issue, as well as others, and the dog, Sport, was the focal point of many of these harsh disputes. While she refrained from training Sport, she would not permit anyone else to do so. Subsequently, the dog nipped two children in the neighborhood. Sally's parents then insisted that Sport be gotten rid of. They were furious with Sally in the way that she had handled the dog and ashamed in hearing complaints from neighbors. It seemed to me in listening to this account that there was a collusion between Sally and her parents in the way in which Sport was handled. Both sides blamed the other, the dog reacting to all the turmoil in the household, perhaps expressing this in his behavior. This was one of the critical experiences of Sally's childhood, and she said, with conviction, that she would never forgive her parents for insisting that Sport be sent away.

In early adolescence she became involved with a boy who seduced her. She subsequently became fascinated with a group of boys from the city (she was living with her parents in the suburbs) and these boys were of a different socioeconomic level and background. She entered outpatient treatment in a clinic, but it ended when her therapist left the area; subsequently, she terminated treatment with another therapist whom she saw briefly. Sometime after this she made a suicidal gesture with aspirin tablets. Later she attended college, although she had expressed a wish to go to a music academy. Her parents vetoed this. Sally stated that she had not eaten a meal with her family for a year and added that her behavior was a direct reaction to her parents' attempt to control her. Sally described herself as a problem eater of long-standing, with a mother who would resort to everything and anything to get her to eat. She felt that all would continue to be just as it was as long as she had close contact with her parents. Her parents were very resistant to Sally's attempts to separate from them. At one point, her mother began giving her clothes away and actually burned some of her personal possessions. A family doctor had suggested that her mother also undertake treatment but she refused. The father and mother finally agreed to support Sally in an apartment near the university.

Sally reported that her mother, a housewife, with a background in accounting, was overly protective of her and felt guilty about and responsible for Sally's troubles. Father, a very successful businessman, saw the patient as a disciplinary problem who needed to be rigidly controlled rather than treated. He had been in the Marines until the patient was about 1 year old. Sally's two siblings, a brother and a sister, were described initially as making good adjustments. Sally's mother said that when Sally was a child she cried easily, was standoffish, clean, fastidious, precocious, and talked and walked at early ages. She was the first grandchild and she was moderately close to her grandmother who was ill with rheumatoid arthritis. Grandmother had become sick at an early age, and Sally's mother stated that she was determined to do for her child what her mother had not done for her. Father's mother had died when he was age 14; he depicted his stepmother as someone who did nothing but cook all day. He was consumed by his business and Sally said that he seemed to feel the children did not need him. He came home for dinner only one night a week. Success was everything to him and it became his obsession to acquire material things. He was not close with his parental family nor with his children, although he had expressed the sentiment that he feels for his family but doesn't show it. He grew up in a cold family and felt that this had made a mark on him, although he was more demonstrative with his son than with Sally.

Sally presented dreams which related to being trapped. One was being trapped in a box, another was being all wrapped up in a blanket. She tried to get loose but couldn't and mother finally released her. She dreamt that she was caught under a carton by a witch and caught in a blanket and tied up in a knot. In another dream, father was pinned to a wall with a sword. She spoke of being sexually promiscuous and had been involved in brief relationships with a number of boys and young men. She stressed an interest in poets, especially liking Walt Whitman and also writers such as Gide and Malraux. She felt that her mother took over the role of both mother and father and with father she felt strongly that his punishment did not fit the crime. Mother reported that when father was "softer" with Sally, she did something to disrupt this, such as taking money from him.

When the patient's mother visited Sally's apartment she wrote to me that the apartment was just impossible, it looked like the tropics, with a cat, dog, and geese and a smell beyond words. She felt that her daughter was unable to sustain friendships with people of her own socioeconomic level, that she was becoming a beatnik, and associated with the "lowest of the low."

During this period, Sally acquired another dog, a Saint Bernard named Chris, and, again, she formed an attachment to the dog, talked about this dog quite a bit, and, while she did not completely own up to being neglectful of the dog, she soon began reporting that the dog had chewed up some of her clothing, was making a "mess" in the house, and had nearly been hurt in some scrapes with cars. On the other hand she reported her concern about Chris's behavior, and said that she took the dog for walks and felt comfortable when Chris was close to her. She would hug him affectionately, and, over time, he began sleeping in her bed, first at the foot, and then lying alongside her. Subsequently, however, this dog also did not work out, and finally, with a mixture of relief and sadness, she gave the dog away.

Continued difficulties were present in regard to her parents' feelings about her psychotherapy and periodically they threatened to stop paying for it. Her dress seemed bizarre according to her mother, and she certainly was very disheveled, much beyond the average college student. At one point she said she wanted to be a child, "not a female," and she wanted to be a little girl so she wouldn't have to "go to bed with her father." She said the only thing between her mother and father was sex. Much later she spent some time, over a summer, working in the Southwest, and she seemed to get along quite well there. She had by then acquired another dog, a mongrel named Rough. She wrote me that Rough had turned into an "outdoor creature" which pleased her very much. She said that she loved being with Rough in these open spaces and that "Rough loves it here." In one letter, her greeting to me was, "To my dearest friend and most consistent comforter." She wrote that she has learned the most from the mountains and the happiest day she has had in many years was the joy she experienced in climbing for miles.

She later mentioned that she had acquired another puppy. "He looks much like Rough but he's going to be a real monster. I'm not quite sure I'm going to keep him, but at present he's here—in my room curled up under the bed with Rough curled up on the bed. They even sleep with the same positions. To acquire a puppy is much better than to become pregnant and when I'm terribly lonely, which I am here, I want nothing more than a child but I haven't regressed that far yet." She also said that she stole something on purpose to get caught stealing and of course was "successful." She went on to say that she hasn't stopped punishing herself for it. She wrote, "The puppy has found a new home, the better for both he and I. I have only faithful Rough." She wrote that she felt "remarkably healthy."

Following her return from the Southwest, and simultaneously with the parents' efforts to stop the treatment, she regressed and experienced significant weight gain. Again her mother described Sally's apartment as a horrible mess with the stench of animals and not fit for human habitation. She wrote to me, saying that the males and females with whom Sally associated "are freaks and beatniks" and that "her morals were sordid." She depicted Sally as living in filthy quarters. Sally's parents again insisted that she come home, and they refused to subsidize her apartment living. When her parents were insisting that she stop treatment, she said that her "father is horribly jealous of you" and father won't support the treatment because of this. Her mother wrote that she felt Sally wanted to be in the apartment so her sex life could be uninhibited, that she was buying diaphragms, that she was posing in the nude, that she had a boyfriend from a much lower social stratum, and that she was promiscuous. Based upon what Sally told me, some of this was true but there was also exaggeration and projection on her mother's part.

Two dreams that were significant in this latter period were of Sally being under the analyst's shirt "as though I was in your womb and you were pregnant. The feeling was one of being warmed and protected." She expressed the realization that relationships were difficult for her to sustain and again she had dreams along the earlier lines of being trapped. She dreamed of a spider web blocking her and the only way she could get out was to kill and squeeze the spider. Associations went to her mother. With all of this travail, she succeeded in graduating from college and got a very good job in teaching.

The patient's mother continued to write to me, for a time every month. In one letter she gave a résumé of Sally's eating habits, from birth to the present day. She began by saying that she tried to breast-feed Sally but it was a sad mistake; the milk supply was inadequate and Sally's first few days of life were spent screaming from hunger. After a few days bottle feeding was instituted. For the first four years of her life mealtime was a nightmare. She was a poor eater. She liked nothing and her mother spent so much time with her at meals she (Sally's mother) began to detest feeding time. It was interesting that she said, as a kind of afterthought, that Sally was a plump and relatively healthy child. When Sally's brother arrived, the eating problem miraculously disappeared. Mother attributed this to the fact that she spent less time with Sally at meals. Subsequently, during Sally's adolescence, as she began going with a boy, she ate excessively. The patient's mother began to harass her about this, and she acknowledged that she did so because she has a revulsion for obesity since she had her own weight problems during her adolescence. Her mother reported that after Sally's boyfriend seduced her Sally began to eat tremendously. Her mother stated that she feels there was a correlation between excessive eating and excessive sex. The mother felt that this was a moral problem for Sally. Later on Sally was taken to various doctors to help her with her obesity and she also saw a therapist for a time. She did improve, in general, and, specifically, with her weight problems. Subsequently, she again gained a great deal of weight and then lost much of it with the aid of prescribed drugs, and she became almost emaciated.

During the course of her psychotherapy with me, there were many references to her dog Rough and subsequently to the puppy, Chris, that she acquired and kept for a time. In many ways Rough seemed to be a representation of herself, and she identified herself with Rough. Rough was scraggly and ill-kempt just as Sally was. Rough assumed the externally tough or "rough" side of the patient while, underneath, she took Rough to be as vulnerable as she was. She was protective of Rough and solicitous of his whereabouts and health; in turn, Rough also served as her protector.

For many months during the course of her psychotherapy, she was agoraphobic and could not come to the sessions without Rough. They sat in the waiting room together and came into the office together. Rough sometimes bounded about the office, but generally sat by her side, and she would stroke Rough as we talked. It was distracting to have Rough there, particularly at those times when he would bark or dart up suddenly if there was a noise, and there were times when he would come over to me and await my attention. However, much of the time he was not friendly, and not appealing to be with, in terms of his poor grooming, smell, and his overall dishevelled appearance. My counter-transference of distaste and withdrawal was similar to how I reacted to Sally at times. At the same time, I recognized that it was with the help of Rough that Sally was functioning as well as she did during this period. I felt gratitude to him for this and appreciated his steady presence in her life. In a sense, he became a cotherapist. It was necessary and very important for Sally to come with him and for him to come with her. During this time, she took him everywhere, since she was fearful of going out alone, and, for a time, she was unable to leave her apartment for any purpose without him. She was attached to him with a visible as well as an invisible tether (Akhtar, 1992). Rough slept in the bed with her and served as a transitional object. He also became her protective and caring parent. She endowed him with the qualities of someone who took care of her and in some measure, such as accompanying her when she left her apartment, he did. Rough protected her as she wished her father had protected her from her mother's suffocating control. He also protected her against her murderous rage toward her mother.

She seemed to attribute much more gentleness and comforting qualities to Rough than were visible to me when I would see him, but clearly he played this role for her. The qualities she attributed to him represented her needs as well as aspects of his actual behavior with her. As her child, she treated him with the attention, acceptance, and consideration that she wished to have from her parents. Simultaneously, there was a sense of her neglecting him, not grooming him, as she did not groom herself, not consistently taking care of him, not being fully attentive to his needs, distancing herself, much the way she experienced her parents in their treatment of her. At times, she would be harsh, excessively controlling, even cruel with Rough. She displaced her anger toward me in the transference and to Rough; contrawise, she displaced anger toward Rough to me. She criticized and reprimanded Rough the way her parents did her.

As the material discloses, Sally had many borderline features. Some of this was played out in a recurrent pattern with puppies whom she adopted. At first, she idealized them, then seemed to became weary in caring for them, and finally totally rejected them in their neediness and then sent them away. She repeated what happened in her childhood when her parents gave away her first dog.

Her therapy was very difficult with an up-and-down course, including consistent intrusions by her parents. At times I felt a sense of hopelessness and despair about the situation. However, I felt encouraged in that there were many features in Sally's difficulties that were common to young adults and to their course of therapy (Escoll, 1987). These included issues of object constancy, separation-individuation (Escoll, 1991), and optimal distance (Akhtar, 1992; Escoll, 1992). Understandably, her parents had every reason to be concerned about Sally in terms of the way she was handling her life, her appearance, her apartment, and her erratic attendance in college. This disorganization represented the intensity of her inner conflicts and her difficulty in regulating herself and her life in a more reasonable way. They also represented defiance of her parents in their powerful attempts to control, epitomized in the early years by a struggle with her mother around eating. Her behavior also represented an attempt to win the attention of her parents and, of course, she was very successful in this. She experienced guilt related to her hostility and defiance. She expressed her masochism in many, many ways. Through her behavior, she was also atoning for her guilt, degrading and humiliating herself.

Through all this, she was able to generally sustain an alliance with me and to work in her psychotherapy, although there certainly were many swings, both in her productivity in the work, and also in her attendance at the sessions. However, she was able to complete her college curriculum and to get a job in teaching. She successfully spent time on her own in the Southwest during which she maintained contact with me by letters. Her parents insisted several times that she stop her treatment, but the patient, with help from me, prevailed upon them to allow her to continue for some time before they finally discontinued her therapy. Follow-up letters indicated that she was still having troubles but basically was doing much better in the way she was feeling, with less depression, more organization of her life, sustaining a job, and beginning to establish, although very tentatively, a better relationship with her parents. Rough was certainly a pivotal creature for her and many of her conflicts were played out in this arena, which were literally brought into the office with Rough's physical presence. He was an important source for her of parental displacement, often as a surrogate for mother and also, in his own way, an object with whom she was able to develop a more consistent relationship than she had with most of the people in her life. He became an integral part of the therapeutic process.

Harry and Hero

Harry, a psychoanalytic patient, described his latency years and early adolescent years as very lonely. His mother and father both suffered serious trauma in their childhoods abroad. They were relatively silent, not only about their early experiences and everything related to them, but they also tended to be silent in everyday discourse at home. The patient's father, trained as a pharmacist, was often unavailable, working long hours to support the family in this country. The patient's mother was timid in using her new language, English.

His sister was nine years older and not available to him. The patient recollected many tender moments with his dog, Hero. He recalled running with his dog, playing with his dog, and throwing balls for the dog to retrieve. All of this seems like standard boy-dog behavior. It went much beyond this, however. As he associated, he recalled Hero as a central figure in the family with whom he could communicate. He remembered going to a corner of the yard with Hero and sitting closely next to him. To Hero, he voiced his most private thoughts, his worries, his anxieties, as well as his joys. He loved athletics and expressed his hopes and dreams of being a sports "hero." He played pretend games of football or baseball with the dog.

Hero was his confidant, and Harry experienced the dog as though Hero could hear him and appreciate and understand what he was saying. This expresses the common idea that a dog, like a human, has empathy, being able to take in what one says and feels, and is nonverbally responsive to it. It was most satisfying and a great relief to Harry that he could say everything and anything to Hero, which he could not express to his parents or to others. This included his sexual fantasies, his experimentation with masturbation, and the questions and doubts that he had about himself in these areas. Harry described hugging Hero, wrestling with him, and clearly there was much pleasurable physical contact involved. Of course, his associations to Hero in all of the above respects also represented some of his transferential wishes toward me. This proved to be a very fruitful aspect of the analysis.

The Family of Mrs. K and Their Dog

There are many families who find it very difficult to live comfortably with a dog and take care of it properly; and the dysfunctional family of Mrs. K is an example of that. She was a widow who bought a large dog. Her two boys were 8 and 10 at the time. Mrs. K found it very difficult to train the dog and it began to leave its excrement all over the house. Mrs. K tended to blame her children for not helping out sufficiently and the children in turn blamed her for this. Mrs. K later tried to set up a system of the children taking the dog out for walks so it could defecate outside. This was followed by many battles about who would do this and whose turn it was, and the family atmosphere became one of accusations and tension.

Mrs. K thought about giving the dog away but could not bring herself to do this since this represented the same kind of neglect and rejection she had experienced from her parents in her childhood. It also went against her ideal of having the dog fulfill her needs for love and companionship which were stimulated in the present by the loss of her husband and strengthened by the troublesome relationship with her children. In desperation, she consulted the service at a veterinary school, which discussed the situation in depth with her, from the psychological point of view. They instituted a kind of family therapy focusing on issues related to handling the dog. This helped a great deal. Mrs. K also entered individual psychotherapy at this time. While there were still many "accidents," the family situation improved to the degree that they were able to keep the dog who proved to be an important companion pet for all of them.

A Widow's Shame

This vignette is about a woman in her seventies, Mrs. Raymond, whose husband, a few years older, had died following a lingering illness of eight months. The patient had no surviving children or siblings and little in the way of friends or related family. She did have a dog, Toby, however, which she shared with her husband, and she counted on the dog for companionship and solace after her husband died. She came into therapy because of depression and feelings of helplessness. She did not know how to drive a car, for example. In psychotherapy, she progressed a great deal, began to take a very forward-looking attitude and began to move on with her life, including finally learning how to drive. This was a significant accomplishment for her about which she was very pleased and proud. As a paper by Settlage (1996) illustrates, a patient in the later years of life can benefit a great deal from psychotherapy or analysis.

Mrs. Raymond began expressing a sense of deep shame about her attachment to the dog. As we explored this, she revealed that she had dreams about Toby, which began after the dog died, six months after her husband died. She dreamed of the dog bounding down the steps, coming to greet her, and barking at her in a happy, excited fashion. She missed the dog's companionship, but her sense of shame about this and about her dreams was very strong. She felt it improper and shameful that she should think so much about her dog. As we discussed this further, it became clear that she missed her husband, also, but because of quarrels and the ambivalence she had about him, her mourning was not undiluted. She acknowledged feelings of relief about his death, even though she missed his presence. Her shame related not so much to this ambivalence, but to the feeling that she was missing her dog more than her husband.

It was difficult for her to come to terms with this shame, and despite interpretations related to her shame, guilt, and other related painful affects, these feelings, including humiliation and self-blame, were unremitting. I finally decided to reveal something personal to help her with her shame: I told her that I had a dog who died and whom I continued to miss a great deal. I told her that I, too, had had dreams about my dog being alive, and running across the front lawn toward me in a familiar way to be stroked and petted. This finally seemed to reach her; she was greatly relieved to realize that she was not alone in her feelings. Her shame and guilt were alleviated. Her short-term therapy progressed to a successful conclusion. She began to expand in new areas of her life, but she began to obsess with ambivalence about getting another dog.

A Collector of Dogs

This analytic patient, a social worker and a therapist herself, had a passion for dogs. She seemed to collect them, both well before the analysis, and during the analysis as well. At one time she had four or five large dogs in the house. The dogs had many significant meanings for her. What emerged most strongly in the analysis related to the dogs as phallic representations. She experienced them as big, strong, and powerful, yet under her control. She felt complete and more acceptable as a person when she was in the presence of the dogs or when she would think about them and picture them. When she was away from them, or for some reason they were less involved with her, she had a sense of deprivation, in part on a maternal, nurturant level, but even more a feeling as though she had been castrated and the phallus represented by the dogs was removed from her. At these times she experienced a sense of loss and depression, which contrasted sharply with her buoyant mood when she and her dogs were engaged in rough play.

Summary

Writing this chapter has brought to my mind many fond memories of my experiences with dogs. Two collies, Buff and Laddie, were an important part of my early years. (Collies run in the family; my wife also grew up with one.) My sisters and I divided the care of our dogs, and competed with each other as to which dog was best. It was a sad and angry time for us when, after a summer, we moved from the country to the city and my parents gave the dogs to a farmer. My interest in dogs was also stimulated by reading adventure books by Jack London. My favorite was *Call of the Wild* (1963), with its heroic sled dog, Buck.

Gaylord, another Collie, played a significant part in the life of our family in my adult years. Gaylord was a handsome fellow, a faithful companion for the children, playful yet maintaining a certain dignified reserve. Following his herder heritage, he would hustle the children on the street into the school bus, including little children who were not yet going to school. Putting Gaylord "to sleep" at 14 years of age was a great loss, accompanied by some guilt. We become attached to certain breeds of dogs; we may also hate, be anxious or fearful about certain breeds. I am wary of German shepherds, having been bitten by one. I also strenuously avoid Rotweilers. I narrowly eluded the hot pursuit of one named Hercules—known as the terror of the neighborhood—whose bite was worse than his bark, a *Hound of the Baskervilles* (Doyle, 1902) type whose personality was not dissimilar to that of his owner.

Dogs are anthropomorphized by their owners and are used as figures for identification and projection of unconscious impulses and wishes. They fulfill many roles and are mentally represented on a broad spectrum, ranging from an unconditionally loving parent to a frightening beast. Dogs are frequently idealized in a stereotyped fashion which is often defensive against other feelings. My personal examples above illustrate that actually we have many different reactions to dogs and a spectrum of internal representations of them. In the therapeutic process in the patients presented, one sees the symbolic meaning of dogs to the patients. For example, dogs are often represented as surrogates for children, siblings, and parents. In these cases, the mental representations of dogs are intertwined in significant ways with the patient's conflicts. As part or full objects, dogs are experienced in a wide variety of important ways. In their role as companions, they take on significance beyond what may appear on the surface.

I was surprised in doing research for this chapter how much literature there is on this topic. Much of it relates to articles about dog phobias in children and to studies and discussions about "pet-facilitated therapy," "the human-animal bond," and the use of dogs in settings, such as hospitals, nursing homes, and with handicapped individuals. I have cited only a small fraction of these papers. The majority of the studies report positive results of exposure to dogs, but some studies suggest the improvement the investigators looked for was not there. Problem areas are certainly present. The effects of loss of pet dogs, for example, through natural death, family circumstances, injury or illness, or being "put to sleep" raise important issues, especially for children. As Freud (1913) pointed out, children and dogs are bound together.

I have attempted to describe the extent of anthropomorphization of dogs and the many pathologic aspects involved in our reactions to them with related mental constructions. This, of course, is not the whole story. Dogs as pets, as companions, as helpers, depending on their temperament and breed, and the interplay with others, are generally available, affectionate, responsive, and loyal. It is understandable that we do become attached to them and value them in their own right. We may attribute human qualities to them, but it is also the fact that they are not human that engages us. They may occasionally defy a command, but they are ordinarily obedient, and they do not otherwise verbally disagree or argue with what we say. They do not judge us, criticize us, or remark on our shortcomings. And we can touch them at any time; usually, they seem to enjoy this. Ordinarily, dogs are friendly and tolerant with children, the elderly, and the handicapped. They participate with them in developmental steps, and do not abuse them. As I noted before, our external and psychic experiences of dogs, therefore, have both adaptive as well as pathologic qualities.

REFERENCES

Akhtar, S. (1992), Tethers, orbits, and invisible fences: Clinical, developmental, sociocultural, and technical aspects of optimal distance. In: *When the Body Speaks: Psychological Meanings in Kinetic Clues,* ed. S. Kramer & S. Akhtar. Northvale, NJ: Jason Aronson, pp. 22–57.
———— (1995), A third individuation: Immigration, identity, and the psychoanalytic process. *J. Amer. Psychoanal. Assn.,* 43:1051–1084.
Alper, L. (1993), The child-pet bond. *Progress in Self-Psychology,* 9:257–270.
Bettelheim, B. (1977), *The Uses of Enchantment.* New York: Vintage Books.
Bonaparte, M. (1940), *Topsy.* London: Pushkin Press.
Buytendijk, F. (1935), *The Mind of the Dog.* London: George Allen & Unwin.
Cusack, O. (1988), *Pets and Mental Health.* New York: Hayworth Press.
de Waal, F. (1996), *Good Natured, The Origins of Right and Wrong in Humans and Animals.* Cambridge, MA: Harvard University Press.
Doyle, A. (1902), The hound of the Baskervilles. In: *The Complete Sherlock Holmes.* Garden City, NY: Doubleday, 1953, pp. 669–766.
Escoll, P. (1987), Psychoanalysis of young adults: An overview. *Psychoanal. Inq.,* 7:5–30.
———— (1992), Vicissitudes of optimal distance through the life cycle. In: *When the Body Speaks: Psychological Meanings in Kinetic Clues,* ed. S. Kramer & S. Akhtar. Northvale, NJ: Jason Aronson, pp. 59–87.

Fraiberg, S. (1951), Clinical notes on the nature of transference in child analysis. *The Psychoanalytic Study of the Child,* 6:286–306. New York: International Universities Press.

Freud, S. (1909), Analysis of a Phobia in a Five-Year-Old Boy. *Standard Edition,* 10:1–147. London: Hogarth Press, 1955.

———— (1913), Totem and Taboo. *Standard Edition,* 13:1–161. London: Hogarth Press, 1955.

Galton, F. (1883), *Inquiries into Human Faculty and Its Development.* London: Macmillan.

Halpert, E. (1980), Death, dogs, and anubis. *Internat. Rev. Psycho-Anal.,* 7:385–395.

Harley, M. (1967), Fragments from the analysis of a dog phobia in a latency child. *Bull. Phila. Assn. Psychoanal.,* 17:127–129.

Heiman, M. (1956), The relationship between man and dog. *Psychoanal. Quart.,* 25:568–585.

Jelliffe, S., & Brink, L. (1917), The role of animals in the unconscious. *Psychoanal. Rev.,* 4:253–271.

Katcher, A., & Beck, A. (1983), *New Perspectives in Our Lives with Companion Animals.* Philadelphia: University of Pennsylvania Press.

Knight, E. (1940), *Lassie Come Home.* New York: Holt, Rinehart, & Winston.

Levinson, B. (1962), The dog as co-therapist. *Ment. Hygiene,* 46:59–65.

———— (1969), *Pet-oriented Child Psychotherapy.* Springfield, IL: Charles Thomas.

London, J. (1933), *White Fang.* New York: Grosset & Dunlap.

———— (1963), *The Call of the Wild.* New York: Macmillan.

Lorenz, K. (1952), *King Solomon's Ring.* New York: Thomas Y. Crowell.

Masson, J., & McCarthy, S. (1995), *When Elephants Weep, the Emotional Lives of Animals.* New York: Delacorte Press.

Meek, C. L. (1982), Dog presence proves salutary in university counseling service. *The Latham Letter,* p. 22.

Morris, W. (1995), *My Dog Skip.* New York: Random House.

Pavlov, I. (1927), *Conditioned Reflexes.* London: Oxford University Press.

Raver, A. (1995), *Deep in the Green.* New York: Alfred Knopf.

Savishinsky, J. (1983), Pet ideas: The domestication of animals, human behavior, and human emotions. In: *New Perspectives in Our Lives with Companion Animals,* ed. A. Katcher & A. Beck. Philadelphia: University of Pennsylvania Press, pp. 112–132.

Serpell, J. (1983), The personality of the dog and its influence on the pet-owner bond. In: *New Perspectives in Our Lives with Companion Animals,* ed. A. Katcher & A. Beck. Philadelphia: University of Pennsylvania Press, pp. 57–63.

Settlage, C. (1996), Transcending old age: Creativity, development and psychoanalysis in the life of a centenarian. *Internat. J. Psycho-Anal.*, 77:549–564.

Sperling, M. (1952), Animal phobias in a two year old child. *The Psychoanalytic Study of the Child*, 7:115. New York: International Universities Press.

Sterba, E. (1935), Excerpt from the analysis of a dog phobia. *Psychoanal. Quart.*, 4:135–160.

Stewart, M. (1983), Loss of a pet—loss of a person: A comparative study of bereavement. In: *New Perspectives in Our Lives with Companion Animals*, ed. A. Katcher & A. Beck. Philadelphia: University of Pennsylvania Press, pp. 390–406.

Storr, A. (1988), *Churchill's Black Dog, Kafka's Mice, and Other Phenomena of the Human Mind*. New York: Grove Press.

Terhune, A. (1927), *Highland Collie*. New York: Grosset.

———— (1966), *Lad, A Dog*. New York: E. P. Dutton.

Thomas, E. (1993), *The Hidden Life of Dogs*. New York: Simon & Shuster.

Tyson, R. (1978), Notes on the analysis of a prelatency boy with a dog phobia. *The Psychoanalytic Study of the Child*, 33:427–457. New Haven, CT: Yale University Press.

Van de Castle, R. (1983), Animal figures in dreams: Age, sex, and cultural differences. In: *New Perspectives in Our Lives with Companion Animals*, ed. A. Katcher & A. Beck. Philadelphia: University of Pennsylvania Press, pp. 148–176.

Veevers, J. (1985), The social meaning of pets: Alternative roles for companion animals. In: *Pets and the Family*, ed. M. Sussman. New York: Hayworth Press, pp. 11–30.

Volkan, V. (1995), Dogman. In: *The Infantile Psychotic Self and Its Fates: Understanding and Treating Schizophrenic and Other Difficult Patients*. Northvale, NJ: Jason Aronson, pp. 175–203.

Watson, B. (1996), *Last Days of Dog-Men*. New York: W. W. Norton.

Young-Bruehl, E. (1988), *Anna Freud*. New York: W. W. Norton.

CHAPTER 6

A Journey with *Homo Aves* Through the Human Aviary

GREGG E. GORTON, M.D.

In memoriam,
Theodore A Parker, 3rd (April 1, 1953–August
3, 1993),
ornithologist *extraordinaire*:
"He knew birds better than any living person."
[John O'Neill, quoted in Sullivan, 1993].

Let us now suppose that in the mind of each
man there is an aviary of all sorts of birds—some
flocking together apart from the rest, others in
small groups, others solitary, flying anywhere
and everywhere.... We may suppose that the
birds are kinds of knowledge, and that when we
were children, this receptacle was empty ...
[Plato, Theaetetus, *The Dialogues*, quoted in
Beck, 1968].

As we contemplate that sanderling [*Calidris
alba*], there by the shining sea, one question
leads inevitably to another, and all questions
come full circle to the questioner, paused momentarily in his own journey under the sun and
sky [Matthiessen, 1973].

Acknowledgments. I wish to thank Matt van de Rijn, Penny Nelson, Mildred Cho,
Andrea Sankar, Dan Cooney, Lynn Peterfreund, Nick and Sam Xenos, Michael Hindery,
John and Roz Brumfield, Carmen Harlan, Paula deLong, Tom Wolman, Richard Sobel,
Richard Beckman, Lisa Henderson, Kevin Muzzio, Clark Terrell, Henry Friedman, Philip
Escoll, Steven Samuel, Tom Reeves, Skip Conant, Lee Zahm, Uranus Knockwood, Salman
Akhtar, Theodore A. Parker, Jr., Tonda Gorton, Jedd and Eliza Sankar-Gorton, and Pamela
Sankar for helpful discussions, suggestions, references, sound recordings, field equipment,

I

Human proclivities toward our avian fellow-travelers are not unlike those we harbor toward other members of the animal kingdom: either we befriend, love, and care for them; fear, hate, and extirpate them; clothe or decorate ourselves with their vestiges; introduce them as characters in our fantasies, myths, stories, heavenly bodies, dreams, poems, music, artworks, and movies—not to say, to discover them lurking in our nightmares, phobias, delusions, and perverse imaginings.

As with other animate objects, birds provide a robust vehicle for the gamut of projective, introjective, and other mental operations, whether benign or pathologic. Yet, birds manifest a constellation of features that, in toto, shape them as unique fodder for our psychic machinations. These features include: the capacity for true flight (shared only by bats and insects); the deliciously primitive predilection for hatching out of eggs; the wondrous, ethereal, and occasionally startling sounds they produce; their unique and exquisitely colorful, feathered vestments; and their seasonal disappearances and returns, sometimes after heroic peregrination from continent to continent or even pole to pole (e.g., the Arctic Tern, *Sterna paradisaea*). Recall also the remarkable intelligence of many species (e.g., parrots, crows, and ravens)—which may in some respects rival our own (Barber, 1993)—as well as the bratty talent a few birds possess for mimicry of our speech (e.g., some parrots, mynahs, magpies, and crows). Add the everyday accessibility of this attractive and diverse group of largely diurnal creatures, which includes nearly 10,000 species inhabiting virtually every ecological niche on Earth's surface, and the Class *Aves* stands alone in evoking our constant wonder, delight, and fondness, yet also our occasional fear, loathing, and even hatred. An intriguing bonus is the hypothesized descent of birds from dinosaurs (e.g., *Archaeopteryx*, discovered in 1861), which, albeit still controversial, only deepens their mystery as we contemplate them.

---

and general edification. Let me be very clear, however, that any egg on my face is solely of my own creation.

I will survey some among the many cultural and mythological meanings of birds, as well as some of their representations in art, dance, theater, film, literature, poetry, and music. As we migrate along, novices discovering our meandering pathway[1] through this rich landscape toward what I hope will be a greater appreciation of the complex relationship between humans and birds, we will stop over occasionally for a diet of various clinical data representative of psychological and psychopathological phenomena involving birds. (This exploratory journey takes the form of a meditation, so I will leave its 17 numbered sections untitled.)

II

Birds have been players among the dramatis personae of the human theater for at least 30,000 years, judging by their painted and engraved representations in Upper Paleolithic cave art (Chauvet, Deschamps, and Hillaire, 1996) and their carved depictions on bone tools from the same period (Page and Morton, 1989). While they originated roughly 150 to 200 million years ago, the archaeological record of humankind's intercourse with birds prior to the Upper Paleolithic reveals only a variety of birds' bones, which either represent food remnants (though birds were not domesticated until about 10,000 years ago) or bone tools or, in a few cases, flutelike instruments.

Then, as if out of the blue, we find a lovely figure of an owl—probably *Bubo virginianus,* the Great Horned Owl—among the stunning images of animals in Chauvet Cave, where the oldest known art in the world was discovered and authenticated in 1994. And in the undersea Cosquer Cave we can marvel at striking 20,000- to 25,000-year-old depictions of now-extinct Great Auks (*Pinguinus impennis;* Clottes and Courtin, 1996). In the New World, the colossal prehistoric earthen mounds of the Hopewell Culture, found in the Mississippi River Valley, include sculpted

---

[1] Since in ancient times birds were perceived to meander anywhere and everywhere, and therefore did not follow existing roads (*vias*), the words *a-ves* and *a-vis*, meaning "without roads," became their chosen name in Latin (White, 1954, pp. 103–104); of course, now we realize that many, though by no means all, species tend to migrate along broad sky-highways known as "flyways."

birds with outstretched wings measuring more than one hundred feet from tip to tip (Spence, 1914). All of these prehistoric depictions of birds may have served a symbolic function, perhaps representing particular seasons, or fertility and birth, for example. Or, perhaps they were intended as gods or totems,[2] symbolic of some imagined higher being or of the social group (Freud, 1913b).

But even more intriguing for our purposes are a number of pictures from the Lascaux Cave, which date back between 15,000 and 20,000 years. Among these are not only a few simple images of birds, but several human figures with bird heads, including the famous painting in the "well" area of Lascaux that shows a human male with a bird head (or mask) lying or falling under a wounded bison. Adjacent to this figure is a bird on a stick whose head is identical to the bird head on the human figure (Marshack, 1972).

This bird-headed man is among the first known representations of any sort of human-animal hybrid, and this and other such images cannot fail to convey the artist's capacity for imaginative interspecies merger—anthropomorphized birds, or *aviomorphized*[3] *humans*, among other such chimerical revisions of the human (animal) form. Perhaps these also were invested with symbolic meanings. Given birds' capacity for flight, such images may have served particular transitional functions, mediating not only between the human and nonhuman, or the earthbound and the free-flying, but between past and present, or present and future. Bird-headed figures might also have represented some imagined journey to or from some faraway place such as a land of ancestors or guardian spirits or gods, or perhaps the realm of death (Marshack, 1972, p. 280). The bird perched on the stick in Lascaux Cave, for example, has been thought by some to portray the bird-soul of the fallen man with the bird head, perhaps about to take flight toward an afterlife (Ogburn, 1976, p. 15).

In a larger sense, such Paleolithic pictures, considered along with Paleolithic bone artifacts engraved with images of ravens,

---

[2] From the Ojibway-Algonquin word *ototeman*, meaning "he is a relative of mine," which is perhaps the most apt way of broadly conceptualizing our relationship with *all* animals.

[3] This neologism is but one instance of "theriomorphism," which refers to the attribution of animal characteristics to some nonanimal entity, such as a god or a human.

owls, cranes, and eagles (Page and Morton, 1989) may reflect an important creative moment in the cultural-evolutionary origin of animal objects' serving transitional psychological functions. After all, transitional objects (à la Winnicott) serve to mediate not only between a child and its maternal caregiver, but also between nature and human culture (Grolnick, Barkin, Muensterberger, 1978). However, it is interesting that bird effigies are only occasionally selected as children's transitional playthings, perhaps because birds lack most mammalian features, such as fur, and perhaps also because they exist largely outside of human control.

Human-animal hybrids, or cave paintings in general, can be conceptualized as residing along a continuum of "magical" objects that mediate between—in Lacanian terms—*the symbolic* and *the imaginary* realms, or "registers," of human experience. Such objects operate between, on the one hand, the symbolic, "named" realm of cultural and linguistic categories, meanings, and names themselves, and, on the other hand, the raw, imagistic "primary" world as we sense and perceive it, and as it is reflected back to us by mirroring objects of all sorts (Lee, 1990; Gorton, 1992).

From a general perspective, objects that serve transitional functions range from the first not-me (nonhuman) precursor object or part-object, to the transitional object proper, to the fetish, to the talisman or amulet (Greenson, 1978) to the linking object (Volkan, 1981), to the totem, and, finally, to the sacred idol (mediating between the human and spiritual realms). The fact that animal images and effigies—and birds, in particular—are deployed in these various transitional functions in many cultures certainly speaks to the degree to which the animal kingdom has been integrated into human psychological and cultural life. But it attests also to the cultural-evolutionary pathway taken by a variety of images and objects that serve higher-order psychocultural functions yet do not rely upon language to transmit their meanings, and therefore, retain a residue of their origins in the realm beyond the boundary of what is knowable in the human world. This boundary is the conceptual limit that demarcates the realm of the *imaginary*, from the realm of pure, unknowable Otherness, or what we sometimes think of as unexplored "Nature" or the

"Universe." This is what is referred to by Lacan as *the real* (Zizek, 1991).[4]

III

Barring time-travel (!), the "true" meaning of prehistoric cultural images must remain forever unknown, so our exploration of the multilayered psychological and cultural relationship between humans and birds may be best served at this point by taking an inventory of the logical categories into which the earliest human representations of birds can be sorted.

First, bird images may be more-or-less *mimetic* representations, which stand in one-to-one correspondence with actual birds of one sort or another, thereby serving either as aids to memory, or as purely aesthetic endeavor, or both. Second, bird images may denote *something else*, and therefore function as *metaphoric* signifiers, symbolic of some aspect of the human experience, for example the arrival of Spring, or birth, or death, or bountiful hunting.

Before proceeding, I should note that signifiers may be of two general types, metaphors or metonyms, though there is inevitably some element of both in any type of communicative discourse (Leach, 1970). Bird (human) images that include *parts* of—or, indeed, are revisions of—the human (bird) form, may function in *metonymic* fashion, albeit with metaphoric overtones. Thus, avian qualities, such as the ability to fly, can accrue to the human form (and vice versa) via *contiguity* of representation; that is, part-for-whole substitution. Examples include not only Paleolithic or Hieronymous Boschian bird-headed figures (see, for example, Bosch's *The Last Judgment* and *The Garden of Earthly Delights*), but also winged part-human figures such as angels, fairies, sphinxes, Japanese fairylike *tengu* (Whittaker, 1989), and winged Victory, among others. Or, consider the manticore, a

---

[4] The real is always, by definition, beyond our senses and our knowledge; therefore, it is that which can never truly be symbolized or defined. For example, it is the unknowable "beyond" that will become the World to the unborn fetus once it takes leave of its mother's interior, but, of course, by then *some other* "place" will have become that which cannot be known.

mythical part-human beast with a flutelike bird voice but no other bird attributes (White, 1954, p. 51).

The mimetic, metaphoric, and metonymic representational categories must have evolved from an ur-cosmology that simply took for granted that humankind and animals—indeed, all parts of the known world—are coextensive and indivisible. This worldview is represented today—though never, ipso facto, truly reproduced—in moments of transformative animal-for-human substitution that have been, and continue to be, highly prevalent in the ritualistic practices of many tribal groups (Spence, 1914; Feld, 1982; Cowan, 1993). Such substitutions are facilitated by means of masks, makeup, tattoos, headdresses, costumes, and the like, so that people construct themselves as *living symbols*. These ritualistic practices occur especially within restricted social spheres, including: healing encounters; rites of passage such as initiations, funerals, or marriages; agricultural or hunting cere-monies; war practices. During any of these, individuals such as shamans, initiates, mourners, or warriors, for example, may dress and behave as birds (Spence, 1914; Feld, 1982; Reina and Ken-singer, 1991).

Analogies to these rituals can be found in various modern artistic practices, such as dance performance. Examples involving birds include the ballet *In Volo* (In Flight), by choreographer Jean-Christophe Maillot (Kisselgoff, 1997), or the modern dance work *Fly*, by Elizabeth Streb, which boasts dancers in harnesses literally flying about the stage. In musical theater, we find *Peter Pan*, with its eponymous protagonist also gliding above the audi-ence, and in opera we find Papageno, the man-parrot in Mozart's *The Magic Flute*. The television program *Sesame Street* has the flightless Big Bird character, who doesn't quite know how a bird should behave, since he has no avian role model. Finally, we can-not fail to note the use of costumed, avian team mascots at mod-ern sporting events, which is perhaps the most ritualized modern American use of avian surrogates (e.g., Baltimore Orioles baseball team, Philadelphia Eagles football team, Temple University Owls, and my alma mater, the West Phoenix High School Thunder-birds).

Ritual involving the illusion of interspecies transformation must itself have evolved from a very early period in human prehis-tory, perhaps at some vanishing point of ur-consciousness that defined the emergence of *Homo sapiens,* the symbol maker, out of what must once have been a purely instinctual, *lived* unity with nature. While ways of life that enact oneness with nature—at one extreme, symbiotic merger—survive now in the form of some Eastern belief systems such as Zen Buddhism (Whittaker, 1989) and the traditional "way" of some Native American cultures (Spence, 1914) they are, in fact, extremely difficult for later-developing groups, such as the dominant cultures of the West, to truly apprehend.

The spread of the notion of a "return to nature," as reflected in the 1960s counterculture, and the rise of ecologically oriented ideologies, as well as hobbies such as birdwatching and birdfeeding, have been, in part, an attempt to capture and disseminate this way of thinking, which suggests the possibility of a vital *reappropriation* of Nature qua Nature by modern society, as against reifying it as an object solely for consumption or piecemeal destruction. The fact that birdwatching, or "birding," has become the fastest growing pastime in the United States, and now is second only to gardening among leisure avocations, testifies to the central role of bird life as a mediating vehicle in humankind's relationship with the natural world. Long after John James Audubon's *The Birds of America* (1840–1844) and Roger Tory Peterson's *A Field Guide to the Birds* (1934)—landmarks of ornithological verve in their own right—the surprising popularity and near cult status in the early 1970s of the long-time bestseller *Jonathan Livingston Seagull,* by Richard Bach (1970), albeit a maudlin allegory of a young gull's romance with the freedom of flight, appears to have demarcated this surge of cultural ornithophilia.

In the purest form of this notion of a "return to nature," a person might in some nearly literal sense *become* a bird, or any of a myriad of other creatures. Among the Kaluli of New Guinea, for example, Steven Feld, in his tour de force of ethnomusicology and ethnopoetics, discerned that a central cultural myth is the story of a boy who is transformed into a bird (Feld, 1982). This tale is fundamentally interwoven into the Kaluli's pervasive ethno-ornithological practices that include the categorizing of birds according to both their morphology and their vocalizations, feather collecting and adornment, and ritualized mimicry of bird songs

during extraordinary melodic-sung-weeping ceremonies performed by Kaluli women at funerals. Feld details how the Kaluli
people's observations of birds—whom they believe to be both
natural and also *ane mama*, the "gone *reflections*" of dead ancestors—have been translated into their understanding of human
behavior, such that bird categories and human categories are
virtual mirror-images (Feld, 1982, pp. 218–219).

For our purposes, such a *lived* relationship with the Avian
Class can be discerned today in Western culture only when we
enter that presymbolic space—as it were, the very surface of the
mirror into which we peer—where the imaginary dominates but
the real lurks, eerily, too close at hand—as in some screen memories and fantasies, dreams, and in psychosis.

IV

Let us make a brief stopover here to note the correspondence
between mimetic, metaphoric, metonymic, ritualistic, and lived
relationships with birds, on the one side, and the three Lacanian
registers of human experience, on the other, since both schemas
offer useful vantage points for our survey and analysis. While each
of the five initially listed categories must, ipso facto, embody some
element of all three of the Lacanian registers—since, by definition, the symbolic, the imaginary, and the real are inextricably
intertwined in a dialectical knot—each may usefully be thought
of as dominated by one of the registers, in particular: the lived
relationship is dominated by the real; the mimetic and ritualistic,
by the imaginary; and the metonymic and metaphoric by the symbolic.

Alfred Hitchcock's film *The Birds* (adapted from Daphne du
Maurier's short story) offers a contemporary example of how
birds can be seen to function in all three registers of human
experience (Zizek, 1991). In the film, we first encounter some
unnamed avian denizens of our world flocking together overhead, in San Francisco, as the heroine stops to gaze at them on
her walk to work in a pet shop. This flock appears to be just like
all of the others we may have noticed, in passing, in our lives,
flying anywhere and everywhere; therefore, it is barely worthy of

reflection. Next, we encounter more feathered creatures, caged and singing endearingly in the shop, where the male protagonist enters seeking a pair of lovebirds. True to their name, this pair of small parrots (e.g., *Psittacula* sp.) will serve as a metaphor for sexual desire—in this case, the mutually wished-for relationship between our hero and heroine. The latter will surreptitiously carry the birds northward on her prankish journey into the couple's as yet unknowable future, where she will encounter a cold, resistant presence in the form of the hero's mother.

A little later, as the motorboat-borne heroine approaches her rendezvous with the man who will become her lover, she is literally struck by something unthinkable—a seagull dips down and strikes her head with its beak in an unprovoked, enigmatic, and wholly uncharacteristic attack that appears at first as a moment of random aberration in Nature's usual, familiar, barely noticed patterns. As Hitchcock builds his peculiar, dread-inducing spectacle, what had begun as a fleeting incongruity—*a breach in the imaginary*—becomes an all-too-predictable and rapacious perversion of nature, albeit symbolized metonymically by birds, themselves a part of nature (Zizek, 1991).

Later, we see many different, typically nonpredatory species flocking together in organized fashion, and then mounting waves of attacks on the populace. Several people are pecked to death. But why? Birds' standard migratory behavior of flocking together both for protection and for efficiency in feeding becomes a metaphor for impending aggression and death that appears in its vivid immediacy to be truly plucked bare of any readily available meaning or explanation!

Shortly after our intrepid heroine's arrival in Bodega Bay, we hear her ask, off-handedly, as she notices some flying birds, "Don't they ever stop migrating?" In effect, she is interrogating the strangeness inherent in what is normally taken unthinkingly, in the quotidian realm of the imaginary, as *perfectly familiar*. Her incisive reperception, which offers a cut in the seamlessness of human experience, prefigures our own perspective as viewers reperceiving *our* relationship with nature through the lens of Hitchcock's dramatic *Entfremdungseffekt*.[5] We begin to wish—with our heroine—that she had never had cause to wonder, or to meddle!

---

[5] This is the term that the dramatist Bertolt Brecht coined to be able to name the "alienating effect" upon the theater audience that occurs with any well-staged breach in what appears as the "natural" order of things. By means of such a device, unacknowledged

We begin to peel away the shell of given meanings to find latent possibilities, and then peel further to glimpse the unknown, with all of its dread and exhilaration. We stand perched (like the human-bird figure in Lascaux Cave?) at the boundary between, on the one side, the symbolic and imaginary registers, and, on the other side, the real, out of which our world has been organized for us by an endless chain of forebears stretching back through caves and forests, and across savannahs, into some asymptotic vanishing point of ur-consciousness that must have marked the emergence of a nascent capacity for symbolization.

Slovaj Zizek, the Slovenian philosopher and cultural critic, has observed, using Lacanian concepts, that:

[The birds in Hitchcock's film represent] the embodiment in the real of a discord, an unresolved tension in intersubjective relations . . . like the plague in Oedipus's Thebes: they are the incarnation of a fundamental disorder in family relationships—the father is absent, the paternal function (the function of pacifying law, the Name-of-the-Father) is suspended and that vacuum is filled by [an] "irrational" maternal superego, irrational, wicked, blocking "normal" sexual relationship (only possible under the sign of the paternal metaphor) [Zizek, 1991, p. 99].

In contradistinction to this "familial" interpretation, another reading of *The Birds,* offered by Wood (1977), is that it depicts a breach in the relationship between an exploited nature and an unnaturally exploiting species, *Homo sapiens*. In this reading, we can discern the drama of the oedipal mother (Earth) striking back through her avian minions at the rivalrous, blonde interloper (representing sexual desire) who would swoop down to snatch her son from her. Indeed, the belief that if a child is not held closely enough or watched "like a hawk," it may be carried off by—a hawk?!—is an ancient fear and source of myth, in many regions. More likely, of course, this reflects parents' ambivalence toward their brood rather than any true threat from above! Indeed, it is the profound union of love and hate—sex

---

assumptions and unconscious ideological biases can be revealed, and alternative interpretations proffered.

and aggression—that represents the ultimate source of what humans tend to project not only onto members of their own species, but onto other animate creatures of all types.

V

Freud was the first to explore the psychological association between sexual desire and birds. He argued that the experience of flying in a dream, for example, accompanied as it often is by a state of blissful rhythmicity, represented infantile desire for sexual fulfillment (Freud, 1913a). Every child, it has been said, has a wish to fly, and most have experienced moments of "flight" at the playful hands of one or another male relative who delights in tossing them into the air. The fundamental fantasy of flight is given form in the story *Peter Pan,* for example, as well as in other artistic endeavors such as Robert Altman's odd film, *Brewster McCloud* (1970), which is constructed around a virginal young man's personal mission to learn how to fly. Yet we may also encounter this wish in the clinical setting.

A 23-year-old patient who had been struggling unsuccessfully to separate from his mother, reported sadly to his therapist that his frequent dreams of flight, in which he would pump his arms up and down in a frantic, but exhilarating, fashion—and which had been his most enjoyable dream adventures—had virtually vanished. This coincided with his beginning both to become aware of his resentment toward his mother and to fantasize about romance with a particular young woman, as well as his beginning to reveal to his therapist his compulsive masturbation, all of which engendered inordinate guilt. He then reported sadness and nostalgia at the loss of his dream-flying, and voiced strong yearnings somehow to have it back. Further analysis of his memories of this joyful mode of transformation revealed that a previously hidden aspect of his exhilaration in flight related to his having felt that he was being gazed at from below by some sort of warm, nurturant *presence* as he flew, although no human figure per se appeared in the dream-tableaux. He was merely a young bird, pumping along, under the watchful gaze of some omniscient or voyeuristic Other. The oedipal, incestuous quality of these dreams, albeit with a preoedipal atmosphere, was manifest.

Alan Wheelis, in his stark and powerful memoir, *The Life and Death of My Mother* (1992), recounts a childhood memory of visiting the market in San Antonio with her, as his father lies dying from tuberculosis. They stop in front of a hot sausage vendor to ponder whether she can afford to buy her son a treat. As the vendor prepares a sausage, he mischievously—but menacingly—wields his knife toward the young boy, and then in the next blink of the eye, whacks the feet off of a pigeon (*Columba livia*) that has suddenly landed on the vendor's cart. With the same mischievous grin, the vendor throws aloft the shocked bird and brushes to the ground the twitching feet. The repetitive, bloody, and futile attempts made by the victimized bird to alight on a branch serve up an awful metaphor for the fantasied fate of the guilt-ridden oedipal son at the hands of a sadistically retaliatory—and nearly psychotic—father-figure.

VI

Freud discerned the close associative link between a fascination with flying, on the one side, and repressed incestuous yearnings, on the other, in his psychobiographic analysis of Leonardo da Vinci (1913a). His insight into this relationship stems primarily from a dreamlike screen memory or infantile fantasy that Leonardo recorded in the midst of some of his scientific musings related to birds and flight—apparently the only time the genius himself wrote of his childhood: "It seems that it had been destined before that I should occupy myself so thoroughly with the vulture [*il nibbio*], for it comes to my mind as a very early memory, when I was still in the cradle, a vulture came down to me, opened my mouth with his tail [*coda*] and struck me many times with his tail against my lips" (Freud, 1913a, pp. 33–34).

Freud argues that this memory-fantasy was woven of Leonardo's memories of being nursed and kissed by his mother—her nipples and lips having been transformed into the tail of a bird in the later recollection. Freud mistakes the bird for a "vulture" due to faulty translation from Italian into German, and then elaborates on the "vulture" as a mother symbol by way of association with the Egyptian maternal goddess, *Mut*, a deity with the head of a vulture (e.g., *Neophron percnopterus*) (Rosenfeld, 1956). According to Freud, Leonardo probably knew of this ancient link (Freud, 1913a). Once we realize that *il nibbio* refers, in fact, to a bird of prey known as a kite, which has a notably sharp, hooked beak and a long tail, the barely disguised maternal association is lost—or is it?

Leonardo's kite may have been the Black Kite (*Milvus migrans*), which is quite vulturelike in appearance when seen soaring overhead, so it is not unreasonable to speculate that the screen elements comprising Leonardo's memory perhaps did encompass the vulture association that Freud mistakenly took for granted, but which later critics have discarded. In addition, the word *nibbio* derives from the same root as that of "nib" and "neb"—both of which connote a bird's beak or bill—and also of "nipple" (*il nipplo,* among other Italian words for this appendage), which is probably from a diminutive of the same root. *Nib* also means snout, mouth, or even *face,* and, in its original usage, the tip of a quill pen, which of course was fashioned from a feather. Thus, through this nesting of associations, the kite image actually serves well as a conveyance of maternal presence. At the same time, with its long tail (*coda*) the kite easily suggests the male sexual organ, and, thus, a fantasied act of fellatio, which Freud argues is Leonardo's true repressed sexual desire. Whatever the validity of Freud's overall analysis, this interpretation is bolstered by the fact that *coda* is also a slang term for penis, as is the Italian word *l'uccello,* the bird. Freud goes on to argue that Leonardo's repressed sexual desire was sublimated not only via his painting, but also his yearning to fly and his design of early flying machines (Freud, 1913a).

Pinpointing the degree to which the inventions that produced aviation, rocketry, hang-gliding, helicopters, etc., were necessarily driven by repressed and sublimated sexual desire, as Freud would have us believe (Freud, 1913a, p. 103), is not, finally, crucial to their understanding. While in some rather trivial sense, the human species' desire to be at one with the birds, the sky, or heavenly bodies, by way of flight, no doubt provided some of the impetus toward early attempts to fly, the very ancient human capacity for imaginative *self-transformation,* whether in dreams, fantasies, delusions—or, in fully lucid waking life—by means of identification with flying life-forms, may offer sufficient psychological explanation for the advent of the aeronautical age.

A modern adumbration of psychodynamic themes related to flight is found not only in *Brewster McCloud,* but also in the film *Birdy* (1985), based on the novel by William Wharton, which depicts a socially avoidant, ostensibly asexual youth who is nicknamed "Birdy" because he is obsessed with birds. In order to be at one with his flock, he alternately strips naked and enters their cage, or fashions a suit of feathers and attempts flight. "As scary as a bird's life must be," he muses, "they always have *that* they can always fly away." He withdraws increasingly, eventually entering a catatonic, yet eerily birdlike state in which he ceases to interact at all in human fashion, as if he has died and been transformed into a bird. His boyhood friend and alter ego, Alfonso Columbato, whose last name refers to the Latin for dove,[6] returns wounded from Vietnam (World War II, in the novel) with his face swathed in bandages, after having been rescued from battle by a huge bird-helicopter. He finds Birdy in a psychiatric ward, and tries to coax him back into the human world, but finally makes contact with his chum only after he himself turns in desperation away from the harsh reality of modern life toward the specular realm of Birdy's oneness with birds.

VII

While attempts to fly during states of delirium, intoxication, or psychosis—often with catastrophic consequences—are by no means unheard of in psychiatric practice, the only published case I know of in which the patient apparently believes himself to *be* a bird is that of "A Little Chanticleer," by Ferenczi (1956). The patient is a 5-year-old boy who suddenly one summer becomes intensely enamored of the chickens in the chickenhouse behind his family's vacation cottage. He ceases to speak in human language and persistently imitates the birds' movements and sounds—clucking, cackling, and crowing, causing his parents to worry that he will lose all capacity for normal speech.

---

[6] According to one of the film's actors, Wharton actually intended Alfonso and Birdy to portray aspects of one and the same person (J. Brumfield, personal communication).

Ferenczi's analysis of the boy, Arpad, reveals that his odd behavior began upon his return to the vacation spa, about a year after he had been bitten on the penis by one of the resident cocks (!). No long after this occurred, he had also been told by a chambermaid who caught him masturbating that she would cut his penis off. The boy has dreams and nightmares about birds, mostly killed cocks and hens, and delights in the slaughter by the cook of such birds for the family table. He displays impulses to obliterate the eyes of the dead birds and quite enjoys plucking their feathers, as well. At times when he does speak intelligibly, he remarks that he should have his *own* head cut off. He also queries his parents about death, and whether angels carry dead children to heaven.

The unfortunate lad is obviously defending against terror at the near-amputation of his penis by the cock, and the threatened amputation by the maid, both of which no doubt reinforced his preexisting unconscious dread either of annihilation or castration by his father. Of course, as Ferenczi notes, one way Arpad can avoid such a fate is to identify with the aggressor and become "cock-of-the-walk" and ruler of the henhouse himself! Unfortunately, Ferenczi does not disclose the outcome of this interesting case—in particular, whether psychological development proceeded toward a manageable neurosis or a full-blown psychosis.

A clear-cut case of birds' entering into a patient's psychotic state is found in Freud's discussion of Judge Schreber's memoir of his mental illness (Freud, 1911). Schreber was in the habit of communicating with "bemiracled relics of former human souls," such as birds, which he referred to as "bird-souls" and "talking birds." He believed that they had been made to repeat "meaningless phrases" that had been "crammed into them," and which, further, they themselves could not understand, even though Schreber *could!* Thus, within the narrative of a mental illness, we discern this lovely commentary on the human experience of birdsong: at times we may feel as if birds are singing directly to us in our own language, though they seem oblivious to the meaning—even the profundity—of their own productions.

VIII

We will return to visit again with Judge Schreber in his asylum cell, but we must not miss an opportunity to touch down first for a rest in the lush region of birdsong and bird language. Of these, much can be said, as the poets remind us. Listen, for example, to the *Nightingales* of Robert Bridges (1929), as they offer up their entreaty:

Our song is the voice of desire, that haunts our dreams,
A throe of the heart . . .
Alone, aloud in the raptured ear of men
We pour out dark nocturnal secret . . . .

Composers of music, ornithologists, birdwatchers, and even psychologists (Ball and Hulse, 1998), are among those *Homo sapiens* whose ears have long been most attuned to the voices of birds. The French composer Olivier Messiaen, for example, often wove birdsongs into his works (e.g., *Quatour pour la fin du temps* and *Oiseaux Exotiques*), thereby creating a magical tapestry crafted from both human and avian aural sources.

The practice of "birding by ear"—locating and identifying birds solely by listening—is an exquisite experience of being at one with the natural world that may involve a virtually addicting, altered state-of-consciousness. A rare genius of this art-science, the ornithologist Ted Parker, who died when his biodiversity survey plane crashed in Ecuador, could recognize roughly four thousand species' vocalizations (Sullivan, 1993). He was truly a master at "reading the world, of turning nature itself into a book" (Rosen, 1977).[7]

The question of who can understand the language of the birds—and who is fated to ignorance of it—is pivotal in many cultures. Those who can are typically seen as closer to the gods,

---

[7] While his legacy lives on in his thousands of field recordings, which are being used to teach a new generation of field biologists so that the world's avifauna and biodiversity might better be conserved, the loss of this youthful "eco-hero," along with his colleague, botanist Al Gentry, will long be felt by all who pose the question of our own and other species' ultimate survival.

or the earth mother, or to some truth—or, even, to immortality.
Thus, Keats, in *Ode to a Nightingale* (1820):

> Thou wast not born for death, immortal Bird!
>   No hungry generations tread thee down;
> The voice I hear this passing night was heard
>   In ancient days by emperor and clown . . . .

Yet others, such as Ivan Cankar, Poet Laureate of Slovenia
(1876–1918), in his story *The Owls*, have clearly felt quite differ-
ently. "The cry soared to the skies . . . so powerful that the stars
shivered. . . . I listened in utter terror—there was an unknown life
beside me, which I could have reached out and touched; it spoke
its own terrible language which I did not understand; and all
secrets, to the very last, were in those voices . . . " (1913, p. 42).

Rabindranath Tagore, the great Indian poet, sometimes discerned meaning in bird song, but at other times was stymied by
these arcane murmurings. He wrote in *Stray Birds*—116 of "some
ballad of the ancient time in a forgotten tongue," but, in *A Flight
of Wild Birds (Balaka)*—36, he reports:

> Many are the human speeches I've heard migrating
> in flocks . . .
> And within myself I've heard
> day and night
> in the company of countless birds
> a homeless bird speeding through light and dark
> from one unknown shore to yet another.
> On cosmic wings a refrain echoes through space:
> "Not here, no, but somewhere, somewhere else!" [Tagore, 1918,
> pp. 327–330].

This "somewhere else" denotes not only other destinations
in this world we share with birds, but, like the "other scene" of
the Freudian unconscious (Freud, 1900), other loci in the chain
of signifiers within the mind of the poet; indeed, it points toward
the whole finely woven net of associations comprising the symbolic register that defines the uniqueness of *Homo sapiens*.

The human subject and human culture are constituted by a
highly elaborated capacity for language, which, while not truly

sui generis (as we are learning through study of other intelligent species), is, nevertheless, so singular that it defines us as the "sapient" Other within the animal kingdom. To this same extent, however, we are also encaged within this linguistic coop as our own kept creature. Indeed, no matter how much, inevitably, we strive to escape into the apparent freedom of the imaginary by altering our conscious states, I will argue (along with Lacan, Chomsky, and others, albeit from diverse perspectives) that *Homo sapiens* is caught always within the invisible "bars" of the symbolic register and the very structure of human language itself. Recall that the "bar" is that principle in linguistic theory—first proposed by de Saussure in 1916, and modified by Lacan—that differentiates the signifer, placed schematically above the bar, from any specific meaning, or "signified," placed below it (S/s; see Gorton, 1992).

The bar also symbolizes the repression barrier, that "mist net"[8] within the unconscious that snags our forbidden fantasies, traumatic memories, hidden meanings, and troubling conflicts—but from which, if we have the strength of ego to breach it bit by bit, such elusive denizens of our psychic depths can also be rescued, collected, and integrated into the collection of experiences that comprises our "self." Thus, the bar also points to the very possibility of finding, remembering, recapturing, analyzing, and finally, knowing—ourself.

In the human effort to understand the language(s) of the birds, then, we come full circle and rediscover our effort to understand ourselves. Plato's metaphor of the receptacle within each of our minds (see chapter epigraph)—at birth, empty, but becoming ever more populated with kinds of knowledge as we migrate through our lives—reveals, on closer inspection, a vessel for specimen collecting that seems to assume the form of that imaginary topological construction, the Klein bottle[9]: a potential space (Winnicott, 1967) that is always (and never) completely at one with the natural world.

This, then, is the structure that inhabits us, and which we inhabit, simultaneously, as both keeper and kept, having

---

[8] Mist nets are finely woven, nearly invisible fabric structures used to catch unsuspecting birds humanely in order to be able to study and band them.

[9] This is a bottle that, paradoxically, opens outward into itself, and is closed inward toward the outside; like a three-dimensional Möbius strip.

evolved—via the emergence of language and consciousness—along a meandering pathway away from enslavement to the
baser instincts, but now tethered within, and just beyond, the
encircling limits of our own, uniquely constructed, human aviary:
truly, *curators of self.*

IX

Humans have long kept birds tethered or in cages (Page and
Morton, 1989), and likely have also long identified with them.
Unlike an injured bird that remains forever unable to fly,[10] the
caged bird can potentially have its free flight restored; thus, it
signifies hope at the promise of release.

Tagore, once again, in his parable "The Parrot's Training"
(Tagore, 1918), tells the story of a parrot that is captured and
caged in order to educate it properly, since "it sang all night but it
never recited scripture." The parable is very explicit: the impious
parrot *is* "culture" that has been trapped and now must be inten-
sively taught so as to rescue it from its benighted obliviousness to
the great and glorious works of (Western) humankind. Eventually, "every creature remotely connected with the cage [espe-
cially, the birds' teachers, and others who had purchased an
interest in the birds' value] was flourishing beyond words," but
one was not—the parrot. Like the "goose that laid the golden
egg," it dies at the hands of its keepers, albeit by then literally
stuffed full with pages of reading material that had been its lessons. The parable is not only an indictment of British imperialism,
but of any and all extreme efforts to deracinate human nature
from its ancient roots in the natural world, and of any misguided
belief that indigenous culture should be obliterated in favor of
what are presumed to be "higher" values and ideals.

Maya Angelou, in *I Know Why the Caged Bird Sings* (1969),
uses the caged bird metaphor to convey the possibility of liberation in her poignant account of an African-American childhood
and youth in a community wholly dominated by whites (Volkan,

---

[10] This powerful image has itself been the basis of aesthetic endeavor (e.g., Michel
Marc Bouchard's play, *Tale of Teeka,* about an abused boy and his pet goose who is unable
to fly [Graeber, 1998]).

1972). And Kate Chopin's classic late nineteenth-century novel, *The Awakening* (1899), opens with a caged parrot who repeats over and over "Allez vous-en! Allez vous-en! Sapristi!"—"Go away, go away, for God's sake!" Originally entitled *A Solitary Soul*, the book tells of its heroine's struggles to fashion an authentic self out of the stultifying, culturally sanctioned feminine roles and values she has been offered in turn-of-the-century New Orleans society. In effect, she struggles to disen*cage* herself so as to seek some new pathway, or, alternatively, to give up and migrate inward. In the end, she escapes to apparent freedom by swimming out into the shining sea to her destiny.

Years later, Hilde Bruch would entitle her masterwork on anorexia nervosa, that disease of bodily "perfection" gone horribly awry, *The Golden Cage* (1978). And Marcel Duchamp, sly provocateur of modern art, would trap sugarcube-sized blocks of marble in a small birdcage, and entitle the result *Why Not Sneeze?* (1923)—as if teasing us into imagining the raw materials of sculpture as living entities that must first be set free—convulsively?—before they can take creative flight as creatures of the artist's desire.

If we dabble long enough among artists, writers, and poets, with their aviary of bird images, we quickly realize that their wish to speak or not to speak—sing or not sing—ventriloquially through the captive prey whom they would stuff full with metaphors and metonyms, in actuality embodies their own uncertain position in the pecking order of worldly things. No surprise! But can it really be that what birds are telling us is simply what we would have told ourselves one way or another, anyway? Or might they be seducing us—Odysseus to their Siren songs—ever proffering that which we desire but cannot quite locate within ourselves—in order, at long last, to be able to set it free: our *own* true voice?

X

In the children's story *Beaky* by Jez Alborough (1990), a "fluffy creature" seeks its identity, having just hatched from an egg that fell from a nest onto the ground while its mother was away. After entreating many citizens of the forest to answer its cry of "What am I?" and being told by a frog that "You must be *something* . . . everything is *something!*" the little creature with a bright blue beak and a curly orange tail, whom the frog names Beaky, hears "something singing softly, far away." It climbs high up in a tree, seeking the source of the joyful song, but becomes lost and falls, only to discover that—lo!—it can fly with its "fluffy flaps," which, of course, are wings. Only then does it see a larger creature flying far above. As Beaky perceives *his* reflection in the mirroring Other, he realizes that he himself is a bird, too! But he is not just *any* bird: he is a Bird of Paradise (Tribe *Paradisaeini*). Thus, in this moment of specular liberation from the descriptive name—"Beaky"—which the frog had temporarily given it/him, he locates his place in the symbolic order of bird names, and finally discovers the possibility of a true self.

XI

In virtually every culture, the names of particular families or species of birds have served as symbols for one or another human attribute or personal quality. Within the Western cultural tradition, much of this lore is captured in a sort of naturalist's scrapbook known as a "bestiary," which is a compilation of stories, legends, and myths relevant to the universe of known and imagined animals. *The Book of Beasts* (White, 1954), for example, is a translation of a twelfth-century Latin bestiary that is believed to have evolved over the prior three millennia, its origins extending back past the Egyptians and perhaps into prehistoric times. Fully two-fifths of this volume (pp. 101–162) is about birds, and the entries even include a mythical, interspecies hybrid called *Ornithanthropus* (p. 262), perhaps a phylogenetic forerunner of my fanciful *Homo aves*. Later, the first printed book on birds, *Avium Praecipuarum* by William Turner, was published (in Latin) in 1544.

It was in this historical context that William Shakespeare acquired his knowledge of birds and their many various associated meanings. He refers to no fewer than fifty species in his works (Goodfellow, 1983), and many of his usages have entered the common language as bird metaphors and metonyms that all of us let fly unwittingly now and again. Examples that are particularly relevant to the "mental zoo" include the clutch of words and phrases that signify craziness or foolishness, such as "crazy as a ... cuckoo" or "... loon" (by way of *la lune* and lunatic, but also reflective of the loon's odd yodeling call). *Turkey, goose,* and *gull,* as well as *odd duck, feather-brained,* and *flighty* can also refer to a foolish person or an idiot. The word *booby,* from the Spanish word *bobo,* meaning dance or idiot, was applied by sailors to a group of tame, slow-witted, seagoing birds, the boobies, who were easy targets when they flew aboard ships. Had it not been for their less accessible nesting places on cliffs and islands, they might have gone the way of the turkey-sized pigeonlike bird, the dodo (*Raphus cucullatus*), whose common name also connotes stupidity, since it too was an easy object for senseless persecution ("dead as a dodo") due to both its flightlessness and lack of fear of man. Finally, "loony bin" and "booby hatch" both refer pejoratively to mental wards.

But what of *Struthio camelus,* the ostrich? Here is another ostensibly foolish bird that is said to stick its head in the sand to avoid reality, though it only appears to do so, perhaps when bending down to its sand-crater nest. And we shan't forget those clown-princes of birds, the ever-so-human penguins (Family *Spheniscidae*), from whom Chaplin may have borrowed his herky-jerky gait. Finally, if someone is "chicken," he (or she) is cowardly, and if he is a "lame duck" (e.g., a late second-term American President) or "hen-pecked," or a cuckold, he is an ineffectual, weak, and perhaps emasculated version of his former self, even if he persists in being, as the French say, "hardi comme un coq sur son fumier" (bold as a cock on his own dungheap)!

In India, labeling someone "the son of an owl" is among the most scurrilous of insults. In Germanic culture, one says "Du hast ein Vogel ins Kopf" or, "You have a bird in the head!" when wishing to tell someone that he or she is crazy or idiotic. In English, we say, of course, "You bird-brained moron!" or the like. Note that here the Platonic metaphor of the aviary of knowledge-birds is turned on its head: a bird that inhabits the mind must be a species of idiocy! But whatever we may guess to be inhabiting a person's own private cranial aviary, perhaps it might not be too unreasonable to inquire, if only rhetorically, whether in a moment of clinical interrogation or loving intimacy: Just what sorts of avian denizens are flying anywhere and everywhere within this head of yours?

XII

Virtually every culture appears to have assigned certain birds to the role of symbolizing badness of one sort or another, while other birds are typically relegated to conveying goodness: consider "hawks" and "doves" in wartime. Particular species not uncommonly carry different valences in different settings, or embody ambiguity. Some birds in the Greek cosmology, for example, were associated with evil, such as vultures, whom the wicked Harpies resembled, yet in Egypt they were maternal symbols. Owls in many parts of India are considered stupid, yet in many Native American tribes and in the United States today they are seen as embodiments of wisdom. The Zuni tribe takes owls as symbols of fertility, but to other Native American groups, the Chinese and the ancient Sumerians (who gave us their owl-bedecked goddess of death Lilith), they represent death (Johnsgard, 1988).

Crows and ravens—or any dark birds—are often associated with bad tidings, death, or evil, as in Poe's *The Raven* (1845), in which a bird (*Corvus corax*) who is perhaps the soul of the narrator's dead lover, Lenore, returns to bedevil him in the "grim, ungainly, ghastly, gaunt, and ominous" guise of that "thing of evil" whose "discourse so plainly . . . little relevancy bore" ("Nevermore"). Among some Pueblo Indians, however, crows and ravens are quite bivalent, signifying bad luck or war, on the one hand, but also standing for dark, gravid rainclouds and agricultural bounty, on the other. And among the Hopis a crow kachina (totemic doll) named Tumas is regarded as the mother of all other kachinas. Yet again, in the *The Birds,* a film originally in black and white that loses some of its impact in the colorized version, crows and starlings are prominent among the squadron of attackers who strafe and divebomb the schoolchildren as they flee their besieged schoolhouse.

Since the advent of the aeronautic age, *all* birds have at times been viewed as embodiments of evil. Flying machines are not only capable of taking wondrous flight "on a wing and a prayer" (consider "The Spirit of St. Louis" of aviator Charles "The Lone Eagle" Lindberg, or aviatrix Amelia Earhart's Lockheed Electra); they are also quite capable of raining down napalm, "smart" bombs, and nuclear genocide (Lutwack, 1994, p. 107). Observe, for example, the dove in Picasso's masterpiece, *Guernica,* perched ironically amid the ruins of a bombed Spanish town with its beak pointing skyward; or, gaze at the stuffed, blindly staring bird specimens kept by the psychotic killer Norman Bates in Hitchcock's *Psycho.*

XIII

Just as Du Maurier and Hitchcock used birds as a collective metaphor to hatch their plot in *The Birds* (1963), the Greek playwright Aristophanes also used *The Birds* as metaphor in his comedic play of the same name in 414 B.C.E. In the play, he refers to no fewer than eighty species of our fine feathered friends in order to suggest a utopian community called "Cloudcuckooland," which he deploys to satirize the foibles and follies of the politicians and hoi polloi of Athens.

Since Greek mythology is replete with birds, it is not surprising that Aristophanes drew so heavily from bird imagery. Nearly every major deity appears to have had one or more species associated with it, including the peacock of Hera, the owl of Athena, the eagle of Zeus, and the dove and swan of Aphrodite. Periodically, these and other gods might assume the form of a bird so as to interact with earthbound mortals. Thus, Zeus raped the maiden Leda while in the form of a swan, producing four offspring, among them Helen of Troy. And Zeus sent an eagle (in some versions, a vulture) to torture the rock-bound Prometheus for his sin of impertinently having given fire to mortals.

Periodically, humans strove to gain the power and freedom of the gods by taking on characteristics of birds, as with Icarus, who perished in his effort to fly too close to the sun, thereby bequeathing us "hubris" as a human foible. Daedalus, Icarus' father, and planner of the labyrinth, was more successful when he fashioned a pair of wings to flee his imprisonment by King

Minos within his own construction. James Joyce drew upon this myth when he named the hero of *A Portrait of the Artist as a Young Man* Stephen Daedalus. Stephen's moment of epiphany as he discovers his identity as a writer occurs when "his strange name seem[s] to him a prophecy . . . a prophecy of the end he has been born to serve . . . a symbol of the artist forging . . . out of the sluggish matter of earth a new soaring impalpable imperishable being . . ." (Joyce, 1916, pp. 168–169). Indeed, the myth that those who can soar are akin to gods has currency even today, as with the "god of basketball," Michael Jordan, who warbles "I Believe I Can Fly" through the voice of the singer/songwriter R. Kelly in Jordan's movie-vehicle *Space Jam* (1996).

Since birds can simply "wing it" whenever they like, they very often symbolize freedom, as with John Lennon's posthumously released *Free as a Bird*," which kills two birds with one stone not only by expressing the general thematic simile of its title, but also by conveying the spirit of the dead Beatle round the world "on the wings of song."

Certain bird-related activities may at times also signify sublimation of yearnings for freedom, as with the breeding of birds (aviculture), and their training, as depicted, for example, in the films *Birdy* (1984) and *The Birdman of Alcatraz* (1962). Volkan (1972) discusses this phenomenon in his musings about the emergence of aviculture shortly after the political partition of Cyprus, and its subsequent decline when boundaries were relaxed.

However, dichotomous possible meanings lurk eerily close here, as well: if boundaries become too fragile, as with the common phobia, "fear of flying," there may emerge a paralyzing anxiety grounded in a wish-fear dilemma that the boundaries of the ego may relax too much, with the potential to unleash aggression or libido that would overwhelm or annihilate the self.

XIV

Thus, while the fact that birds fly about freely, and may appear without warning, provides inspiration to some people, to others it is cause for fright. Particularly when birds mass together and make a noxious clamor, not to mention voraciously consuming precious crops and discharging their feculent offal, or divebombing us to protect their young, they may evoke loathing, dread, and murderous hatred.[11]

In my experience, actual "ornithophobia" is probably more common than is usually appreciated. One man reported a lifelong fear of birds that he attributed to his extreme childhood myopia. As far back as he could recall, he had feared that a bird might suddenly appear and peck at his eyes. He said, "You never knew what they were going to do—they have such quick movements!" On the other hand, a woman's lifelong fear of birds, also without remembered traumatic etiology, had to do with *their* eyes, which were eerily frightening to her: "Something about those eyes—I don't know—I get a chill just thinking about birds' eyes!"

Peto postulates that "terrifying eyes" represent a visual, archaic forerunner of the superego, which incorporates the experience of having been under a "destroying, annihilating" parental gaze "before which there is no secret and which sees . . . what is going on in one's own body" (Peto, 1969, p. 204). Perhaps this hypothesis can elucidate young Arpad's delight in destroying the eyes of his tormentor, the chicken![12]

Another sort of fear may be seen in a dream reported by one of Grolnick's patients. The dream had occurred just prior to the patient's impending separation from his girl friend: "I was watching a man, a bird and a horse. The bird attacked the horse's testicles with his beak. Then I turned around and heard a sawing sound. When I looked, something was sawing away at the horse's penis" (Grolnick, Barkin, and Muensterberger, 1978, p. 222). This seems to be a very different sort of attack than what is feared in the two cases above!

In all of these cases, an attack by a bird is at issue: the ornithophobic child fears either an attack on his eyes—organs through which he gazes at his mother and at the world, or an attack upon her (the female patient) *by* the eyes of the parent; while the man

---

[11] Another bivalent image, the scarecrow, is, of course, designed to prevent birds' destroying the fruits of our labor.

[12] I should not fail to acknowledge that birdwatching, the practice of spying on birds—by means not only of the naked eye, but of binoculars and telescopes—so as to identify and study them, is a consummately voyeuristic practice that gives the term *scopophilia* an added dimension!

with separation anxiety and resultant retaliatory anger and guilt
dreams of an emasculating attack on genitalia—organs that differentiate him from the female object and with which he can penetrate and impregnate her. Notably, in Hitchcock's *The Birds*, the
single most gory moment is a close-up of a dead man's bloody
eyesockets. The visceral fear evoked by the movie largely derives
from its powerfully eliciting early childhood fears of being horribly maimed, eviscerated, or annihilated, more so than later fears
of castration.

Deutsch, in "A Case of Hen Phobia" (1931), describes a 20-
year-old man who as a 7-year-old boy had become fearful and
avoidant of all hens in his family's farmyard. He had previously
been the victim of an ostensibly playful homosexual attack by his
grown-up brother, who grabbed him from behind as he stooped
down, held him around the waist, and shouted "I'm the cock and
you're the hen!" Despite the boy's squawking protestations, the
brother would not let him go until the terror/excitement had
crescendoed terribly. The phobia eventually resolves when his
brother leaves two years later. Through her analysis of the man's
sexual difficulties, Deutsch comes to understand that the hen "is
a sort of mirror of [the patient's] feminine tendency," from
which he must flee in order to manage his passive homosexual
wishes.

Thus, birds may enter us, take leave of us, attack us, watch us,
or haunt us (as I write, a strain of Hong Kong avian flu threatens a
world pandemic). But some of us may also try to enter *them*, and
not just by wearing a cloak made of their feathers (Reina and
Kensinger, 1991) or stuffing their carcasses for our table! Instances of sexual congress with birds occur now and again, as
recorded in Krafft-Ebing's *Psychopathia Sexualis* (1886, pp. 180,
375–380) and in John Water's crude filmic catalogue of perversi-
ties, now a cult anticlassic, *Pink Flamingos* (1972). There, in one
of the truly Boschian, or Rabelasian, moments in modern cinema,
a man and woman perpetrate the bloody rape of a chicken in
what can only be called a *sauvage à trois*. This has nothing to do
with using peacock plumes for sensual delight in the popular
image of bondage and sadomasochistic sexual teasing!

Instead, the sadistic imagery of the cockfight comes to mind.
Cockfighting, as both "sport," spectacle, and betting activity, has

been practiced at least since Roman times, and remains popular, though sometimes illegal, in many parts of Latin America, the United States, and elsewhere. Geertz, in his anthropological classic about cockfighting in Bali, examines the many cultural meanings of this activity (1973), which is but one among the many ways that birds have been exploited to one degree or another to serve a vast range of human desires and needs.

Some of the other more intriguing uses to which birds have been assigned include: foretelling the future as is ornithomancy, a form of augury through observation of bird behavior, which was common in many cultures, including China and ancient Rome, and from whence is derived the word "auspicious," from the Latin *avis* (bird) and *spicere* (to see). There is oomancy, divination through examination of birds' eggs or their contents. There is hunting (e.g., falconry), and fishing with birds (e.g., in Japan, where, for centuries, tethered cormorants with gullet rings that prevent them from swallowing their catch, have been used to catch fish). And the dead are disposed of by exposure to vultures in "sky burials" in India, Tibet, Iran, Mongolia and some Native American cultures (Weidensaul, 1996). Birds are also used to transmit messages (e.g., carrier pigeons), provide energy (guano, produced by Guanay cormorants in Peru), and detect danger (e.g., poison gas sensitive birds in mines and World War I trenches). Domestic fowl are used as earthquake predictors in China. Birds are used also in the manufacture of vaccines (e.g., viral culture using hen's eggs) to facilitate studies of "imprinting" behavior and learning (e.g, Nobelian Konrad Lorenz's study of goslings and Niko Tinbergen's study of gulls); and to indicate the relative health of Earth's ecosystem (e.g., bird-banding, bird census-taking, and field-ornithologic biodiversity studies).

XV

Meanwhile, Judge Schreber, still ensnared within his delusions, communes with birds, and a century later, halfway across the world, a quite schizotypal female patient, having withdrawn from most human contact, *literally* communes with them by rescuing the sick, injured, and orphaned of the ornithine community, whom she then allows anywhere and everywhere in her squalid Philadelphia apartment. "They are all my children," she says, though she refuses to name them. Schreber gives his "bird-souls" girls' names, the better they might evolve into symbols of a feminine aspect of God and of the Heavens. Recall that one of Schreber's principal delusions is that he has been transformed into a woman in order "to redeem the world and restore it to its lost stage of bliss" (Freud, 1911). In this way, his delusional system facilitates his being able to imagine sexual union with a paternal figure without at the same time being conscious of the forbidden homosexual nature of this transaction.

Freud adds an interesting postscript to the case that illuminates Schreber's proclivity for staring at the sun. His belief that it would talk directly back to him parallels the mythology of the eagle (e.g., *Haliaeetus leucocephalus*), which in many cultures is held to be the only creature able to be so visually intimate with the sun, and, thus, closest also to royalty. Freud notes that young eaglets are said to be pushed prematurely from their sky-scraping eyrie to an early death if they cannot look into the sun without blinking, a sort of test of the purity of the aquiline lineage. This link to eagle mythology provides for Freud further confirmation of Schreber's special bond with this heavenly body, which must surely represent a sublimated relationship with the principal father-symbol in the human cosmology. We might imagine what sort of young child, in the absence of grandiose delusions, is able to meet his father's stern gaze with his own without flinching —presumably, one strongly identified with the aggressor, such as a psychopath or a future king![13]

Thus, certain birds have done service as go-betweens moving between humankind, in its search for its voice, and the cosmos, whether construed as the place of gods, or more simply, and profoundly, as the Great Beyond—another one of our many names for the *real*. The group of birds known as raptors, which includes eagles, hawks, falcons, buzzards, kites, and the like, has served as a particularly intriguing flock of "messengers of the

---

[13] There may be more here than meets the eye regarding Freud's own penchant for focusing his awesome analytic capabilities unwaveringly upon even the most daunting of analytic challenges.

gods'' for humankind, and, therefore, has been particularly generative of myths and fantasies. These powerful, swift, rapacious
birds possess an awesome ability to vanish upward, becoming
mere specks in the sky, or even to disappear altogether in apparent merger with the airy nothingness (Weidensaul, 1996).

Yeats, in his allusion to the decline of Judeo-Christian culture
in *The Second Coming*, draws upon falcon imagery to provide the
central metaphor of the poem:

> Turning and turning in the widening gyre
> The falcon cannot hear the falconer;
> Things fall apart; the centre cannot hold;
> Mere anarchy is loosed upon the world. . . [Keats, 1820, p. 187].

The interspecies communication breakdown—falconer to falcon,
or God to man, or Man to nature—that occurs with spiritual
anomie prefigures destruction of the established order, not unlike what is foreshadowed in Hitchcock's *The Birds*.

Shakespeare refers to falconry, or ''hawking,'' many times in
his plays and poems (Goodfellow, 1983). It was first practiced
about four thousand years ago in China and Persia, and was popular among the royalty and aristocracy of Shakespeare's day. As a
gentleman, with his own coat-of-arms, he would have been entitled to fly a goshawk (*Accipiter gentilis*), which would have been
trained to recognize *his* voice, and none other. Thus, with birds,
it is not simply a matter of our learning to understand what *they*
have to say—imagine a young goshawk charged with learning to
comprehend and obey no one else but William Shakespeare![14]

XVI

In Egyptian mythology, the gods Horus and Ra are both pictured
with falcon heads on human bodies, a fact that Freud knew well.
As a child, he had seen Egyptian funerary scenes in his family's

---

[14] St. Francis of Assisi (1182–1226), patron saint of birds and other animals, turned
away from his curatorship of a human flock, and took to preaching directly to a truly
feathered ''flock'' in order to teach them spiritual lessons, presumably of the sort Tagore's
caged parrot was *supposed* to have been studying.

copy of Philippson's richly illustrated translation of the Old Testament into German, and these images almost certainly provided some of the material for his "Egyptian Dream," which he recounts in *The Interpretation of Dreams*: "In it, I saw my beloved mother, with a peculiarly peaceful, sleeping expression on her features, being carried into the room by two (or three) people with birds' beaks and laid upon the bed. I awoke in tears and screaming and interrupted my parents' sleep. . . . I fancy [the figures] must have been gods with falcons' heads from an ancient Egyptian funerary relief" (p. 583).

Freud interprets the dream, which perhaps contains elements of a primal scene experience, as depicting his mother's dying, but he determines that his anxiety at the dream's images is due not to his fear of her death, but to his repressed incestuous desire for her. He notes that the German word for bird, *Vogel*, gives rise etymologically to a vulgar term for sexual intercourse, *vogeln* (to "bird"), a term Freud had learned from a boy named Philip, whose name, in turn, provides an associative link between sex and the bird-figures by way of Freud's memories of the falcon-headed images in the *Philipp*son's Bible.

Rosenfeld (1956) argues cogently that this dream from Freud's seventh or eighth year provided the crucial paradigmatic "totem" for his life's work—not the bird, but, of course, *Homo sapiens*, a hybrid of man and beast, an interspecies merger of lower, primitive instincts and a "civilized" veneer. Freud's huge collection of archaeological artifacts, many of them Egyptian—and not a few depicting bird-headed gods and birdlike figures (Gamwell and Wells, 1989)—further attests to this theory. Rosenfeld's spadework also turns up a fascinating link between the Philippson funerary illustrations and Freud's later elaboration of the Oedipus complex, of which the Egyptian dream is most certainly a primordial elaboration: one of the funerary tableaux in Philippson's is labeled as being from Thebes, which is not only a city in Egypt, but also the town in Greece where Oedipus' father reigned and later, of course, was slain by the son who would then marry his own mother.

Now it should be clear why Freud repeatedly stressed the sexual symbolism of birds, as if their beaks, eggs, and Springtime arrival followed by nest building, often elaborate courtship dances, and quite public copulations did not adduce reasons enough! With their beaks, they are phallic in visage: words for the penis include, of course, "pecker," but also "cock" and *l'u-cello*, as mentioned earlier. One man, newly a father, dreamt of "a beautiful woodpecker with a red head that suddenly flew out of my bathrobe, which was hanging on the wall." After initially being "startled and surprised," he "marveled" at it. His wife had recently given birth to his namesake, and while clearly a proud papa, perhaps the fact that part of him—in the form of his infant son—was now pecking at his wife's breast, was in no small measure emasculating ("a bird in the hand is worth two at the breast"?). At the same time, perhaps he felt as if he himself had been the one to give birth—to a marvelous little *pecker!*

Yet birds are also universally taken as female symbols, as is made explicit in the British slang term for a young woman, "bird." Thus: breasts (turtledoves, pigeons); vulva, mons, and pubic triangle ("bird" and "nest"); sexuality ("the birds and the bees"); birth (storks); motherhood (in ancient Egypt, the vulture; also "mother hen"); purity and beauty (swans); love and faithfulness (doves, lovebirds, nightingales, larks); rebirth (the phoenix); and life itself (in Mayan myth, the resplendent Quetzal, *Pharomachrus mocinno*). Note also that the word *incubus*, which refers to a mythical male demon who seeks sexual union with sleeping women, derives from the Latin word for incubation, meaning to lie upon and hatch eggs. And, remarkably, the word *nightmare* derives from the Anglo Saxon *mare*, from the Sanskrit *mara*, both of which refer to an incubus, which was once believed to be the nocturnal demon that caused nightmares. Finally, "flipping a bird" or "giving the bird" refers to a familiar, aggressively sexual gesture with middle finger extended, perhaps because this posture of hand and digits suggests the outline of a bird.

Not surprisingly, then, stories and myths regarding reproduction and creation from many cultural groups around the world have been informed and nourished by human experiences with birds. In a Greek myth, for example, primordial Chaos begets "black-winged" Night, who lays an egg from which is born winged Eros (primordial desire), who mates with Chaos to produce the world, the first generation of birds, and the first family of gods (Schmidt and Benardete, 1980). In Native American myth, Raven is the wise creator of the world, and also sometimes the Trickster, who, in a moment of boredom, impulsively adds genitals to all his creatures, thereby inventing what the stories call "Raven's greatest game," from whence spring all subsequent generations of creatures of the earth (Savage, 1995).

And in a lovely, contemporary poetic "myth" entitled *St. Kevin and the Blackbird,* the Irish poet Seamus Heaney (1996) offers an image of a saint's allowing a blackbird to nest in his outstretched hand, which rests palm up just outside the window of his narrow cell. As he feels the warmth of the bird incubating its eggs, St. Kevin finds

> himself linked
> Into the network of eternal life. . . .

Except,

> now he must hold his hand
> Like a branch out in the sun and rain for weeks
> Until the young are hatched and fledged and flown [p. 20].

While we wait, with him, keep in mind that the image of the nest has been a fecund source of metaphor for human behavior: the "empty nest" syndrome, the "nesting instinct," "feathering one's own nest" and "fouling one's own nest," for example. And eggs, too, have offered a rich harvest of sayings and metaphors: "to walk on eggshells," "hard-boiled" (as in "tough"), a "nest egg," "to lay an egg," "an egghead," and "Don't count your chickens before they hatch!"

As St. Kevin patiently participates in the creation of a miracle,

> A prayer his body makes entirely
> For he has forgotten self, forgotten bird
> And on the riverbank forgotten the river's name.

It is as if "the shut-eyed blank of underearth" has "Crept up through him" and "there is distance in his head. . . ." He is "Alone and mirrored clear in love's deep river" (Heaney, 1996, pp. 24–25).

XVII

While across the Atlantic, Emily Dickinson, peering out through the window of her darkened room, but profoundly unblinkered, manages to coax that most treasured of all birds into the shape of words: "Hope is the thing of feathers/That perches in the soul" (Dickinson, 1862, p. 79). And the artist Marsden Hartley, too, finds feathered emissaries of desire to populate the blank canvas of his soul: "All warblers of the world have come/to me, and are in me living—" (Hartley, 1923, p. 831).

The Norse God Odin, it is said, would send forth two ravens, Thought and Memory, to encircle the world by day and return at night to bring him all he needed to know (Savage, 1995). While, in *The Far Field*, Theodore Roethke prays for all of us: "to come upon warblers in early May [is] to forget time and death . . ." (1964, p. 785).

Birds are much more often balm than abomination. Through them, within us, upon their wings—and ours—we hear the air they embroider with song. We commune with them, nesting in our feathered beds, enjoying flights of fancy. We chase wild geese, and give them names. And we read the bird-ciphers in the text of our mirroring mother, Earth. For, the human aviary is as wide as earth and sky, and even if, as *Homo aves*, we find ourselves kept within its confines, still, it cannot encompass the ever-stretching field that is the mind of our caretaker and keeper—*Homo aves*—whose imagination is as boundless and timeless as Nature itself.

Until, at long last, we flutter down to land in an unknown, familiar place—a shore by the shining sea—after our long, first journey to this precious harbor, to moult and spend a season.

I close now with a haiku entitled *Reflection*, which I wrote in 1988 as I found myself contemplating another life from afar, paused momentarily in my own journey under the sun:

Bird on the wing
                    in endless sky:
                                darting pupil
                                            of an awesome eye.

REFERENCES

Alborough, J. (1990), *Beaky*. Boston: Houghton Mifflin Co.

Altman, R. (1970), *Brewster McCloud*. MGM [Distributor].

Angelou, M. (1969), *I Know Why the Caged Bird Sings*. New York: Random House.

Aristophanes (414 B.C.E.), The Birds. In: *Four Greek Plays*, ed. & tr. D. Fitts. New York: Harcourt, Brace, 1960.

Audubon, J. J. (1844–1846), *The Birds of America*. New York: Macmillan, 1946.

Bach, R. (1970), *Jonathan Livingston Seagull: A Story*. New York: Macmillan.

Ball, G. F., & Hulse, S. H. (1998), Birdsong. *Amer. Psychologist*, 53:37–58.

Barber, T. X. (1993), *The Human Nature of Birds*. New York: St. Martin's Press.

Beck, E. M., Ed. (1968), *Bartletts' Familiar Quotations*, 14th ed. Boston: Little, Brown.

Bridges, R. (Nightingales) 1929 In: *Modern British Poetry: A Critical Anthology*, ed. L. Untermeyer. New York: Harcourt, Brace, 1942, p. 59.

Bruch, H. (1978), *The Golden Cage*. Cambridge, MA: Harvard University Press.

Cankar, I. (1913), *My Life, and Other Sketches*. Lubjana, Slovenia: Vilenica.

Chauvet, J. M., Deschamps, E. B., & Hillaire, C. (1996), *Dawn of Art: The Chauvet Cave: The Oldest Known Paintings in the World*. New York: Henry Abrams.

Chopin, K. (1899), *The Awakening*, 2nd ed. New York: W. W. Norton, 1994.

Clottes, J., & Courtin, J. (1996), *The Cave Beneath the Sea: Paleolithic Images at Cosquer*. New York: Harry N. Abrams.

Cowan, J. G. (1993), *Messengers of the Gods: Tribal Elders Reveal the Ancient Wisdom of the Earth*. New York: Bell Tower.

Deutsch, H. (1931), A case of hen phobia. In: *Neuroses and Character Types: Clinical Psychoanalytic Studies*, ed. H. Deutsch. New York: International Universities Press, 1965, pp. 84–96.

Dickinson, E. (1862), Hope is the thing with feathers. In: *Selected Poems and Letters of Emily Dickinson*, ed. R. N. Linscott. Garden City, NY: Doubleday/Anchor, 1959, p. 79.

Feld, S. (1982), *Sound and Sentiment: Birds, Weeping, Poetics and Song in Kaluli Expression*. Philadelphia: University of Pennsylvania.

Ferenczi, S. (1956), A little chanticleer. In: *Sex in Psycho-Analysis*. New York: Dover, pp. 204–213.

Frankenheimer, J. [Director] (1962), *The Birdman of Alcatraz.* MGM [Distributor].

Freud, S. (1900), The Interpretation of Dreams. *Standard Edition,* 4. London: Hogarth Press, 1953.

———— (1911), Psycho-analytic notes upon an autobiographical account of a case of paranoia (dementia paranoides). *Standard Edition,* 12:1–79. London: Hogarth Press, 1958.

———— (1913a), Leonardo Da Vinci and a Memory of His Childhood. *Standard Edition,* 11:1–55. London: Hogarth Press, 1957.

———— (1913b), Totem and Taboo. *Standard Edition,* 13:1–161. London: Hogarth Press, 1955.

Gamwell, L., & Wells, R. (1989), *Sigmund Freud and Art: His Personal Collection of Antiquities.* Binghamton, NY: State University of New York.

Geertz, C. (1973), Deep play: Notes on the Balinese cockfight. In: *The Interpretation of Cultures.* New York: Basic Books, pp. 412–453.

Goodfellow, P. (1983), *Shakespeare's Birds.* Harmondsworth, U.K.: Penguin Books.

Gorton, G. (1992), Book review. *The Seminars of Jacques Lacan,* Books I and II. *Psychoanal. Books,* 3:491–508.

Graeber, L. (1998), A story of a boy and his goose. *NY Times,* January 30, p. E41.

Greenson, R. (1978), On transitional objects and transference. In: *Between Reality and Fantasy: Transitional Objects and Phenomena,* ed. S. A. Grolnick, L. Barkin, & W. Muensterberger. New York: Jason Aronson, pp. 205–209.

Grolnick, S. A., Barkin, L., & Muensterberger, W. (1978), *Between Reality and Fantasy: Transitional Objects and Phenomena.* New York: Jason Aronson.

Hartley, M. (1923), Warblers. In: *An Anthology of Famous English and American Poetry,* ed. W. R. Benet & C. I. Aiken. New York: Random House, 1945, p. 831.

Heaney, S. (1996), St. Kevin and the blackbird. In: *The Spirit Level.* New York: Farrar, Straus & Giroux, pp. 24–25.

Hitchcock, A. [Director] (1963), *The Birds.* MGM [Distributor].

Johnsgard, P. (1988), *North American Owls: Biology and Natural History.* Washington, DC: Smithsonian Institution Press.

Joyce, J. (1916), *A Portrait of the Artist as a Young Man.* New York: Viking Press.

Keats, J. (1820), Ode to a nightingale. In: *An Anthology of Famous English and American Poetry,* ed. W. R. Benet & C. Aiken. New York: Random House, 1945, p. 263.

Kisselgoff, A. (1997), Dance review: Old bird duet is back, with some new tricks. *NY Times,* November 8, Section C, p. 9.

Krafft-Ebing, R. (1886), *Psychopathia Sexualis,* tr. F. S. Klaf, 12th ed. New York: Stein & Day, 1965.

Leach, E. (1970), *Claude Lévi-Strauss.* New York: Viking.

Lee, J. S. (1990), *Jacques Lacan.* Amherst: University of Massachusetts Press.

Levi-Strauss, C. (1963), *Totemism.* Boston: Beacon Press.

Lutwack, L. (1994), *Birds in Literature.* Gainesville: University of Florida Press.

Marshack, A. (1972), *The Roots of Civilization.* New York: McGraw-Hill.

Matthiessen, P. (1973), *The Wind Birds.* Shelburne, VT: Chapters, 1994.

Ogburn, C. (1976), *The Adventure of Birds.* New York: William Morrow.

Page, J., & Morton, E. S. (1989), *Lords of the Air: The Smithsonian Book of Birds.* New York: Wings Books.

Parker, A. [Director] (1984), *Birdy.* Tri-Star Pictures [Distributor].

Peterson, R. T. (1934), *A Field Guide to the Birds.* Boston: Houghton Mifflin, 1980.

Peto, A. (1969), Terrifying eyes: A visual superego forerunner. *The Psychoanalytic Study of the Child,* 24:197–212. New York: International Universities Press.

Poe, E. A. (1845), The raven. In: *The Unabridged Edgar Allan Poe.* Philadelphia: Running Press, 1983, pp. 1043–1046.

Pytka, J. [Director] (1996), *Space Jam.* MGM [Distributor].

Reina, R. E., & Kensinger, K. M., Eds. (1991), *The Gift of Birds: Featherwork of Native South American Peoples.* Philadelphia: Museum of the University of Pennsylvania.

Roethke, T. (1964), The far field. In: *The Norton Anthology of Modern Poetry,* 2nd ed., ed. R. Ellman & R. O'Clair. New York: W. W. Norton, 1988, p. 785.

Rosen, J. (1977), Why I am for the birds. *NY Times Book Review,* June 15, p. 55.

Rosenfeld, E. M. (1956), Dream and vision: Some remarks on Freud's Egyptian bird dream. *Internat. J. Psycho-Anal.,* 37:97–105.

Savage, C. (1995), *Bird Brains: The Intelligence of Crows, Ravens, Magpies and Jays.* San Francisco: Sierra Club Books.

Schmidt, J., & Benardete, S. (1980), *Larousse Greek and Roman Mythology.* New York: McGraw-Hill.

Spence, L. (1914), *The Myths of the North American Indians.* New York: Dover, 1989.

Sullivan, R. (1993), Theodore Parker, Alwyn Gentry, biologists, die in airplane crash. *NY Times,* August 6, Section C, p. 11.

Tagore, R. (1918), The parrot's training. In: *Rabindranath Tagore: An Anthology*, ed. K. Dutta & A. Robinson. New York: St. Martin's Press, 1997, pp. 327–330.

———— (1997), *The One and the Many: Readings from the Work of Rabindranath Tagore*. Calgary, Alberta: Bayeux Arts.

Tinbergen, N. (1953), *The Herring Gull's World: A Study of the Social Behavior of Birds*. Garden City, NY: Doubleday/Anchor, 1967.

Tyler, H. A. (1991), *Pueblo Birds and Myths*. Flagstaff, AZ: Northland Books.

Volkan, V. (1972), The birds of Cyprus: A psychopolitical observation. *Amer. J. Psychother.*, 26:378–383.

———— (1981), *Linking Objects and Linking Phenomena*. New York: International Universities Press.

Waters, J. [Director] (1972), *Pink Flamingos*. New Line Cinema [Distributor].

Weidensaul, S. (1996), *Raptors: The Birds of Prey*. New York: Lyons & Burford.

Wharton, W. (1978), *Birdy*. New York: Knopf.

Wheelis, A. (1992), *The Life and Death of My Mother*. New York: W. W. Norton.

White, T. H., Ed. & Trans. (1954), *The Book of Beasts*. New York: G. P. Putnam.

Whittaker, C., Ed. (1989), *An Introduction to Oriental Mythology*. Seacaucus, NJ: Chartwell Books.

Winnicott, D. W. (1967), The location of cultural experience. In: *Playing and Reality*. Harmondsworth, U.K.: Penguin, 1971, pp. 112–121.

Wood, R. (1977), *Hitchcock's Films*. New York: A. S. Barnes.

Yeats, W. B. (1921), The second coming. In: *The Collected Poems of W. B. Yeats*. New York: Macmillan, 1933, p. 187.

Zizek, S. (1991), *Looking Awry: An Introduction to Jacques Lacan Through Popular Culture*. Cambridge, MA: MIT Press.

CHAPTER 7

Snakes and Us

D. WILFRED ABSE, M.D.

Throughout history, the relationship of man and snake has been complex and paradoxical. On the one hand, the snake has been emblematic of wisdom and empowerment, procreation and longevity, even the hope of rebirth and immortality. On the other hand, it has represented death and disease, sin, lecherous temptation, and cunning duplicity. Thus the golden, snake-intertwined heraldic staff of Hermes or Mercury constitutes the caduceus, signifying healing power and medical art in ancient Greek and Roman mythology, whereas Medusa, the mortal daughter of the Gorgons, in venerable legend dallied with Poseidon in Athena's temple whereupon the outraged goddess changed the offender's hair into serpents framing a viperous malevolent face so awful to behold that any viewer would turn to stone. As far back as the Old Stone Age, man was already fascinated with the shape of the snake. Thus at the Dome of Serpents at Rouffignac in central France, deep under the earth on the curved clay ceiling of a massive cave, hundreds of intertwining, serpentine markings are displayed. Moreover, Paleolithic man sometimes engraved his tools and weapons with images of snakes.[1]

---

[1] In the children's board game *Snakes and Ladders*, the player slides down the numbers when the snake is encountered and rises in the numbers as a ladder indicates. In such a game the snake activates descent and symbolizes misfortune. No doubt the folkloristic basis resides in the widespread experience of toxic snake bite, often fatal before the era of scientific medicine and the availability of antivenom. The ups and downs which punctuate the fate of human beings are illustrated in children's games as they are in the most sophisticated of modern novels.

In ancient Greece there were many established sites for oracles, the most famous being that at Delphi, near the foot of the south slope of Mount Parnassus. Following rites of purification and sacrifice to an earth goddess at the shrine, a priest or priestess imparted her response to bewildered suffering human questioners. Sometimes a duly entranced supplicant emitting ecstatic cries was utilized in this responsive process to another by means of the priest's interpretation of his or her vehement glossolalic utterances. Gaea was worshipped especially for her capacity to facilitate fertility, and rites were often conducted by priestesses who themselves became possessed and then gave forth oracular utterances. These states of altered consciousness followed frenzied orgiastic rites and sometimes were associated with the worship too of chthonic deities presiding over night and darkness. Hera, the queen of heaven, sent a monstrous serpent, a female python, to incarnate Gaea, the earth goddess, in order to facilitate her being adequately worshipped. However, Apollo, one of the Olympian gods, later killed this python. Thereafter, the Pythean games celebrated his victory over her every four years with song and poetry and athletic contests. Slater (1968) relates these and other elements of Greek mythology to the structure and dynamics of the classical Greek family of the ruling class in the fourth and fifth centuries B.C.E.

According to Morris and Morris (1965), the snake figures more than any other animal form in myths, legends, and folklore throughout the past. It is notable that the fascination with or aversion to snakes, one way or another, shown by humans is hardly reciprocated. The snake shows no attachment even when kept as a pet; it is doubtful whether it ever learns even to recognize the person who feeds it regularly and expends loving care in handling it. Any snake, moreover, however docile, will strike immediately in self-defense if accidentally hurt or startled. Clearly, the relationship of man to snake is, however intense, a very one-sided passion. In connection with this intense interest, conscious and unconscious, it is to be borne in mind that the word *fascination* is itself derived from the Latin vulgarism *fascinum* denoting the penis. It is the shape of a snake and especially the pattern of its movement which provoke so much human attention and strong feelings of attraction or of repulsion (or both) far beyond its food value or the danger of snakebite.

All over this planet, the appearance of the snake makes a forceful impact on the human being; sometimes this impact can best be described as a *tremendum.* Thus in the Hokkaido Ainu of the Saru River region there is a type of Arctic hysteria instigated by any sudden confrontation with the reptile (Ohnuki-Tierney, 1980). Characteristically this occurs in females during late adolescence or at menopause. As detailed by Foulkes (1972), there is a sudden onset of shouting of obscenities, with later echopraxia, echolalia, heightened suggestibility, and wild dancing; and sometimes then jumping into water or into a fire. Such symptomatic behavior is stereotyped and repetitive, the Ainu woman being in a hypnoid state of altered consciousness. She would often loudly curse her husband, such as she would not dare to do ordinarily, deterred by fear of violent retribution. Ainu women typically have a great fear of snakes which are regarded as having supernatural powers. An encounter with one in actuality, or sometimes only in a dream, would readily precipitate the hysterical attack. Usually such an episode is regarded as possession by an alien spirit, so that any hostile behavior is discounted in the heavily male dominated society. It is, however, evident that such a spirit comprises protest otherwise absolutely forbidden.

The battle of the sexes is indeed not confined to the circumpolar peoples, but stretches from pole to pole and all around the equator. Often it is confined to a pleasurable thrill in the sexual encounter of a couple. The sudden appearance to a woman of a snake may then be simply startling, and the cause of a mere frisson.

PERCEPTION AND SYMBOL ACROSS CULTURES

According to Gestalt psychology, the earliest figure-ground structuring of visual and other sense perception is instinctually embedded in the inborn dynamics of human brain physiology. In Gestalt principles of organization the law of similarity—the counterpart of Aristotle's law of association—indicates that similar items (for example, those alike in form and color) or similar transitions (those alike in the steps separating them) tend to form groups in perception. The law of proximity, as the Gestalt psychologists call it—the counterpart of Aristotle's other law of association by *contiguity*—indicates that perceptual grouping is favored according to the nearness of the parts. Other important principles are derived from Gestalt studies: the law of *closure* indicates that closed areas are more stable than unclosed ones and therefore form figures in perception more readily; and the law of *continuation* indicates that perceptual organization tends to occur in such a manner that a broken straight line appears to continue as a straight line, a partial circle as a circle, and so on, even though many other kinds of perceptual structuring would be possible. *Closure* and *continuation* are aspects of articulate organization. In accordance with these principles a major function of the perceptual apparatus turns out to be the stripping away of redundant stimulation and the encoding of incoming information in an economical form useful for the organism. Organismically, perception is governed by the law of *prägnanz*, which provides that when patterns of stimuli offer many possible interpretations, the one most economical and useful to the organism at that time will be selected. Gestalt psychologists offer many figures to illustrate the principles adumbrated, among them the widely known and classically ambiguous one of an urn the edges of which can also be interpreted as two faces looking at each other. "Urn or profile, one is master for a while and figure will change into ground. The two perceptual matrices are reciprocal, alternation determined by unconscious physiological processes" (Köhler, 1930).

In psychoanalytic amplification of Gestalt findings, the perceptual-conscious organization as outlined above in the service of reality adaptation enlists augmentation and sometimes distortion preconsciously in subliminal perception and especially by endopsychic interaction with repressed unconscious phantasy. This is a process corresponding with the hidden order in art's substructure as elaborated by Ehrenzweig (1967), for, after all, the primary process like the secondary one is not only relatively so but has its own organization which makes more liberal use of displacement, condensation, and symbolism. The shape and movement of the snake resonates with the experience of and the phantasies connected with the penis and comes to be a representation of or symbol for it. Morris and Morris (1965) note that the extraordinary importance often given to a snake is not only a result of lack of understanding of its enigmatic character, but is due to an unconscious symbolic equation of the snake with the phallus. This results in many qualities, both real and imagined, which associatively belong to the male organ of copulation, being projected onto the snake. Certainly with its ever open eyes and expressionless face, and its swift and slithering movements, the snake gains attention and readily provokes mythic elaboration in man, and this is replete with phallic symbolism. Down the ages too men have been impressed by the reptile's ability to change its skin, appearing thus to renew its youth, and at the same time wonderfully seeming to increase in size and strength.

Africa has provided many interesting examples of snake worship which flourished worldwide in the nineteenth century. Hambly (1931) noted that ideas concerning resurrection and fecundity were shared in the various belief systems of numerous African snake cults. Variants of python worship spread across the continent and reached a peak of concentration in Dahomey and Nigeria. European visitors to Dahomey in the nineteenth century were astonished that large numbers of snakes in villages were better fed and cared for than the human inhabitants. A special house was provided for them, to which they were carefully returned if they strayed away. Catching sight of such a reptile, a Dahoman immediately would prostrate himself on the ground in obeisance. The python was treated with profound respect and addressed as "master, father, mother and benefactor." The snake god Danh-gbi of Dahomey was attended by a large priesthood headed by the king who allegedly consulted the python about problems in government. The snake periodically appeared to young women who then became possessed by a rush of ecstasy. Later many entered the service of the snake temple. On some ceremonial occasions they would dance around with earthen pots on their heads shortly before human sacrifices were made, a sacred ritual apparently designed to bring rain. Morris and Morris (1965) write:

> Numerous wives were provided for the python. When the millet began to sprout, the old priestesses rushed round the village seizing and carrying off young girls between the age of eight and

twelve to be his brides. Some pious parents deliberately left their female offspring out in the streets. After due instruction, the snake's wives took part in licentious rites with the priests and eventually became public prostitutes whose services were eagerly sought by the male worshippers when crops were germinating. Since the god directed his wives' activities, which were thought to assist him in his efforts for the community's welfare, no disgrace was attached to their profession. The snake's wives were not allowed to marry and any children born to them belonged to the god. To molest or kill any python, even by accident was to invite severe punishment. Formerly the penalty for this crime was death by fire, but by the nineteenth century the sentence had been commuted to a severe ordeal, which was still likely to prove fatal unless the culprit was lucky and had distributed adequate bribes. M. Oldfield Howey [1928] tells us that "the offender was placed in a hole under a hut of dry faggots, thatched with grass that had been generously greased with palm oil. Sometimes a dog, a kid and two fowls were placed along with him, and he himself drenched with palm oil. The hut was set aflame, the doors of light wicker and grasses fastened, and the snakeslayer had to break out and rush through the fire to the nearest running water, followed by the Serpent priests, who beat him mercilessly with sticks and pelted him with clods." A service of commemoration in honour of the python was held thirteen days later [p. 28].

Correspondingly, Joseph Conrad's *Heart of Darkness* (1902) projected an image of Africa as "the other world," the antithesis of Victorian European civilization. But, of course, the other world lies within, as demonstrated by the unfolding fate of Mr. Kurtz in the novella, in his descent from humanism to barbarism.

The ambiguity of the figure offered by Rubin (1915) is obviously limited in its value because it does not encompass the many configurations of unconscious symbolism. The very word *symbol* indicates etymologically a throwing or flowing together, and though a snake is an animal and may be perceived objectively as such exteroceptively, inwardly it is apt to quickly recruit emotionally laden and multiple figurative meanings. The herpetologist in his quest for objective knowledge is required to shed from his mind any effects from such primitive indirect and perturbing representations. As Jones (1916) noted in his famous seminal essay, some important symbolic modes of thought are very primitive, both ontogenetically and phylogenetically representing a reversion to earlier stages of mental development. Outside Africa, snake worship remains perrsistently entrenched in India. Many temples are dedicated to the hooded serpent, the cobra, the totem of the early Dravidians in pre-Vedic India. Oldham (1905) noted that it was to those ancient deities, rather than to the great gods of the Brahmins, that the Hindu people turned in times of flood or famine or other natural disasters. Thus to the snake god they prayed in times of pestilence; and in times of drought they prayed to him for rain. To cobras they offered the first milk of their cows, and the first fruits of their harvest, in ceremonial reverence and appeasement. The phallic Hindu god Siva is also known as "King of Serpents" and snakes are found entwined about cult objects connected with the worship of the male principle of generation which he above all represents.

Nowadays some villages in southern India have several days of festivities celebrating the cobra god. Following the monsoon season, the rivulets and rivers become swollen and flood the surrounding earth, incidentally flushing out hundreds of cobras. Some of these are carefully captured by trained personnel and taken into the village in capped urns. Later at an appointed time in large gatherings drums are noisily beaten and colored banners hoisted. Some suitably trained individuals then prod the liberated snakes which raise their head and strike at other people who have shields to protect themselves. There is competition to be the snake handler who gets his snake to raise his head the highest, and also for the person who has captured the fattest snake. Soon after such games, the priests among them conduct a religious service. Later the snakes are carefully returned to the locations where they were found and there they slither away. In the religious services, the snake god is thanked for bringing rain and thus water to flood the rice fields sufficiently. Reversing the actual causal sequence, the cobras are regarded as bringing the rain.

The emperors of China down the centuries had claimed to be the sons of dragon gods, the dragon being an evolved form of the snake, according to many Chinese scholars. Similarly, Quetzalcoatl, the Aztec God, the exotic feathered serpent was called "rattlesnake," and priests were named after him. Morris and Morris (1965) note that Quetzalcoatl promised his people after the fall of Tulla that he would return one day. They write: "On sighting the Spaniards resplendent in their shining armour sailing in from the east, the priests informed the Aztec ruler Montezuma that Quetzalcoatl had come back. The invaders were greeted with presents which included a feathered cloak and snake mask set with turquoises, the emblems of the god" (p. 41).

The novel *The Plumed Serpent (Quetzalcoatl)*, by D. H. Lawrence (1926), is a vivid evocation of Mexico and its ancient Aztec religion. Here the serpent expresses the Nietzschean idea of the powerful superman which the author nurtured and in which he found the illusion of power which protected him from feeling helpless.

Monaghan (1995) discusses the Nuyootecos who dwell in southwestern Mexico, and who are typically very concerned with the effects of malicious envy (*Yatuni*). They speak of *Yatuni* as something that exists between groups of people as well as between individuals. The noxious effects can result in serious physical illness, sterility, and death of individuals as well as a wide range of antisocial consequences. The Nuyootecos tell of a golden age in the distant past when rainfall was always abundant, at least two ears of corn sprouted on every cornstalk, and humans grew tall and strong. Among them at that time were "Rain People," the tenuvi, members of another tribe who served to mediate Nuyooteco relationships with rain spirits. However, some Nuyootecos grew envious of the tenuvi and denounced them as exploitative, so that many others threatened them and they departed. It then stopped raining, and drought ensued causing the harvest to be lost. Within a short time, animals died of thirst and people starved. The Nuyootecos sent out a commission to plead with the exiles. Only two returned. Though these two relieved the drought, Nuyootecos never again enjoyed the same level of prosperity. Thus by allowing *Yatuni* to influence them into driving some neighbors out, they destroyed the basis of their own well-being.

The focus of Nuyooteco thinking about *Yatuni*, according to Monaghan (1995), is the *Tachi*, the demon of sacred envy, and there are many polluting animals the result of his union with women, including snakes, buzzards, toads, scorpions, and lizards. Monaghan (1995) writes: "The snake is the foremost of the children of Tachi. There are many kinds of snakes in the region, and each—even the smallest and most harmless—is feared. One reason is that snakes make them ill. For example, snakes may give people the evil eye just as people who feel Yatuni may give others the evil eye" (p. 139).

Anent snakes, he adds:

> One kind of snake merits special mention, the *koo tuun*, "black snake" or *tilcoate* in Spanish. I bring this up not only because it is the most fearsome of the children of Tachi, but also because people encounter it when they have illicit sexual affairs. Some say the snake coils around its victim, sticks its tongue in the victim's ear, and lashes him with its tail. Alternatively, it may hang the victim upside down from a tree branch. This is significant because it shows that Tachi is a tangible presence in human interaction. Thus, Nuyootecos say that when a *tachi tiu*, or whirlwind, passes through a group of people, they will begin fighting, and the course of the fight will trace the path of the whirlwind. Similarly, people tell the story of a blind man who saw a tachi step into a jar of pulque from which several men were drinking, and the men then began to fight with one another [p. 140].

As is well known in Europe and the United States, in legend St. Patrick, the patron saint of Ireland, banished snakes from the country in the fifth century. Thus the legend attempts to dramatize the riddance of evil, notably including malicious envy, by the introduction of Christian charity. Schoeck (1970) pointed out that all peoples, not only those of the most primitive peasant cultures, have continued to have considerable problems with social envy. Chaucer (1394) in *The Parson's Tale*, describing seven sins, wrote that envy was the worst of all, and "flatly against the Holy Ghost." The snake, the lowly creature that goes upon its belly, is also a fitting symbol for malicious envy. Are we not proud of our upright posture?

THE PASSIVE PHALLUS AND THE PHALLIC WOMAN

Though saturated with phallicism, since ancient times snakes have also been important female symbols, especially representing the malevolent mother. The witch with the broomstick is of course an allied and familiar symbol. Berke (1988) elaborates:

> In fertility cults phallic objects have been represented with snakes coiled around them. The encircling snake represents clinging vines, possessive arms, and dominating, insatiable women. And because the snake devours its object whole, it has also been associated with mothers' devouring breasts, eyes, mouths, vaginas, wombs and psyches. Finally because the snake gets into things, it has been linked with the female phallus, which "knows what is going on" [p. 348].

In his major work, Freud (1900) showed that the sexual organs were often represented in the manifest dream reported by the patient through isomorphic figures; and of these, the snake, he asserted, was the most important symbol of the male organ. Indeed the perceived shape and movement of the animal readily resonate with elements of the body-image, especially the penis and the tongue. The snake's predilection for penetrating into crevices or holes in the earth, extending and retracting its body, sometimes secreting a potent fluid, certainly facilitates such body symbolisms. However, as symbols are condensations with multiple references which are overdetermined, we must in different contexts be ready to acknowledge many aspects of serpent symbolism which jar a mechanical notion of a simple equation of snake = penis. Indeed in many instances, a symbol may represent two or more inconsistent elements. Such is the condensed nature of unconscious phantasy; and thus it is in fertility cults encircling snakes can represent the female of our species, as noted by Berke (1988) above with reference to the "Phallic Woman." This woman is endowed in phantasy with either a penis or a phallic attribute. The former may be part of her anatomy externally, or internally hidden inside herself. The basis for such an image is rooted in the phallic libidinal phase of development in which both male and female were viewed by the child as having the same sexual executive organ. This mistaken theory was brought to light in the analysis of adults when the castration complex became elucidated, and was later confirmed by experience with children. Preceding that phallic phase is that of anal sadism, or the cloacal stage. The word *cloaca* (Latin for "drain") indicates a hole at the posterior end of the body of a vertebrate into which the intestinal, urinary, and reproductive ducts open. In most mammals it is a transient structure in embryonic development. The snake, like other reptiles, has a persistent cloaca in the adult form, that is, it has no septum such as exists in mammals with rectovaginal and rectourethral separations. The image of the snake, it is interesting to note, sometimes oscillates between cloacal and phallic symbolism and at other times in different contexts represents a confluence of both "bad" and "good" stuff. Bonaparte (1953), writing of the development of sexuality in humans, suggests it would be more correct to term the sadistic-anal stage of infantile psychosexual development in male and female, the *sadistic-cloacal* since it partly reflects and repeats preceding unfolding embryonic events. In regard to the female of our species, she writes:

> In this stage where the vagina is still only adumbrated as an adjunct to the anus, which in fact it is, it is the whole cloacal opening which dominates the libidinal organisation. The *hole* seems to assert itself, so to speak, through all the libidinal organisation before the *protuberance*, and Freud long ago recognized the dominance of oral, as of anal erotism, as preceding that of phallic erotism. . . . The hole, however, will stay female, and the protuberance establishes the male. Thus the cloacal stage will remain the substratum of the *feminine*, and in the history of libidinal development, it is the feminine which exists before the masculine [p. 34].

Bonaparte draws attention to the passive phallic phase which follows the cloacal, and which is followed and overlaid by the active phallic phase in the active positive Oedipus complex. She elaborates upon the long, passive prehistory of the phallus, and writes:

> At the beginning, what every small boy wants to get from his mother is that she titillate and touch that pleasurably sensitive organ and, only later, will he want to push and pierce actively with it. This first stage of development, or what should rather be called passive phallic awakening, which always doubtless precedes the active phallic flowering that ends in the Oedipus complex, would

be that in which many semi-impotent males will linger or to which they will regress; such for instance, as those masturbators who find their phallic masturbation phantasies all-sufficient, or men who, though able to exercise object choice, demand only masturbation or fellatio from women and have no need for penetration. All degrees of retardation, in this attitude, however, may be met with, as well as every amalgam with the active phallic position which would challenge it, since certain men need but a few preliminaries by way of passive stimulation to be able to pass to active penetration. But here it would be best to define what we ourselves mean by the passive phallus. Some analysts, indeed, object that the phallus is always active when in erection, and however that may come about. By active phallus, therefore, we mean the phallus that is able to enter into erection and want to penetrate, whether spontaneously, through excitation of the central nervous system, or by sight or thought, for instance, of the love object. The passive phallus, however, needs localized peripheral excitations in order to function and then, in extreme cases of passivity, may even achieve orgasm without erection [p. 43].

As regards female sexuality, the long passive prehistory of the phallus, given the essential passivity of the female, pursues its course in the little girl with much significance for her fate. But she too, of course, had the genital region cleansed, attended to, and involuntarily caressed by the mother. It was the mother who awakened the child's passive and phallic-cloacal sensitivity.

These considerations enlarge the understanding of snake cults and of snakes as pets. Those who handle the snakes enjoy the mother's privileges, and thus attempt to overcome and overcompensate for feelings generated by infantile helplessness and passivity, in this dramatic activity with docile snakes.

THE FUNDAMENTALIST SNAKE CULT OF THE BIBLE BELT OF SOUTHERN UNITED STATES

Weston La Barre (1969) described the dangerous snake-handling cult that arose in the late 1940s and early 1950s among the rural mountain people displaced from remote parts of southern Appalachia into the industrial Piedmont of the New South. The founder of this cult, one George Hensley, had pondered a text from Mark 16:17–18 (King James Version) which purports to be a report of Jesus Christ's injunction following his resurrection:

17. And these signs shall follow them that believe; In my name shall they cast out devils; they shall speak with new tongues;
18. They shall take up serpents; and if they drink any deadly thing, it shall not hurt them; they shall lay hands on the sick, and they shall recover.

The emphasis George Hensley put on the message conveyed in these verses appertaining to snakes became a very circumscribed development within the fundamentalist Christian faith of the rural South which had long been a stronghold of low-church sects like the Baptists, the Methodists, and the Holiness and Pentecostal churches. The more general view, however, strictly followed that of the early chief exponent of the Christian movement in the first century C.E., a Syrian Jew from Tarsus named Paul. In *Man and His Gods*, Homer W. Smith (1952) wrote:

[Paul] was possessed of "a thorn in the flesh, a messenger of Satan" which has been interpreted as epilepsy. As described in the Acts of Paul and Theda he was "of a low stature, bald on the head, crooked thighs; handsome legs, hollow-eyed; he had a crooked nose; full of grace." This was apparently spiritual grace, for Paul was always acutely conscious of his physical infirmities. Argumentative and even querulous, he was given to alternating fits of violent rage and severe depression, and in his seizures he emitted inarticulate sounds, i.e., spoke "in an unknown tongue . . . unto God." In such moments he experienced ecstatic visions which he prized above all waking realities. According to his own account he had persecuted the followers of the Messiah until one day, on the road to Damascus, he had fallen to earth and had been caught up into the third heaven and heard words which it was not lawful for a man to utter; thereupon he repented of his persecution, and became convinced that he had been personally charged to spread the faith, and to warn people of the coming Doomsday. Impelled by the fear that the last trump would sound before he had fulfilled his mission, he traveled about the empire propounding that the Messiah, whom he called Jesus, had *already* come, had suffered a sacrificial death by crucifixion and had ascended unto heaven. He proclaimed that the Day of Judgment would be next week, or the week after, and that those who wished to be saved should repent and be baptized and protect themselves by participation in a eucharistic meal [p. 178].

The minority sects in Appalachia, small in number, which actually "took up serpents" in their ritual performance, subscribed to the basic tenets of faith advocated by Paul but besides taking up serpents they also emphasized the phenomenon Paul himself experienced of speaking in tongues. They believed that the Holy Spirit confers supernatural gifts such as this ability to speak in tongues (lalling) and to heal by prayer, the laying on of hands, and anointing with oil. Paul had praised lalling as a way to edify the spirit of the speaker in private prayer, or as a sign to impress unbelievers, and he permitted its use in church if followed by "interpretation." Among some of the snake-handling cults were those who thought they were speaking to God in ancient Hebrew!

Kildahl (1972) found among such creeds which put an extreme emphasis on individual religious peak experience a pervasive belief that the few who thus transported could speak in tongues were likely to possess in abundance other charismatic gifts including those of interpretation and prophecy. As La Barre (1969) insisted, the phallic symbolism of the snake, that is, its unconscious representation to man of both the male genital concretely and of generative power more abstractly, though preeminent does not exclude a multiplicity of other kinds of body-image symbol formation. In particular, the snake also is replete with oral and anal symbolisms, including notably, and probably, in my opinion, only second in cathexis to the penis, the human tongue.

As regards other oral symbolisms, La Barre (1969) notes the most persistent and wholly false but widespread folk belief that snakes suckle at the human breast. Among other instances he cites the Welsh tradition that the mythical flying snakes had drunk women's milk spilt on the ground and had then eaten sacramental bread. In a footnote he compares this quaint symbolic doublet to the flying (i.e., phallic) snakes of old Semitic and modern Egyptian folklore. He writes: "Flying snakes are of course just as

unreal as suckling snakes; but once we employ the snake to sym-
bolise man, then it is inevitable (because of human anatomy and
man's universal familial nature) that everywhere we will first find
snakes suckling women and then returning later as flying serpents, having incorporated the father's masculinity, "power,"
creativity, immortality . . ." (p. 95). Incidentally, these remarks
illuminate the origins of the Welsh national flag, as well as other
flying dragon banners, notably in China.

Audition of glossolalics, from a developmental perspective,
reveals that the subject reverts to the actual prestages of word
language, babbling and lalling; and conversation with him later
often shows that he felt elated and suffused with omnipotence
and was speaking effectively in many languages, including ancient
Hebrew and Greek, despite the evident babyish performance.

But the accompanying glossolalia of those who religiously
take up snakes is just one index of regressed mentation in a group
context, a regression in which the snake innocently arouses affective reactions based on an infiltration of cryptophoric symbolism in an altered waking state similar to that in dreams. The
cryptophoric symbolism of nighttime dreaming in the sleeping
state often replaces a part or a function of the body by the visual
image of an external object. Thus the male organ may be replaced
by a snake or airplane, the female breasts by peaches, the female
genitals by a jewel case. The visual cryptophoric symbolism of
dreams largely pertains to the expression of sexual and aggressive
strivings and anxieties, the symbols substituting for sexual objects
and relations.

La Barre maintains that the snake handler, as does the severely neurotic, wanders in a jungle of unconscious symbolism
about which he concludes:

> The snake has a cleft tongue, says folklore, because he tells lies, a
> literal kind of double-talk. But whose is the *double-entendre* of the
> innocent conscious—and guilty unconscious—sly symbolism? Pro-
> jectively we say the *snake* lies (denies oedipal guilt); all the while
> it is we who so deny. Thus it is the projected discrete serpent that
> is the Devil, or the instrument of the Devil (sexual or incestuous
> desires); hence he (snake, phallus) must be spurned and killed
> (as must these desires), lest we be killed. Therefore, to handle the

snake, without the punishment of death, means either (1) that God the father is being royally hoodwinked in this dangerous game, or (2) that God grants genitality to the (incestuously) guiltless. Snake-handling is then an anxious testing and abreaction of guilty terror. To "dominate" the snake is to dominate guilty and dangerous sexual desire. But neurotic symbols "eat their cake and have it too," for snake-handling is itself obviously erotized. The snake is both the ancestral or oedipal father, giver of life, God—and the phallic Devil, instrument of God. The snake is both death and life, and immortality as well; the godhood of the father and the sinfulness of the son; the instrument both of pleasure and of its punishment. As the prime symbol used by human beings, the snake must always and everywhere be preoccupied with man's basic concern: the human body image and its life and death or immortality. The snake represents every modality of our body's guilts and needs [p. 108].

Indeed, once selected as a body-image symbol, the snake can express singly, or condense, every psychosexual modality of the body, including in anal-symbolism "bad stuff" to be rejected and expelled as snake shape and movement emulate the formed stools of defecation. In the Christian West, the emphasis is apt to be on the putative evil of the animal whereas in the Hindu East, it shifts toward the sacred good. Nowadays, the more objective aspects sometimes get commercialized, the skins of rattlesnakes being put to use as leather bags, wallets, and purses, and suburban gourmet restaurants serving such delicacies as pizza with rattlesnake meat. Here too a thrill resides in associated phallic and oral symbolism, a thrill produced by anxious but omnipotent and elated feelings generated by devouring this animal. For the unusual meat evokes oral-sadistic phantasies of eating up the terrible and ambiguous object which once inspired such awe, but is now completely mastered and assimilated.

Recently, Kimbrough (1995) has given a sympathetic account of current religious snake handlers of eastern Kentucky. He took part in three hundred such religious services in twenty-five snake-handling churches. It is evident that the followers of George W. Hensley remain active in Appalachia and mountaineers remain impressed with ancestral preaching methods laced with snakes. Due to snakebite deaths, legislation has attempted to stop the practice without notable success.

Kimbrough describes an episode in 1939. He writes:

In 1939 George Hensley was evangelizing in Florida. During one service a doctor from New York approached Hensley and asked him if he would handle his serpent. Hensley replied, "If the Lord moves on me, I will." The physician returned later that evening accompanied by seventeen doctors and thirty-five nurses. In his possession was a seven-foot snake, which some believe to have been a cobra. The people in attendance stated that anyone bitten by the serpent would perish in thirty seconds.

As the service progressed, Hensley finally went to the snake box and started handling the giant serpent. The snake struck Hensley in the palm of his hand. The congregation believed that he would perish at any moment. Hensley started to dance almost frantically and to talk in tongues. The physician who owned the serpent examined Hensley, because he felt that the great evangelist was in danger of losing his life. The doctor allegedly reported, "His pulse is actually getting stronger." The doctor also spoke many languages. When he listened to Hensley speaking in tongues, he began to cry and said, "I don't know any of this." Park Saylor says, "When Hensley was full of the spirit he would handle any snake put in front of him. . . . If you are living right, like God would have you to live, and walk like God, live holy and honest before God, that snake might as well bite on a dogwood stick. God is not going to put you in jeopardy. A few years ago there was a man who said he had the faith of "blue steel." He was killed by a rattlesnake. Faith isn't enough. You have to be anointed to handle snakes" [pp. 113–114].

Hensley at the age of 75 in 1955 had apparently lost none of his zeal and ability to preach the gospel. In the summer of that year, however, in a service in a shed near the community of Altha in northwestern Florida he met his death. Kimbrough (1995) describes the occasion:

When the Spirit moved him, he went to a lard can that held a large eastern diamondback rattlesnake. Hensley opened the container and removed the snake. For fifteen minutes he handled the serpent in various ways, placing it on his head, rubbing it in his face, and wrapping it around his neck. When Hensley began to put the snake back in the can, it suddenly turned and struck him

on the wrist. His arm became swollen and turned black. He began
to vomit blood. Many of the spectators tried to persuade Hensley
to seek medical attention, but he refused. Calhoun County Sheriff
George Guilford asked Hensley to visit a hospital, but he responded, "I'll be saved by my faith. I won't go to a hospital for
anything." Early Monday morning, George Hensley died. His wife
said his final words were, "I know I'm going. It is God's will"
[p. 133].

THE TRIUNE BRAIN

The patient, a young military man, presenting with a problem of
sustaining a relationship with a woman, recounted in the middle
phase of his psychoanalytic therapy, his acquiring a garter snake
at the age of 12. At last he felt then he had found a means of
intimidating his domineering and "control freak" mother. He
tenaciously clung to this pet for several months, one which he
assured me was "really utterly harmless" as his father had knowl-
edgeably but reluctantly agreed despite the mother's specious
persistent arguments. He complained that when it once got free
in his absence at school his mother had sought the aid of a neighbor who caught and dispatched the snake to its freedom in the
woods nearby where he had formerly found it. He thought the
snake itself was "utterly mechanical" and, unlike his dog, boring
as a pet, but he had anyhow clung to it when he realized how
terrified his mother was of it—as a means of retaliation, he now
supposed. Later in treatment after pursuing his anxious phantasies of controlling and castrating phallic women, he talked
about the snake which had at first fascinated him. He had named
it "Dick" (a vulgarism for the penis among his pals), and expati-
ated on its inability to relate to him as his dog did, and on its
autonomy and complete resistance to control unless carefully
boxed. From these reflections we were able to go on to discuss his
intense feelings and exuberant phantasies about his own genitals
especially during his pubescence.

Many such experiences as this in analytic sessions illustrate
the ramifications of ophidian symbolism in the relationships of
man and woman. As is so well known in Western Judaeo-Christian

culture, the snake is incriminated with Eve and Adam in Original Sin. While St. Paul took the view that celibacy was superior to marriage inasmuch as it imposed no worldly obligations that interfered with devotion to the Lord, yet he did not contest the view that marriage could be sanctified by Christ. However, the church fathers of the fourth century developed the more extreme view that sex anyway was an experiment of the serpent and marriage thus a foul and polluted way of life. Tannahill (1980) aptly sums up:

> It was Augustine who epitomized a general feeling among the Church Fathers that the act of intercourse was fundamentally disgusting. Arnabius called it filthy and disgusting. Methodius unseemly, Jerome unclean, Tertullian shameful, Ambrose a defilement. In fact there was an unstated consensus that God ought to have invented a better way of dealing with the problem of procreation. Augustine, retrospectively offended by his own experiences, set his mind to the problem and concluded that the fault lay not with God but with Adam and Eve [p. 141].

In the Hebrew Bible it is clear that the serpent "more subtil than any beast of the field" (Gen. 3:1) takes major blame for he persuaded the woman to eat the forbidden fruit of the tree of knowledge, claiming that "in so doing then your eyes shall be opened, and ye shall be as gods, knowing good and evil" (Gen. 3:5).

Now our eyes are more truly opened to the role of the serpent brain in the evolutionary development of human nature. MacLean (1973) maintains that man's brain retains the hierarchical organization of three basic types which, in ascending order, are the reptilian, paleomammalian, and neomammalian. These three brains are like biological computers, each with its own peculiar subjectivity, sense of space and time, intelligence, and memory. In particular, the reptilian brain forms the matrix of the upper brain stem and comprises much of the reticular system, midbrain, and basal ganglia. Behavioral observations of ethologists and clinical neurological and experimental findings suggest that the reptilian brain in mammals is fundamental for such genetically constituted forms of behavior as selecting home sites, establishing territory, engaging in display, hunting, homing, mating, breeding, imprinting, forming social hierarchies, and selecting leaders. With the exception of hunting, all behaviors impressed me as a boy of 12 when I kept homing pigeons whose reptilian antecedents are less overlaid than ours, though insofar as they are, their notable capacity for sustained pairing and caring attachments within their own kind is remarkably different from that of the snakes. MacLean (1973) notes:

> The reptile brain seems to be hidebound by precedent. Behaviourally, this is illustrated by the reptiles' tendency to follow roundabout, but proven pathways, or operating according to some rigid schedule. Customs of this kind appear to have some survival value and raise the question as to what extent the reptilian counterpart of man's brain may determine his obeisance to precedent in ceremonial rituals, religious convictions, legal actions and political persuasions [p. 10].

MacLean makes it clear that superimposed on the reptilian brain is the primitive cortex of the old mammalian brain, or limbic system, the neurologically embedded circuits of which subserve emotions and insure self-preservation more adequately through feelings, fighting, and self-protection. Appearing much later in evolution is the neocortex which reaches its culmination in man—and enables us to speak and read and write and calculate arithmetically as well as we do. However, this compound of three brain types presents special difficulties of intercommunication between its parts because of differences in chemistry and functional anatomy. Insofar as interaction between the parts can obtain in the human animal, MacLean locates the material basis of the further development of empathy. The reptile entirely lacks this capacity—and man has also the capacity to block off imaginative sympathy. Burrow's (1958, 1964) studies of the tensions of men in groups led him to posit that these tensions were an expression of human psychic aberration. The alienation Burrow repeatedly discussed was man's increasing tendency with biological and cultural evolution to rely excessively on words, often as mere symbols of unity and coordination, and thus increasingly to substitute make-believe communication for the fellowship that can only be developed out of the totality of organismic processes. His distrust of semantic speech and his belief that salvation lay in more direct contact among grouped individuals arose from his developing the view that civilized man became lost in the world of the "corticosymbolic"—in MacLean's neomammalian brain part. Thus man became, according to Burrow, cut off from his "thalamosplanchnic" system—MacLean's paleomammalian part of the brain. Certainly empathy is grounded in the intercommunication of the limbic system and neocortex. Beneath these parts of the triune brain is that of the snake and the crocodile which unfortunately is so ready to dominate under conditions of group regressions, as in war.

METEMPSYCHOSIS

All mythological systems encompass a variety of notions concerning the transformation of man into beast and vice versa. In the stories of the ancient Greeks, gods often changed into animals in order to facilitate their designs with greater speed, security, and secrecy. In Scandinavian mythology, Odin changes himself into the shape of an eagle, Loki into that of a salmon. Eastern religions coagulate moral preachments with myths of transformation. The embodied human soul, with its self-consciousness, is often in these stories regarded as existing previously in an animal. Dreams and hallucinations in this context are considered as gleams of memory, recording acts in a former animal state of existence. In the Upanishads, Hindu beliefs adumbrate the absorption of the soul into the immanent Brahma after death in the most favorable instances, where in the worst case scenario the self sinks in the scale of creation to be degraded to animate a brute. The religious doctrine of metempsychosis related such sequences to rewards and punishments administered by Brahma in accord with prevailing mores. Baring-Gould (1973) writes:

> It was not merely a fancied external resemblance between the beast and man, but it was the perception of skill, pursuits, desires, sufferings, and griefs like his own, in the animal creation, which led man to detect within the beast something analogous to the

soul within himself; and this, notwithstanding the points of contrast existing between them, elicited in his mind so strong a sympathy that, without a great stretch of imagination, he invested the beast with his own attributes, and with the full powers of his own understanding. He regarded it as actuated by the same motives, as subject to the same laws of honour, as moved by the same prejudices, and the higher the beast was in the scale, the more he regarded it as an equal [p. 155].

Certainly it was not unchecked, unconscious projective identification which enabled Jane Goodall (1986) in her patient work with the chimpanzees of Gombe to convince herself, and us, that these near relatives of ours share very similar emotions to our own.

In any event, among the abundant superstitions which concern transformation, three shapes are preeminent: that of the serpent, that of the avian, and that of the wolf. Thus Baring-Gould (1973) notes that ancient peoples saw the forked and writhing lightning and supposed it to be a heavenly fiery serpent. Even now, in the folklore of the North American Indians, lightning remains the great serpent and thunder is often supposed to be his hissing noise. More generally in theriomorphosis, the dragon is likewise a condensation of the serpent and avian forms.

It is remarkable that ancient Greek mentation moved back and forth, often bewilderingly, between the two poles of *logos* and *mythos*. In the fable of the Trojan horse, the Athenian warriors are hidden in a humongous wooden equine. Here a middle position between such oscillations and one of cynical deception is represented. For the Greeks built this vehicle to engage with and exploit the Trojan cult of horse worship. Laocoon, the priest of Apollo, opposed the consensus of making a breach in the wall, to let the wooden horse in, warning the Trojan leaders that there were soldiers in it. However, when Laocoon was about to offer a sacrifice to his god on the shore, two monstrous serpents came out of the sea, and strangled him and his two sons. In the story, this was a punishment ordained by Apollo for a prior act of sacrilege, but the Trojans took the view that he was punished for his opposition. They pulled down part of the wall and brought the wooden horse into the city. The following night Sinon, the infiltrated Greek spy who had pretended he was in flight from his compatriots because they had chosen him as a sacrifice to the gods, freed the warriors inside the horse and gave the agreed torch signals to the Greek ships off shore. The soldiers then succeeded in holding off the Trojans so that they could open the gates to the rest of the Greek army. And so Troy was taken thousands of years ago, as a result of a disregard for the disfavored and discredited priest of Apollo who was killed by the sea serpent (cf. *Larousse World Mythology*, 1965, p. 164). These malicious serpentine mammoths of the deep persist worldwide in popular imagination; the most notorious of them now in the Western world is known as the Loch Ness monster.

In the highlands of Scotland, south of Inverness, is a deep, tranquil lake surrounded by yew, birch, and fir trees on gentle hills that roll down to the water. This lake contains a vast amount of peat particles in suspension, rendering its brownish waters mysteriously opaque. Inhabiting the murky depths since the sixth century, transcending the boundaries of time, and parts of its body appearing sporadically on the surface, is according to persistent legend, the Loch Ness monster, perhaps the most illustrious of all Western cryptozoological creatures. Ellis (1995) writes:

> To place the most common descriptions of the monster in a historical (or more accurately, a prehistorical) perspective, let us conduct a paleontological search for the creature that fits the descriptions most often applied to the Loch Ness monster. During the Mesozoic era, a period that lasted approximately 100 million years, the dinosaurs ruled the world—and, it would appear, the oceans as well. A large group of long-necked plesiosaurs swam with broad, paddle-like flippers, and because they were air-breathing reptiles, they poked their heads out of the water to inhale. A plesiosaur looks much like the creature that most cryptozoologists conjure up when they try to place a long-extinct animal in Loch Ness: a dinosaur that looks, as the nineteenth-century amateur paleontologist William Conybeare wrote, "like a snake threaded through the body of a turtle." However, until the "sightings" of the nineteenth and twentieth centuries of the various plesiosaurs (there is fossil evidence for some eight or nine species, divided into two groups, the plesiosaurs and the shorter-necked, larger-headed pliosaurs), there was no reason to believe that they had not died out, along with all the other dinosaurs, by the end of the Cretaceous period, some 65 million years ago [pp. 23–24].

A belief in herpetic monsters is not confined to ancient Greece, and is there embedded in mythology, or to the lochs of modern Scotland. Such a belief is more or less conspicuous among all races of all times, the literate and preliterate, in writings, folklore, and artifacts. Mountford (1978) has given a vivid account of the various beliefs of Australian aborigines in creatures, often of immense size, which live in deep water holes. Usually highly colored like a rainbow, they have manes and beards and long projecting teeth with which they destroy their victims. In general, the aborigines are afraid of these huge creatures whom they seek to appease in their rituals before drinking at their respective water holes. If they break the taboos associated with slaking thirst, the rainbow serpent will, they think, rise in the air and create havoc through storms so heavy that all will drown. Essentially, the rainbow serpent is the spirit of the water and any sign of fire, its opposite element, drives them deep into it. Thus, the drinkers protect themselves apotropaically when drinking at a water hole either by carrying a burning stick, or lighting a small fire nearby.

Slater (1968) noted that the serpent often represented the umbilical cord quite explicitly in ancient Greek religious practice. The omphalos, the navel of the earth, was guarded by a female python coiled on a stone while the priestess prophesied in peaceful coexistence, as is shown in many vase paintings. Thus, Slater suggests, the serpent may often constitute a threshold symbol separating the world of life and consciousness and the realm of death and unconsciousness. But the serpent antithetically appears often too as a link between these two worlds. To increase ambiguity the serpent may also be cast in the role of a Boundary Violator in some mythological as in some psychopathological contexts. In this latter connection, Slater (1968) wrote how monstrous the snake as penetrating penis symbol can become:

> For individuals in whom narcissistic anxieties are severe, the sexual act shatters the body image of both male and female. The boundary between Me and Not-Me crumbles, since the female is penetrated and part of the male disappears inside of another. In addition, psychological boundaries are obliterated through orgasm. The ego dissolves, inundated with impulse, and this may

be experienced as a kind of death—as complete submersion in unconsciousness. . . . At the oral level, ecstasy is feared as a bursting or disintegrating of the boundaries of the self. . . . Finally, physiological changes do occur, particularly in the case of impregnation, and in oral fantasy these assume grotesque proportions. At this level all orifices are mouths, all sexual conduct impregnating and boundary-shattering [p. 101].

OPHIDIOPHILIA AND OPHIDIOPHOBIA

Some individuals are exceptionally apprehensive of snakes. The bites of a few species are indeed venomous and warrant the arousal of human fear. Thus in temperate North America, there are four poisonous snakes—the water-moccasin, the copperhead, the rattler, and the coral and they are all very dangerous. However, beyond transient startle, which, incidentally, confers a readiness to deal with the possibilities of objective danger, some sensitive people are plunged into overwhelming anxiety and other dysphoric emotions such as horror and disgust, on account of the unconsciously symbolic role of a snake, however harmless it might be in reality.

From the analysis of neuroses of adult patients, Freud drew the well-known inferences of the general occurrence of the Oedipus complex in childhood, of the ubiquity of castration anxiety, and of the profound significance, too, of extragenital erotogenic zones of the body. He had checked these inferences in the famous case of Little Hans (Freud, 1909), a 5-year-old boy with a phobia of horses. Freud (1895) had earlier mentioned that there were many common phobias, that is, avoidances to prevent loading with displeasure or painful emotion. Thus many people detest some events such as funerals which incite fears of death, or nighttime solitude which excites forbidden phantasies, or some creatures such as spiders and snakes. Some people have more specific avoidances such as those of open or closed spaces or of heights. The phobias, common or specific, can also be classified psychodynamically in terms of the degree of displacement in the symbolism utilized, or in terms of developmental fixation, that is, the depth of regression involved in the illness. Sperling (see chapter 9) shows that spider phobia often reflects a pregenital fixation with pronounced anal-sadistic features and, unlike Freud's case of Little Hans, a much more ambivalent relationship to the mother than to the father. Moreover, such a case of spider phobia may represent much symbolic displacement inasmuch as there had never been any exposure to an actual spider bite.

As with spiders and horses, so with snakes. Ophidiophobia may coexist with hysterical symptoms at a predominantly oedipal level of psychopathology or it may be the result of deeper regression and pertain predominantly to paranoid anxiety. The illness may then comprise more primitive mechanisms of defense including massive disowning, projection, denial, and splitting as well as repression and displacement.

The psychotic core of human adult anxiety has its roots in the phantasies and imagination of the child. This in turn has much of its foundation in ancestral experience as mythology attests. Griffiths (1935) in her study of the imagination in early childhood utilized drawings, ink-blot tests, story-telling, and dreams of children from London and Brisbane. These 5-year-olds were prompted to imagine terror-inspiring situations. Serpents, spiders, and wolf-snake hybrids figured most frequently in death-threatening contexts. Sometimes biting dogs appeared. Koppitz (1968) evaluated the responses of children from 6 to 12 years to requests to draw the human figure. Many of them drew animals instead, including a sea serpent, a dangerous looking mordacious snake, a two-headed dragon, and a poisonous lizard. Hall and Van der Castle (1966) in a study of the dreams of thousands of urban adult Americans found that the serpent figured considerably more often than any other animal, excepting the familiar dog. That the snake image has impacted heavily on the human psyche is evident in the most ancient literature, including the archaic Sanskrit Brahminic and the Buddhist Pali writings; and it is evident in Indian fables and fairy tales and in Indian paintings and sculptures down the ages. Vogel (1972) asserts that though we may safely assume that Indian orphiolatry had its foundation in the dread inspired by poisonous reptiles, even in the earliest sources real snakes are described side by side with mythic serpents which haunt the earth and the sky. To the native mind, he deduces, these imaginary monsters possessed as much reality as the creeping snakes of the earth which constantly endangered their lives. Vogel (1972) quotes the *Yajurveda:* "Homage be to the snakes whichsoever move along the earth. Which are in the sky and in heaven, homage be to those snakes. Which are the arrows of sorcerers and of tree-spirits, and which lie in holes, homage be to those snakes. Which are in the brightness of heaven, which are in the rays of the sun, which have made their abodes in the waters, homage be to those snakes" (p. 7).

Werner and Kaplan (1963) in their famous book on symbol formation suggest that there is considerable similarity in the level of differentiation of cognitive constructions among children in more advanced cultures and among adults in more primitive ones. Moreover, Jones and Jones (1928) showed that humans and chimpanzees never previously exposed to snakes reacted very fearfully in much the same way. It is on a phylogenetic as well as ontogenetic basis that primitive forms of symbolism can be facilitated and then utilized in symbol formation. Even in an urban environment where the snake is generally conspicuous by its absence, the image of the reptile is prevalent as a symbolic vehicle. While snake phobia is widespread, the avoidance of snakes does not usually result in obvious maladaptation in an urban environment. Yet it is of course always significantly related to any development of frankly neurotic disability in an individual due to sexual and hostile conflicts precipitated by events in his or her life cycle.

Snake worship, being a collective phenomenon, affects human manifest behavior markedly and directly as such. Many nations have known or still practice this form of animal worship. Vogel (1972) writes:

It would be difficult to quote another instance in which it takes such a prominent place in literature, folk-lore, and art, as it does in India. Nor would it be possible to name another country where the development of this cult can be studied during a period which may be estimated at no less than three millennia. During so vast a space of time the deified serpents have haunted the imagination of the people of Hind. But even more astonishing is the endless variety of aspect under which the Nagas appear in Indian literature and art. We meet, on the one hand, with the primitive type of reptile endowed with the magic properties which we are wont to associate with the dragon of Western fable. On the other hand, the Naga frequently has the character of a water-spirit. Again, he may be able to assume any form he chooses, and commonly appears in human shape. In Brahmanical legend he may become a pious ascetic, in Buddhist lore he may even develop into a self-denying saint. Very often these various types appear strangely blended [p. vi].

It is especially the cobra which is held to be sacred. Deified as Naga, the cobra is worshipped today in large parts of India. The Naga of Indian mythology and folklore is the cobra or other sacred snake raised to the rank of a divine being, deva, or higher still, God. Besides the uncanny properties ascribed to all snakes and the sudden and terrible action of its venom, the cobra is conspicuous by its hood with its peculiar spectacle marks. Thus it is called *serpent à lunettes* in French. According to a common legend the spectacle marks are the footprints left by Krishna on the heads of the Naga Kaliyah. After his victory over the eagle, Krishna as shepherd-god, addressed the serpent. "When Garuda seeth my footprints marked on thy head, the enemy of thy race will not assail thee" (p. 27).

Garuda is the deified eagle who feeds on Nagas. The Garuda of legend is thus consonant with the eagle of nature who preys on snakes. Charpentier (1922) maintains that legendary stories of the combat of snake-mother goddess and eagle god in various versions, and notably in the opening book of the great epic poem, *The Mahabharata,* belong to a class of folktales, portraying wagering animals. Generally, the animal apparently least likely to win does so by recourse to deceit, such as in the Western fable of the race of the hare and the tortoise. In its Indian epic form concerning eagle and snake it serves to explain why Garuda is allowed to feed on the Nagas. It is a favor bestowed on him by Indra as a reward for his courage despite the deceit practiced by the Nagas, and indeed the deceit constitutes a justification for the eagle's voracity. In this and other numerous stories and sculptures pertaining to the theme of Garuda attacking Naga, derivatives of primal phantasies, including notably those of primal scene origin, are manifest.

In the great Pali collection of birth stories, the Jatakas, relating to the previous existences of the Buddha, there is a rich harvest of *Naga* lore. In one such tale, it is recounted how a Naga and Garuda (or "Suparna") were reconciled through the holy influence of a hermit. The anchorite turns out to be a prefiguration of the Buddha.

The snake all over the world arouses intense human emotions ranging from what is evident in the Hebrew Old Testament where a bad serpent represents Satan, the embodiment of evil, to that evident in Hindu scriptures where a good, nurturing all-powerful thousand-headed one supports the earth; or in Egyptian religion where good reptiles serve to protect the sun god.

It has been pointed out by Marshack (1977) that the serpentine/meander designs of Upper Paleolithic man may also represent continuity and of happenings occurring in cycles. They are abstract symbols of experiences of recurrent birth and death, alternation of day and night, seasons, phases of the moon, bodily metamorphoses in time, and changing events in general. Above all, the ouroboros, the snake that bites its own tail, is symbolic of perpetual rebirth and recurrence of the fundamentals of human existence in the grip of cosmic forces. In a similar vein, Maddock (1974), discussing the Rainbow Serpent of Australian aboriginal mythology, considers that the curvilinear imagery of the snake aptly expresses the abstract notion of cyclicity embedded in the structure of aboriginal thought. Concurring with this hypothesis, Knight (1991) holds that the visually striking image of the snake aptly expresses the logic of alternation, metamorphosis, and of perpetually incorporating within itself its own opposite: wet season and dry, the highest and the lowest, male and female. But Knight contends that the snake, at another level, is identified with "the symbolic force of menstrual synchrony" (p. 31). Writing of the snake as a phallic power symbol, he notes that over much of the world, encounters with a dragon are featured in male initiation rituals, and in inauguration ceremonies whereby young men acquire masculine power and leadership. In native Australia, such power is achieved by the penis being cut along the underside, the wound producing a flow of blood. During subsequent rituals the scar of the wound is reopened so that bleeding occurs. The more sacred the particular ritual, the more bloody it becomes—and the more taboo it is for women. He writes further:

> In 1937, Ashley Montagu first put forward the theory that "subincision" in the male was originally instituted in order to cause the

male to resemble the female with respect to the occasional effusion
of blood which is naturally characteristic of the female. He admitted that the idea "must appear fantastic" but provided ample
supporting evidence. According to Róheim, the secrecy surrounding subincision ritualism acts "like a simple inversion of the
menstruating taboo, the men saying 'We are not allowed to see
your bleeding so we shall not allow you to see ours.' " The Pitjand-
jara call the subincision hole a "penis womb. . . " [p. 31].

   If the operation is so painful, why do men do it? In keeping
with the view of cultural origins which informs this analysis, I suggest that culture begins with a tendency toward menstrual synchrony, and that when—in certain regions or during certain
epochs—the synchrony breaks down, its formal structures are ritu-
ally preserved by men, whose tendencies toward dominance cannot now so effectively be checked [pp. 31–32].

According to Knight, a "bad snake" notion comprises the
menstrual synchrony and power of women, and in the ritual
events the evils of womankind are mastered and replaced with
a more benign symbolic substitute under the power of males.
Masculinist myths alongside such rituals justify the usurpation of
women's menstrual power by describing the female version in
lurid terms as a cannibalistic monster from which humanity has
to be rescued. Such a concatenation of ideas adheres, sometimes
subliminally, to the reptilian dragon of world-wide mythology in
its many different versions. In the legend of St. George, for instance, the hero succeeds in subduing a dragon that infested a
pond in Libya and fed on the dwellers in the neighborhood. The
beast possessed a princess who was about to be eaten. St. George
slew the monster after he had wounded it, and after the princess
had led it home in triumph by her girdle. Perhaps in this way,
she dramatized her overcoming the formerly overwhelming phallic mother.

   In his discussion of the "World-Dragon," Knight (1991) argues his view that patriarchal power is a usurpation of an original
matriarchy. Whether or not this is grounded in phylogenetic
events as he supposes, certainly there is no doubt of its ontogenetic authenticity. He is of the opinion that the usurpation and
simultaneous political inversion of women's menstrual powers is
what such dragon-slaying or monster-vanquishing initiating experiences are really all about.

Psychoanalytically considered, all these rituals and mythologies are saturated with the ramifications of the male castration complex, especially as they relate to early mothering. However, individual emotional experience accompanying perception or imagination of a snake depends on the cultural and the internal context including, of course, unconscious phantasies. McDougall (1936) notes that primary emotional qualities may be blended. Thus in discussing admiration, he considers that both wonder and submissive feelings are involved, the former revealed partly by the impulses of curiosity—to approach and to contemplate the admired object, the latter by some degree of incitement of humility. By analogy with chemical interaction, McDougall considers admiration a binary compound. However, the impulse to approach, to draw near humbly may be impeded by an impulse to withdraw, or even run away, because of fear, as a result of which we may be suspended as it were in the middle distance. When this occurs we experience the emotion we call awe. This may be further compounded by gratitude, itself composite and including tender feelings, when reverence is generated. Anger may complicate further this chemistry of the emotions. Here it suffices to recognize that compound emotions are aroused in ophiolatry, and awe and reverence may be dominant and magnified in a group context. Who can doubt that a crucial aspect of this emotional arousal is connected with the infantile mode of relating to the phallic mother, she who gives of or refuses to give of her strength, and who must be obeyed?

Keuls (1985) proposes a concept of "phallocracy" to explain social dynamics in ancient Greece, a cultural system symbolized by the image of the male reproductive organ in permanent erection. This concept connotes dominance of men over women not only within the private sphere of sexual intercourse, but also a successful claim by a male elite to general power, buttressed by a display of the phallus less as an organ of union or of mutual pleasure than as a kind of weapon, a spear or war club, and a scepter of sovereignty. On the pictorial evidence furnished by vase paintings and other figure monuments, she bases her view of phallocracy, and of its function as an antidote to an obsessive fear of women. She emphasizes the importance of the motif of the rebellion of the Amazons for the ancient Greeks. This expressed men's gynophobia, as did other Greek myths. Moreover, their drama, their laws and customs also fulsomely "document the same view of women, as caged tigers waiting for a chance to break out of their confinement and take revenge on the male world" (p. 4). Keuls also discusses another Athenian foundation myth, and the residual, nighttime ritual of the *arrhephoroi*, "bearers of the sacred objects," which partially echoed it, concerning the disobedient daughters of Cecrops. They had been told not to open the basket they were entrusted with, which contained the baby Erichthonius. Impelled by their curiosity the two girls opened it, to look inside, whereupon they saw not only the infant but also a large snake. The snake jumped out in pursuit of the frightened girls who threw themselves off a slope of the Acropolis to their death.

According to Neumann in *The Origins and History of Consciousness* (1954), the circular serpent, the oruboros, represents man and woman, begetting and conceiving, devouring and giving birth, active and passive, above and below at once. A disciple of Jung, he sees it as a basic symbol of life's wholeness. In *The Great Mother* Neumann also expounds a darker vision. Thus he avers that all Aztec policies were subordinated to the wars that were waged for the purpose of taking prisoners to be sacrificed to the cult of the Snake Woman who yielded fertility only when satiated by terrible blood sacrifices. He also suggests that in incest with his mother the hero begets himself. It is evident that much unconscious phantasy is condensed in snake symbolism, and there is much interpenetration of opposites, a characteristic which generates the *mysterium tremendum* of religion. However, as La Barre (1969, p. 131) has emphasized, the "*mysterium tremendum* of religion is really the naively unexamined human mind which has forgotten the individual formative history of its longings." It should be added, it is not only the longings but the correlative phantasies and fears which engender and shape collective beliefs.

Neumann conceived the primordial image of the snake as rooted in the collective unconscious. He asserted that the circular snake, the primal dragon which engages with its own tail, is the archetype of creativity, the self-begetting ouroboros. Mudkin (1983), however, objects to the excessively speculative nature of

Neumann's views, and especially what he regards as the unscientific methodology upon which they are built. Yet he acknowledges "remarkable parallels in biological and psychoanalytic theory" (p. 269).

Silberer (1912) discussed several different kinds of visual symbolism which displaced more or less logical word symbolism when the mind was functioning in a state of apperceptive insufficiency, that is, when endeavoring to process data and solve a problem in a state of fatigue or drowsiness, or when an individual was not yet able to grasp an idea which some day in the future he might. Among other categories he noted "functional phenomena" which indicated the way in which the mind was functioning (quickly, slowly, lightly, fruitlessly, strainedly, etc.) and "material phenomena" in which what the mind was engaged in thinking about is visually represented when in a state of apperceptive insufficiency for one reason or another. The first mentioned above, is related to the subjective process of mentation, the second to generating adequate ideation concerning an objective problem. These considerations are apposite when reflecting on the remarkable creative accomplishment of Kekulé. Koestler (1964) writes:

As a last example in this chapter I shall quote the dramatic cases of Friedrich August von Kekulé, Professor of Chemistry in Ghent, who, one afternoon in 1865, fell asleep and dreamt what was probably the most important dream in history since Joseph's seven fat and seven lean cows:

"I turned my chair to the fire and dozed," he relates. "Again the atoms were gamboling before my eyes. This time the smaller groups kept modestly in the background. My mental eye, rendered more acute by repeated visions of this kind, could now distinguish larger structures, of manifold conformation; long rows, sometimes more closely fitted together; all twining and twisting in snakelike motion. But look! What was that? One of the snakes had seized hold of its own tail, and the form whirled mockingly before my eyes. As if by a flash of lightning I awoke.... Let us learn to dream, gentlemen."

The serpent biting its own tail gave Kekulé the clue to a discovery which has been called "the most brilliant piece of prediction to be found in the whole range of organic chemistry" and which, in fact, is one of the cornerstones of modern science. Put in a somewhat simplified manner, it consisted in the revolutionary proposal that the molecules of certain important organic compounds are not open structures but closed chains or "rings"—like the snake swallowing its tail [p. 118].

In this remarkable moment of truth, Kekulé, who had wrestled long with the problems of carbon compounds, especially benzine, suddenly was enabled to develop the ring theory. In this example, the creative mode of mentation and the solution to the chemical problem were both simultaneously visually represented by ouroboros in an altered state of consciousness.

REFERENCES

Baring-Gould, S. (1973), *The Book of Werewolves.* New York: Causeway Books.

Berke, J. H. (1988), *The Tyranny of Malice.* New York: Summit Books.

Bonaparte, M. (1953), *Female Sexuality.* New York: International Universities Press.

Burrow, T. (1958), *A Search for Man's Sanity—The Selected Letters of Trigant Burrow,* ed. Committee of Lifwynn Foundation, E. Galt, Chairman. New York: Oxford University Press.

——— (1964), *Preconscious Foundations of Human Experience.* New York: Basic Books.

Chaucer, G. (1394), The parson's tale. In: *Canterbury Tales.* Baltimore: Penguin Books, 1952, pp. 509–512.

Conrad, J. (1902), *Heart of Darkness,* ed. R. C. Murfin. New York: St. Martin's Press.

Ehrenzweig, A. (1967), *The Hidden Order of Art.* Berkeley & Los Angeles: University of California Press.

Ellis, R. (1995), *Monsters of the Sea.* New York: Knopf.

Foulkes, E. F. (1972), *The Arctic Hysterias of the North Alaskan Eskimo.* Anthropological Studies No. 10. Washington, DC: American Anthropological Association.

Freud, S. (1895), Obsessions and phobias: Their psychical mechanism and their aetiology. *Standard Edition,* 3:64–82. London: Hogarth Press, 1962.

——— (1900), The Interpretation of Dreams. *Standard Edition,* 4&5. London: Hogarth Press, 1953.

——— (1909), Analysis of a phobia in a five-year-old boy. *Standard Edition,* 10:1–147. London: Hogarth Press, 1955.

Goodall, J. (1986), *The Chimpanzees of Gombe*. Cambridge, MA: Harvard University Press.

Griffiths, R. (1935), *A Study of Imagination in Early Childhood*. Westport, CT: Greenwood Press, 1970.

Hall, C. S., & Van der Castle, R. (1966), *The Content Analysis of Dreams*. New York: Appleton-Century-Crofts.

Hambly, W. D. (1931), Serpent Worship in Africa. *Anthropological Series*, Vol. 21, No. 1. Chicago: Field Museum of Natural History.

Howey, M. O. (1928), *The Encircled Serpent*. London: Rider.

Jones, E. (1916), The theory of symbolism. In: *Papers on Psycho-Analysis*, 4th ed. London: Ballière, Tindall & Cox, 1938, pp. 129–186.

Jones, H. E., & Jones, M. C. (1928), Fear. *Childhood Ed.*, 5:136–143.

Keuls, E. C. (1985), *The Reign of the Phallus. Sexual Politics in Ancient Athens*, 2nd ed. Berkeley: University of California Press.

Kildahl, J. P. (1972), *The Psychology of Speaking in Tongues*. New York: Harper & Row.

Kimbrough, D. L. (1995), *Taking Up Serpents*. Chapel Hill: University of North Carolina Press.

Knight, C. D. (1991), On the dragon-wings of time. In: *Maidens, Snakes and Dragons*. London: Kings College, pp. 7–49.

Koestler, A. (1964), *The Act of Creation*. New York: Macmillan.

Köhler, W. (1930), *Gestalt Psychology*. London: Bell.

Koppitz, E. M. (1968), *Psychological Evaluation of Children's Human Figure Drawings*. New York: Grune & Stratton.

La Barre, W. (1969), *They Shall Take Up Serpents*. New York: Schocken Books.

Larousse World Mythology (1965), New York: Prometheus Press.

Lawrence, D. H. (1926), *The Plumed Serpent (Quetzalcoatl)*, ed. L. D. Clark. Cambridge, U.K.: Cambridge University Press, 1987.

MacLean, P. D. (1973), *A Triune Concept of the Brain and Behavior*. Ontario: University of Toronto Press.

Maddock, K. (1974), *The Australian Aborigines: A Portrait of Their Society*. Harmondsworth, U.K.: Penguin.

Marshack, A. (1977), The meander as a system: The analysis and recognition of iconographic units in Upper Paleolithic compositions. In: *Form in Indigenous Art*, ed. P. J. Ucko. London: Duckworth, pp. 286–317.

McDougall, W. (1936), *An Outline of Psychology*, 7th ed. London: Methuen.

Monaghan, J. (1995), *The Covenants with Earth and Rain: Exchange, Sacrifice, and Revelation in Mixtec Sociality*. Norman: University of Oklahoma Press.

Morris, R., & Morris, D. (1965), *Men and Snakes.* New York: McGraw-Hill.

Mountford, C. P. (1978), The rainbow-serpent myths of Australia. In: *The Rainbow Serpent: A Chromatic Piece,* ed. I. R. Buchler & K. Maddock. The Hague & Paris: Mouton Publishers, pp. 23–97.

Mudkin, B. (1983), *The Cult of the Serpent.* Albany: State University of New York.

Neumann, E. (1954), *The Origins and History of Consciousness.* New York: Pantheon Books.

Ohnuki-Tierney, E. (1980), Shamans and *Imu:* Among two Ainu groups. *Ethos,* 8(3):204–229.

Oldham, C. F. (1905), *The Sun and the Serpent.* London: Constable.

Schoeck, H. (1970), *Envy: A Theory of Social Behavior,* tr. M. Glenny & B. Ross. New York: Harcourt Brace & World.

Silberer, H. (1912), *Von den Kategorien der Symbolik,* Vol. 2. Zentralblatt für Psychoanalyse.

Slater, P. (1968), *The Glory of Hera: Greek Mythology and the Greek Family.* Boston: Beacon Press.

Smith, H. W. (1952), *Man and His Gods.* New York: Grosset & Dunlap.

Tannahill, R. (1980), *Sex in History.* New York: Stein & Day.

The Upanishads (c. 400 B.C.E.), Harmondsworth, U.K.: Penguin Books, 1965.

Vogel, J. P. (1972), *Indian Serpent Lore, the Nagas in Hindu Legend & Art.* Varanasi, India: Prithivi Prakashan.

Werner, H., & Kaplan, B. (1963), *Symbol Formation.* New York: Wiley.

CHAPTER 8

Spider Phobias and Spider Fantasies

MELITTA SPERLING, M.D.

Although spider phobias and spider fantasies are by no means a clinical rarity, only a few psychoanalysts have reported on them (Abraham, 1922; Gloyne, 1950; Sterba, 1950; Azima and Witt-kower, 1957; Little, 1966a, 1967; Newman and Stoller, 1969). To those who, like myself, have encountered these phenomena in work with patients, these contributions have been of great interest. There are no references in the literature to psychoanalytic observations of such phenomena in children, nor reports of follow-ups on patients in whom such phenomena have been observed during treatment.

I had an opportunity to study analytically spider phobias and fantasies in three children, two adolescents, and three adult patients. In one case I could observe a spider phobia in its early stages in a prelatency child and follow up the vicissitudes of this phobia during latency and adolescence. In one adolescent patient, the spider phobia and fantasies which had been of long standing, came to light only at the beginning of the third year of analysis and reappeared toward the end of the fourth year when they became a central point in her analysis. Two adult patients resorted to spider symbolism in critical emotional situations. In both, these remained single occurrences. In one patient it appeared as a nightmare and in the other patient as a kind of delusional experience. These and similar observations convinced me that the presence of spider phobias and fantasies may be of specific diagnostic and prognostic value. I therefore wish to take up this and other aspects of these phenomena which have not received sufficient consideration thus far. I should like to present case material upon which my thoughts and suggestions are based and shall begin with my youngest patient, 4-year-old Ruth.

CASE 1

Ruth was referred to me because of a severe sleep disturbance of some two years duration. From the age of $1^1/_2$ years, following tonsillectomy and the birth of a baby brother, Ruth was up every night for most of the night. She had frequent nightmares and was particularly frightened by one recurrent nightmare in which she saw a spider crawling on her bed wanting to take her to the hospital. She could not shake off the hallucinatory quality of this nightmare even after awakening. Once when talking to me about this nightmare, she showed me how the doctor had cut off her pussy "because I am very bad," adding, "I and my mommy have a big one. My brother and my daddy have a little one." "I could cut my brother's pussy off." Climbing up on me, she said, "I am the doctor and I'll cut your nose pussy off."

In her play sessions Ruth also brought out her intense oedipal resentment against her mother. Her wish to kill her mother came out with particular clarity in a game which she played incessantly. In this game I was the mother who wanted to sleep, but Ruth would not let me. I would then be so sick that the doctor who came, and whose role Ruth played, would tell me that I would soon have to die because I did not get enough rest. The mother's constant complaint to Ruth was that she didn't let her sleep and rest. By her sleep disturbance Ruth managed to separate her parents at night, and because the mother had to take care of the baby, the father attended to Ruth during the night. This arrangement only intensified Ruth's oedipal conflicts and her sleep disturbance.

The mother had weaned Ruth abruptly at 9 months of age and, in anticipation of the new baby, had accelerated her bladder and bowel training. Envy for the breast and penis, both of which she did not possess but which her mother gave to her little brother, had greatly intensified her oral-sadistic impulses. She dealt with this internal danger in a phobic way by externalization and projection onto the mother and displacement onto the spider. From her dreams, her play, and her verbalizations, it became clear that the spider represented the dangerous mother who had taken her to the hospital for a tonsillectomy as a punishment for her oral-sadistic impulses. But what had prompted the choice of the spider as the symbol of the dangerous mother?

In a similar situation, that is, following a tonsillectomy and the birth of a younger brother, I could study in a 2-year-old child the onset of an animal phobia which first occurred only at night but then carried over into the daytime (Sperling, 1952). This little girl, Linda, was referred to me because of a sleep disturbance associated with attacks of paroxysmal tachycardia. Linda, too, suffered from intense breast and penis envy, and she, too, dealt with her oral-sadistic impulses directed against her mother's breast and her brother's penis in a phobic way by externalization and projection onto the mother, and displacing it first to a fish and then to cats and dogs. The first nightmare about a fish, in which she screamed that a fish was biting off her finger, occurred after Linda had watched her mother cutting off a fish's head. In Ruth's case, however, neither the child nor the mother could trace the onset of the acute spider phobia to an actual experience.

Play analysis brought, within a few months, such dramatic relief of Ruth's sleep disturbance that the parents, for whom this had been the only disturbing symptom, were ready to withdraw her from treatment. I had already at that time, more than twenty years ago, expressed the belief that severe early sleep disturbance even in the absence of other clinical symptoms, could be an early indication of possible psychotic development (Sperling, 1949, 1955b). The parents consented to let her stay in treatment for two more months until the family moved into a new house in another community. I tried to use this short time to bring about a modification of the relationship between Ruth and her mother, but the mother was not available for active participation in the treatment, and this goal could not be accomplished.

I heard from Ruth again when she was 9 years old. According to the mother, Ruth had done very well up to about six months earlier when a very marked and progressive deterioration in her behavior took place. She had a recurrence of the sleep disturbance with nightmares. She appeared withdrawn, she had unmotivated outbursts of temper and spoke incoherently. She could not concentrate in school, and the teacher had indicated that the school would not be able to keep her in her present condition. Ruth was obviously suffering from a schizophrenic disorder. This clinical impression was confirmed by psychological testing which in summary stated that this was a case of severe schizophrenia with marked paranoid features and a poor prognosis regarding therapy and recovery.

It is not possible, within the framework of this paper, to deal with the dynamics of her illness or with the therapeutic techniques which led to a complete recovery with a follow-up to adulthood. For my present purposes, I have selected some fragments from her treatment during the schizophrenic phase which are directly related to the spider phobia of her early childhood. Among her many bizarre psychotic productions, a recurrent theme about a character which she called "Tiddy Ray" is of particular relevance. Tiddy Ray was a lady who devoured people. She did not eat with her mouth, but put people into a hole under her breast (Tiddy meant breast) or in the middle of her body. Tiddy Ray caught people who snooped around and came close to her. There were many elaborations with anal and phallic elements added, but the essential fantasy was a condensation and projection to Tiddy Ray of Ruth's oral-sadistic impulses. Ruth also had visual hallucinations; she saw Tiddy Ray and her gang hiding behind doorways or the venetian blinds signaling to the men to catch her.

In working through these fantasies, Ruth recalled her spider phobia and was now able to trace its onset. She remembered an incident when she was between 2 and 3 years of age. Some children with whom she played told her that spiders kill and eat people. She was not sure whether they had shown her a picture or had threatened her with a spider, but she knew that since then she had been terrified of spiders.

The spider fantasy which had played such a role in Ruth's fantasy life during childhood was a forerunner and the matrix for the later schizophrenic Tiddy Ray fantasies. The schizophrenic breakdown at $8^1/_2$ was preceded by the birth of another brother which to Ruth was a repetition of the trauma that had precipitated the sleep disturbance at age 2.

The onset of puberty, when she began to develop secondary female characteristics, decidedly altered Ruth's already considerable conflict concerning her sexual identification into the direction of the male. She was awkward and tall and had a deep voice, which only increased her feelings that she was not a real girl. The birth of the brother had reactivated and intensified her penis envy and feelings that she could never please her mother as a girl, that is, without a penis. Ruth had already expressed in her play and fantasies at age 4 the displacement from mouth to genitals. She had experienced the tonsillectomy as an oral castration inflicted upon her by her mother. The spider, which expressed Ruth's oral-sadistic impulses directed toward her mother's breasts and her brother's penis, indicated her confusion of nipple with penis, and mouth with vagina. The oral-sadistic and the bisexual meanings of the spider were expressed later in the cannibalistic persecutory, but human Tiddy Ray symbol. Exposure and working through of the spider phobia and of the underlying fantasies and impulses would seem to account for the change in the symbol used for the expression of her basic conflicts from all developmental levels (Sperling, 1961).

CASE 2

Leslie was 13 years ago when she began treatment. Extremely infantile and withdrawn, she had great difficulty in school and socially. Many fears beset her and she daydreamed almost perpetually. She was suspicious and silent, and at first it was difficult to make contact with her. In the second year of treatment she began to reveal some of her fears and fantasies. She had a very marked preoccupation with spiders. She saw spiders, even when they were not there. She looked for spiders at night and searched her bed for them. Later in her analysis she revealed that she lay awake for hours during the night, afraid to close her eyes for fear a spider would fall into her mouth. She said she had the same feeling about spiders as she had about her mother. She disliked them intensely, but she looked for them all the time. "She is always on top of me," Leslie would say. She felt that her mother was always rushing her. She had a fantasy and a fear of spiders being on top of her. This was an important and elaborate fantasy which she revealed fully some three or four years later in her analysis.

She felt strongly about being touched by a spider. This was exactly how she felt about her mother touching her. Often when she found a spider, she crushed it with a vengeance. She would keep stepping on it even if it was dead on the first step. She talked about her feelings on watching her mother eat. The sight of her mother's teeth when she ate an apple, the crushing noise, nauseated her. She also complained about a specific smell, especially when in the car with her mother, to which she is very sensitive and to which she reacts much as she does to the sight of a spider. When she saw a spider on the ceiling one night, she thought about her parents and that they were together in their room while she was alone trying to do some homework. She suddenly felt very hungry and went into the kitchen to get some food. When she saw a spider she had the sensation of fear and immediately thought of her mother. She could feel a sensation on her skin like spiders' feet or like fingers touching her. The sensation was a mixture of anxiety and sexual feelings. In her fantasy there were now an enormous number of spiders, and she had the feeling that the spider legs were tying her up so that she was in the power of the spider, "my domineering mother," she said.

Leslie had suffered from a very severe sleep disturbance since early childhood. She was afraid to fall asleep and kept herself awake by remaining on a spider watch practically all night. Analysis revealed that this sleep phobia had a protective function beyond the conscious fear of a spider falling into her mouth during sleep. To sleep in her state of mind was too dangerous because she might succumb to her thoughts and impulses and wake up crazy. As it was she had great difficulty in maintaining some sort of mental balance even in her waking state, and in her analysis she was still on guard against revealing the full extent of her "craziness."

Leslie was now 16 years old and for the first time dating a boy. The resurgence of the spider feelings and fantasies at this time were related to her intense anxiety about going out with a boy. After her first date she was preoccupied with spiders all night.

She had actually seen a spider, killed it, and then hallucinated spiders all over the place. She felt completely engulfed by them. Then she thought about what we had discussed about the spiders, namely, the spider symbolizing mother and her own homosexual desires for mother. She was afraid of boys and heterosexuality. The sensation of being touched by a spider was the same as being touched by her mother, and she was at this time phobically avoiding any physical contact with her mother.

She had fantasies of spiders coming toward her bed and attacking her. She also had fears and fantasies of being attacked by men. When she returned to her analysis after the summer vacation she noticed a change in her attitude toward spiders. "They have gone," she said. In explanation she added "maybe they have actually gone, but really I am not preoccupied with them anymore, but I am now preoccupied with wasps and bees." She was more afraid of the wasp than of the spider. Spiders she could kill, herself, but she was unable to do anything about a bee or wasp, and she had to call her mother for help. Her mother actually did once kill a wasp for her. She associated the wasp with her father. She was not afraid of bugs when they sat quietly and didn't move, only when they started moving and coming close to her, especially toward her face, or rather her mouth.

Her spider preoccupation returned in full force after a short time. She had a dream about a spider web over her head. It was not round like a spider web usually is, but straight, and went from one side of the room to the other. She thought of her mother and that this meant that her mother was on top of her. She was aware of the sexual meaning of this and of her wish for her mother to be with her at night when she felt lonely and frightened. She talked about the change in her feelings concerning her father and her mother. Although she still hated her mother, she felt closer to her now than to her father whom she regarded as weak and inadequate.

We were dealing now with her fears of growing up, of boys and heterosexuality, of being queer and of hating and needing her mother, and her feelings of being rejected. She had become aware that she was establishing with girls a similar relationship as with her mother. She had succeeded in graduating from high school and was now attending and living at a college, which made it possible for her to continue treatment. She had dated several boys casually, but had felt awkward and afraid. In dreams, she would be in bed with a girl when all the other girls slept with boys. She had changed roommates and felt that her new roommate got all the attention and was controlling her.

During this period of treatment (Leslie was now 18 years old), she had been sleeping rather well and there had been no signs of any spider preoccupation. But now again her sleep became disturbed, she had nightmares of a paranoid, homosexual nature involving particularly her roommate. In these dreams, her roommate was coming into her bed to attack and kill her. In some dreams Leslie had posted signs in her bed, "Don't touch me. Don't do it." She was afraid to sleep because of what she might do during sleep to her roommate. She also had such thoughts and fears during the day. She felt very dependent upon this roommate and didn't dare to say anything to her. In fact, she had lost her voice on occasions, and even in her dreams could not talk, but had the written signs.

She had an unexpected date with a young man who was visiting. That night she looked for spiders again, and in her following session she was preoccupied with spiders. In class they had talked about a fable in which a man was transformed into a spider. She again had the sensations of soft spider legs touching her and spiders being all over her. She talked about not knowing what people really do in intercourse. She was very frightened of it because to her intercourse had something to do with strangling and killing. When she thought of her parents having intercourse, she thought of them having their legs wrapped around each other like spiders. She felt like killing her mother. She then remembered that it was not a man who was turned into a spider, but a woman who had been spinning. A goddess turned her into a spider hanging in the web. She had a recurrent fantasy in which she saw a spider caught in the web, hopelessly entangled and unable to escape. This fantasy she had had since childhood. She suddenly thought of a story a girl had told her about people who were turned inside out. In her next session she again talked about her roommate—her fear that this girl would attack and kill her or that she would attack and kill the roommate. She said that in her mind sex was tied up with attack and with spiders. It had something to do with being held down and unable to scream, with strangling and being strangled, but also with eating and being eaten. To squash a spider reminded her of a penis and the juice that comes out. Being eaten related to the vagina but also to having a spider in her mouth. Her roommate had told her that she once ate or swallowed a spider. But Leslie knew that her fear of spiders was very old and that even as a small child she could not sleep because she was afraid that a spider from the ceiling would fall into her mouth.

The release of these fantasies apparently facilitated the recollection of relevant early childhood experiences and related affects. She remembered how lonely and afraid she felt as a child. Unable to sleep, she would go into her parents' bedroom during the night and watch them silently. The silence also reminded her of a spider. She remembered the rage and humiliation she felt when her father once reprimanded her for pulling at her dog's penis. She thought of the clicking noise of her mother eating apples or chewing with her mouth open. Her roommate did this too, which made Leslie feel very uncomfortable. While talking about it she experienced sensations in her throat like choking, like having something stuck in her throat. The clicking noise had an association to licking, and she recalled that as a child she had been licking her dog and her dog licking her. She then thought of something that happened when she was 2 years old. She had been bitten on her mouth by the neighbor's dog. She had to be rushed to the hospital to get stitches and shots. Her mother recently spoke about it, so she knew this actually happened. Her mother had also mentioned that she had had a miscarriage around that time. When her mother said this, Leslie had a visual image of going upstairs into her parents' bedroom and seeing blood on a white sheet. Leslie knew that her mother had not wanted any more children, and she connected her fears of pregnancy and childbirth with this.

She had her menarche at 12 years of age. Her menses had been irregular and very painful until the latter part of her analysis when she had been able to work through some of her feelings concerning femininity and female functions. She recalled with much affect an experience when she was very young. She could see herself sitting on the floor and looking up at her mother. She could see the black pubic hair, she had the feeling that the origin of her spider phobia was related to this experience. Her parents always slept in the nude and would walk nude to the bathroom. She was always very much interested in looking. She talked about some of her activities during puberty. She and one particular girl used to get undressed and look at and touch one another. Leslie had very strong voyeuristic impulses. Talking about this made her think of a spider who was silently and intently watching its prey. Which is how Leslie had observed the primal scene as a small child.

Her fear of genital intercourse became more apparent when she began to date more frequently and engage in sex play. She was to see a gynecologist because of a vaginal discharge. She was very worried, afraid of what he might find. She considered the secretion an indication of something very bad, but was reluctant to speak about her thoughts and fantasies. She had felt nauseated on the way to her session and now her nausea returned. With signs of disgust and anxiety, she admitted to having the crazy idea that she had a horrible thing in her vagina, a spider which must have gotten into her vagina when she was very young and had just been staying there all this time. She had the idea that the secretion was the stuff that came out when squeezing a spider. She was afraid the gynecologist would find it, and yet she wished that he would remove the spider from her vagina because she considered this the cause of her fear of sexual intercourse. After releasing this fantasy, her nausea cleared instantly. In her next session she reported that the vaginal discharge had stopped. We were able in subsequent sessions to work through her wishes for a hidden penis-nipple in her vagina-mouth which had been manifested in her spider fears and fantasies.

Leslie was suddenly able to understand her anxious preoccupation with spiders when she was called on to visit and help a young relative who had given birth to a baby. She managed to get a sore throat and thus avoid the visit. The thought of seeing the baby nursing (her relative was breast-feeding her child), as well as the thought of holding the baby, made her anxious and nauseated. Her oral-sadistic impulses and fears of eating and being eaten had been expressed in her spider preoccupation.

These excerpts from the analysis of an adolescent girl were selected to demonstrate that the spider symbol originated early in life, probably before the third year, together with the sleep disturbance. In Leslie's case, as with Ruth, the spider symbol contained the psychotic core of her personality. Leslie, too, had suffered an early injury to her mouth, the dog bite, and surgical intervention, and she too had externalized her dangerous oral-sadistic impulses, projected them onto her mother, and displaced them to the spider. The spider had served to express her earliest as well as the subsequent conflicts. Because of this fixation and the intense narcissism, ambivalence, and hate associated with it, oedipal wishes and conflicts became particularly threatening and were expressed in the spider preoccupation. The spider had become the symbol for the primal scene (the parents wrapped around each other in intercourse) and for her bisexuality and homosexual wishes. Leslie's long analysis (six years) succeeded in bringing about an integration of her personality with resolution of the potentially psychotic core which had manifested itself in her spider preoccupation.

CASE 3

In this connection, a dream from the treatment of the third patient, a severely phobic woman (and a transference fantasy of patient No. 4) are of particular interest. Patient No. 3 had been treated in early adolescence for a severe school phobia and behavior suggestive of psychosis. She made a remarkable recovery, returned to school, held a job, got married, and was even able to travel, but she had apparently not resolved the phobic core, that is, her relationship with her mother. She came for treatment after her youngest child had started school because she felt anxious and feared a return of the earlier phobic behavior. We found that she had in part transferred her relationship from her mother to her husband, and that raising three children had helped her to disguise the remnants of her phobia. When, in treatment, we were uncovering her resentment and death wishes against her husband and her oedipal conflicts and hatred for her parents which had been completely denied and overcompensated for by a very dependent and affectionate daughterly attitude, she had a nightmare about a big black spider. She had never before had any spider dreams or fantasies nor did she have a spider phobia. She thought of a clay sculpture she had seen the previous day that looked like a female genital, legs open and the vulva visible. It was an ugly thing and that was really what the spider reminded her of.

She talked about death and about being abandoned. Her husband had mentioned a pain in his chest and jokingly told her to prepare to take care of herself. She felt anxious that morning coming to her session and had asked her husband to follow her in his car, at least up to where the roads parted. When he pulled away in his car she had the feeling of being all alone and completely abandoned. While talking, she was putting her hand over her mouth and at that moment thought of the spider. She thought of anesthesia, a mask put over her mouth, the tonsillectomy, of suffocating, and of her mother. She was visibly shaken and expressed a fear of losing her mind. She thought of a psychotic relative who had recently been hospitalized. This led her to recall and to relive with much affect the very traumatic circumstances of her tonsillectomy at age $11^{1}/_{2}$. Her mother had taken her to the doctor for a physical checkup. Without the patient's knowledge, he recommended and arranged for a tonsillectomy to be performed the next day. When she got up that morning to go to school, her mother told her she was going to have a tonsillectomy and took her to the doctor's office. Her mother held her hand when the mask was put over her face, but she knew that her mother had left and the nurse had taken over before she became unconscious. "How could they do this to me," she cried in my office. "How could I trust anybody?" A few months after the tonsillectomy, her mother gave birth to a baby brother. It was shortly thereafter that she developed an incapacitating school phobia.

In subsequent sessions these associations were followed by memories and affects that led to the reconstruction of the events preceding the acute onset of the phobic behavior at age 12. She had shown signs of phobic behavior from the age of 3. When she was 3 years old a sister was born, and from that time on she had begun to cling to her mother. She had episodes of school phobia and reaction to changes, but was able to maintain herself until a brother was born when she was not quite 12 years old. She experienced the tonsillectomy which preceded the birth of her brother as an oral castration, inflicted upon her by the mother. This reactivated her intense breast and penis envy at the critical pubertal phase, when she was to relinquish both her preoedipal and oedipal hold on the mother in order to establish a proper sexual identification and accept herself as a female.

Her associations to the spider dream led her further back to early childhood. They used to spend summers in the country where she could overhear her parents quarrel and then have intercourse. She disliked this house, later rationalizing this with a dislike of some relatives who also vacationed there. She remembered seeing spiders there, but she never had any conscious preoccupation with or fear of spiders. The spider dream which eventually led to the resolution of the core of her severe and long-standing phobia, indicated that the spider symbol must have formed early, about the time that her phobic clinging to her mother began, but it had been split off and remained latent until it was brought to the fore under the impact of analysis. She had never wanted to be pregnant and give birth to children because it was fraught with the idea of death. She had married a man she knew was sterile. She had adopted three children and had done a remarkable job with them, outdoing her mother without having been a "real" mother herself.

She had been talking about sensations in her vagina. She had a slight discharge and a fear that she might experience a burning sensation. She was unduly concerned about feeling as if she had a bubble there. We had talked in previous sessions about her penis envy and her bisexual wishes. She could now analyze these sensations herself and also understand why she had been so afraid and had avoided gynecological examinations. She left the session saying "I want to be a woman, not a spider." As with Leslie, the sensations in her vagina and the vaginal discharge completely disappeared after this session. The spider had been the symbol for her oral sadism (her intense breast and penis envy) and for her bisexuality, as well as for the primal scene and her oedipal hate. Multiple severe phobias and psychosomatic symptoms, especially nausea and headaches as defenses against the breakthrough of her destructive and perverse impulses, had enabled her to keep the potentially psychotic spider part of her personality under repression. Analysis mobilized, brought into focus, and resolved this danger.

CASE 4

Case 4 highlights the role of psychosomatic symptoms as defenses against and expressions of pregenital oral and anal-sadistic impulses and of bisexuality. This material is from the analysis of an adolescent girl in treatment because of ulcerative colitis and anorexia nervosa. At the time of the episode reported here, the third year of her analysis, many of her fantasies underlying the ulcerative colitis and the anorexia nervosa had been brought to the fore. The somatic manifestations of the ulcerative colitis and anorexia had subsided, and she was dealing now with her symbiotic needs and wishes to engulf and completely control her objects. One of her basic colitis fantasies was of having little people in her colon. Cannibalistic and coprophagic fantasies and impulses had been a major dynamic factor both in her anorexia and the ulcerative colitis.

During one analytic session she suddenly saw in fantasy a spider pulling her strings one after another and eating her children. We had in previous sessions discussed her need to manipulate people like puppets and pull them on strings. She projected this need for magic control to her analyst and often suddenly sat up on the couch to watch me in paranoid fashion. She had fantasies of surprising me, of catching a glimpse of my magical "instruments." Sometimes, as she came into my office, she thought of "Come into my parlor," said the spider. Like Ruth, she felt she could never please her mother without a penis. She carried a boy's name, and as a child felt that she looked and was treated like a boy. Although she had clinging relationships with one girl at a time, she did not think that she could be a lesbian. She considered herself a "homosexual," that is, a boy who likes boys, whereby she could merge and act out the fantasy of being both boy and girl in one.

She used to have an intense fear of crawling bugs, terrified lest the bugs eat her up. Once as a child she saw a bug crawling into her room. She screamed in terror, waiting for it to attack her. Her father, alarmed by her screams, came into the room, killed the bug, and threw it into the toilet. During her analysis she had many dreams of bugs, especially of leeches. She believed that leeches were poisonous, that they were not supposed to be pulled out or the poison would get into the body. They had to be cut out. At this phase of her analysis she had gained sufficient ego strength to be able to tolerate such fantasies consciously without fear of succumbing to them in reality, that is, of becoming manifestly psychotic.

In this case both the oral and anal fixations were particularly intense and played their respective parts in the somatic manifestations of anorexia and colitis and the unconscious fantasy life underlying these somatic symptoms. Her intense breast (a sister had been born when she was 2 years old) and penis envy, her pregnancy and birth fantasies, and her conflict of sexual identification and bisexuality had been elaborated mainly somatically, preventing their expression in overtly disturbed behavior.

CASE 5

Case 5 again illustrates the use of the spider symbol as a transference manifestation in a pregenitally fixated patient who also employed somatic symptoms for the expression and release of her pregenital impulses and as defenses against a breakthrough of such impulses in a manifest psychosis. In this patient, the spider symbol also appeared during the later stages of her analysis when she had gained sufficient ego strength to tolerate and to deal with her fantasies and impulses consciously.

The patient, a 35-year-old woman, had been in analysis because of severe, chronic ulcerative colitis. Concomitant with the subsiding of the somatic symptoms, her oral- and anal-sadistic impulses and fantasies came to the fore. She had dreams and fantasies about wild animals: tigers eating up people, cats swallowing birds (Sperling, 1960). By this time we had worked through some of her infantile sexual fantasies of oral impregnation and anal birth, her intense penis envy and primal-scene reactions, and were now analyzing her latent homosexual relationship with her mother. She had transferred this relationship in part to her husband and now to the analyst. During this phase of her analysis, fantasies about her analyst as a spider emerged. She had a fantasy that the analyst was in bed with her as a big spider engulfing and gobbling her up with a big mouth. She dreamed that she was at the analyst's office on a bed. The analyst was putting her arms around the patient's neck in a tricky way. The patient bit the analyst in the neck, near the jugular vein, and drew blood. Of interest is the fact that this patient had had bleeding with every bowel movement during her ulcerative colitis. Her mother had told her that she had been a difficult birth, that if it had taken any longer, the doctor would have had to cut her up into pieces. The patient had a fantasy that children, in order to get out of the amniotic bag, had to bite their way out. Sometimes when looking at the analyst she had the idea that the analyst was gobbling her up, pulling her thoughts and everything out of her, and taking her inside into her body. She, similar to the adolescent patient, had fantasies that little people were in her colon. She had a very strong unresolved homosexual attachment to her mother and intense bisexual conflicts. One of her oral impregnation fantasies was that the baby got inside mother by being eaten up by mother, the same way that the patient would have wanted to obtain her husband's penis. She often expressed amazement that her husband was not afraid to put his penis into her mouth.

The experience with this patient would seem to support my belief that spider fantasies are not readily disclosed because they related to the patient's most guarded and feared impulses. This may be a reason for the paucity of spider material in the psychoanalytic literature.

CASE 6

A 7^{1}/$_{2}$-year-old boy was referred for treatment because of encopresis. The case was found to be not one of true encopresis, but of a peculiar bowel ritual. He had never defecated into a toilet. Instead he deposited his feces in a special place in the house, a corner of the bedroom near his mother's bed. His mother then inspected and disposed of them. But this behavior was not really why his mother had brought him for treatment. Peter also suffered from an intense phobia of black widow spiders. There had been some talk of black widow spiders having been seen, when his phobia began, but not in the vicinity of where he lived. He was also afraid of being poisoned by the fertilizer used on the lawn.

His mother impressed me as a borderline psychotic with marked paranoid trends. It was difficult to obtain information about Peter's early development. According to his mother it had been very satisfactory except for his refusal to use the toilet at home. Unfortunately, I could study Peter for only a few months because his mother withdrew him from treatment with the rationalization that he had sufficiently improved, and was no longer in need of treatment. The mother herself was not accessible to treatment and obviously was not able to tolerate the intrusion into her very pathological relationship with her son.

Peter's fears of being poisoned revealed themselves as manifestations of his pregnancy fantasies and of a very strong feminine identification. We had just begun to uncover wishes and fantasies of poisoning; that is, impregnating his sister and mother with his feces—fertilizer. The release of some of these fantasies had remarkably decreased his spider phobia and preoccupation with being poisoned, the behavior which had disturbed his mother much more than his encopresis. In fact, it appeared that Peter's special way of delivering his feces to his mother was in response to her pathological needs. There was no opportunity, however, to investigate this further.

In Peter's case the anal elements and the anal significance of the spider symbol predominated. The black widow spider was the symbol of Peter's very strong but consciously rejected feminine identification and his anal (perverse and destructive) sexuality, externalized and projected upon his mother and displaced to the black widow spider. It would seem that in the male, the anal fixations and anality are the more significant factors in the genesis of bisexual and homosexual development.

CASE 7

This role of anality and of anal fixations in the choice of the spider symbol as a representation of the patient's bisexual orientation and pregenital sexuality is further illustrated with Case 7,

Paul, whose long and successful analysis was conducted under my supervision. The diagnosis was that of a severely disturbed boy with flat affect and defective object relationships. He was a bed-rocker and very accident-prone. Paul was 6 years old when he started analysis. At the time of the episode to be reported here, he was in the fourth year of analysis.

He came in for his session sucking on an ice cream cone. He was holding it up so that it dripped into his mouth. This reminded him of sitting on the toilet and dropping feces. In this connection he thought of the many (repetitive) drawings he used to make of attacks from above and below, of planes dropping explosives and of antiaircraft shooting up and destroying planes. For years his play and fantasy dealt primarily with machines rather than humans. He then talked about an old fear of spiders coming up from the toilet. He once saw a movie of a giant spider. For a long time he was afraid that he would be bitten by a spider and be immobilized. This led him to talk about experiences with his mother. In order to prevent him from rocking, his mother used to tuck him in so tight that he could not free himself. He would wake up and become panicked. His mother's hand and fingers tucking him in, that is, immobilizing him, suddenly reminded him of a spider and it became clear to him that the giant spider he feared was his mother.

Paul's childhood had been inordinately traumatic. His mother had a depression when he was an infant, and when he was 3 years old, acted out severely before and after her divorce. His father, alternately seductively overindulgent and rejecting, also had many affairs. There had been actual seduction by an older brother, and sex play in which holding down and immobilizing the partner was a factor.

CASE 8

I will confine myself here to relating an episode which took place in the third year of her analysis. Her mother died when the patient was not yet 6 years old, and she was raised by an aunt. The episode relevant to spiders occurred the day of that aunt's funeral, which the patient did not attend. Her analysis revealed that she had not accepted her mother's death, and that she entertained fantasies of her mother returning to life. The night of the funeral, the patient was alone in the house, thinking about her aunt, when she saw a spider on the window. She was convinced that the spider was a reincarnation of her aunt. This patient had occasional acoustic and visual hallucinations all of which related to her fantasies about her dead mother.

DISCUSSION

As dissimilar as these cases may appear clinically, there are certain genetic and dynamic similarities between them which are of great significance for the thesis of this paper. All these patients experienced maternal rejection in their childhood, together with a high degree of overstimulation particularly in the visual spheres. In cases 1 and 2, where the onset of the spider symbol and also of a severe sleep disturbance could be traced back to the age of 2 or 3 years, the maternal rejection was particularly marked. In case 1, this could be clearly established during the second phase of treatment when she was overtly psychotic. Her mother confided that she had felt threatened and appalled by Ruth from birth on, that she had thought there was something wrong with her, that she was not like a real girl. These feelings related to the mother's unconscious rejection of her own femininity projected onto Ruth. Ruth's feelings that she could never please her mother as a girl, her intense rivalry with her brothers, her confusion and conflict over sexual identification had some basis in her mother's unconscious feelings concerning her. The mother's identification of the child with an unconsciously hated and rejected part of herself is an important genetic factor in the development of psychosis in the child (Sperling, 1954, 1955a, 1963). Severe, intractable sleep disturbance in a young child may sometimes be the first and only clinical indication of a later psychotic development (Sperling, 1949, 1958, 1969).

In the case of Leslie, the mother's rejection was on a conscious level and quite apparent. The mother, sensing that her relationship with Leslie was very unsatisfactory and that Leslie was not developing properly, had sought treatment for herself

when Leslie was not yet 4 years old. After a short period of treatment, the mother was advised to leave the care of the child to
someone else. She could not accept this advice and broke off
treatment. An attempt to treat Leslie when she was 8 years old
failed. She was found inaccessible and unresponsive. At the same
her parents approached me, Leslie was 10 years old, and the
psychological testing suggested a schizophrenic development.

I worked with the mother for more than three years in preparatory analysis before undertaking to treat Leslie. In analyzing
the mother, it could be established that Leslie represented to her
not only the rejected "crazy" part of herself, but also of her own
hated, psychotic mother. Leslie's mother had not wanted any
children; Leslie was an unwilling concession made to her husband. Without the preparatory treatment of the mother, in which
a modification of her attitudes and feelings toward Leslie could
be achieved, Leslie, in my opinion, had no chance of recovery.
As in Ruth's case, credit must be given to Leslie's mother; without
her help the surprisingly successful outcome could not have been
accomplished.

In Peter's case there were indications that he was identifying
with his mother who appeared to be suffering from a paranoid
psychosis. With Paul, the pregenital, especially the anal, fixations
were marked, and the diagnosis pointed to the development of
a severe narcissistic character disorder. The third patient, who
had the single nightmare about a black spider, had used an incapacitating phobia with the mechanisms of denial (of the internal
danger), of externalization, and of displacement—first to the
school, then to any situation that entailed separation from
mother—in defense against her overwhelmingly strong pregenital
impulses. She, similarly to patients 2 4, and 5, also had used somatic pathways for the immediate discharge of such impulses.
Patients 2 and 3 primarily used nausea, severe headaches, and
cramps, whereas patients 4 and 5 had ulcerative colitis and anorexia. When the phobic mechanisms as well as the somatic defenses were invalidated by analysis, the split-off pregenital and
potentially psychotic core symbolized by the spider appeared. The
spider was a highly condensed symbol containing the core fantasies and conflicts from various developmental levels, in particular,
breast and penis envy, primal-scene reactions (murderous and

suicidal impulses), bisexual and homosexual wishes and fantasies. The spider also represented both the patient and the mother in these feared and deeply repressed aspects.

It is my contention that the use of the spider symbol by these patients in times of stress was an indication that they felt threatened by an imminent breakthrough of these warded-off pregenital, "crazy" perverse impulses. The spider fear, fantasy, or preoccupation served the function of preventing the flooding of the ego with these pregenital fantasies and impulses. By displacement to this specific symbol, a total break with reality was avoided. Here the similarity with the dynamic and economic function of single phobias and obsessions is apparent (Sperling, 1952, 1967). Unless subjected to analysis, the psychotic core represented by the spider remains unchanged, and these fantasies and conflicts retain their pathogenicity, constituting a continuous threat to the patient's emotional equilibrium. In this connection, the patient described by Azima and Wittkower (1957) and the contribution by Newman and Stoller (1969) are of particular interest.

The patient of Azima and Wittkower was a man who suffered from an incapacitating fear of spiders and was treated with anaclitic therapy using drugs. The spider phobia dated back to childhood, but had been precipitated in an acute, intense form by the birth of a son. The material which the patient produced and his behavior during the regressed state was overtly psychotic, dealing mainly with oral-sadistic attacks and counterattacks upon the spider-mother-breasts, that is, with biting and being bitten, with devouring and being devoured.

Newman and Stoller's patient was a woman with hermaphroditic genitalia, who, during a psychotic episode, developed the delusion that her genitalia were a spider. The authors found that the spider also represented the patient's mother and the patient herself as a hermaphrodite. This patient had been preoccupied with spiders from early childhood.

A review of the remaining literature on spider symbolism regarding the type of patients and problems encountered might be of interest. Abraham (1922) stressed the bisexual aspects of the spider symbol. His patient, who had fears of being transformed into a woman and his mother into a man, would, I believe, by present psychoanalytic criteria be considered a severe character disorder. Foulkes (1943) dealt specifically with this fantasy of sexual transformation. His patient developed a paranoia with a delusion of an operation which would transform her into a male. Sterba's paper (1950) is of particular interest because of his discussion of a short story by the German novelist, H. H. Ewers. The story deals with three men who succumb to an acute delusional spider psychosis and commit suicide by hanging. The last man, who kept a diary describing his delusion about a spider-woman, was found dead with a spider crushed between his teeth. Sterba's patient had attempted suicide by hanging. Little (1966a,b, 1967) stressed the pregenital aspects of spider symbolism. The mother of one of his patients was a borderline psychotic; the mother of another patient had committed suicide. He mentioned a colleague who, after learning of his interest in spider phobias, confided that he had a spider phobia as a child which had not been uncovered in her personal analysis. I cite this as confirmation of my experience that spider phobias and spider fantasies are revealed only with great reluctance and usually late in treatment. Gloyne (1950) described mass hysterical reactions to the fear of being bitten by the tarantula during the Middle Ages, reactions characterized by a dancing mania leading to mass suicide. This tarantism, related to ancient cults and rites, was of a decidedly sexual character.

Most investigators would seem to agree that the spider is a representation of the dangerous (orally devouring and anally castrating) mother, and that the main problems of these patients seem to center around their sexual identifications and bisexuality. However, that this concept of the mother is the result of the child's projection of its own denied oral and anal-sadistic impulses and of the specific relationship with the mother has not been emphasized; nor have the roles of the childhood climate and of the traumatic experiences been sufficiently elaborated. There has been no convincing explanation of why these patients chose spider symbolism in particular for the expression of their conflicts and impulses. The type of patients and problems described in the literature on spider symbolism is not at all uncommon nor is the sight of spiders; spider symbolism, however, seems to be rather uncommon. While preparing the discussion for this paper, I spoke to many colleagues with long and extensive clinical experience and was surprised by the apparent rarity of this phenomenon in clinical practice. I agree with Little's (1967) observation and thinking: that patients do not readily reveal their spider phobias, and because of the distaste attached to the subject (Little refers in this connection to Freud's [1919] paper "The Uncanny"), analysts do not seem particularly interested in it.

I should therefore like to point to some of the factors which, in my opinion, contribute to this specific symbol choice. Even young children have a variety of choices available for the symbolic expression of dangerous impulses and wishes. The choice of insects, and in particular of spiders, is not only an indication of the nature of these impulses and the defenses adopted by the child's ego against them, but is also related to the developmental phases and the quality of the mother-child relationship at that time.

It is my contention that the choice of the spider symbol indicates a fixation to the pregenital and in particular to the anal-sadistic phase in a very ambivalent and predominantly hostile relationship to the mother, with an inability to separate from the hated mother. Here again, Leslie serves as a good illustration for the tenacity of such a relationship.

While she was at college (she was able to live away and function somewhat independently from mother by this time, although she still went home for weekends and telephoned her mother frequently), her parents went abroad. Leslie's separation anxiety had dominated the analysis for some time preceding this event, which occurred during a short holiday from school. The day before her parents departed, Leslie went out of town to visit a friend. In the past, whenever her parents had taken a trip, it was during the summer when Leslie was in camp. They always returned in time for visiting days. Leslie reduplicated this situation by visiting the friend. She could not tolerate the awareness of actual separation and the feeling of being left.

She returned to her parents' house with a friend the next day to fetch some things she had left in the study. While there she suffered a severe anxiety attack. She felt that a giant spider was coming out of the wall, engulfing her and tying her up with many legs, so she could never free herself and escape. She screamed in terror for her friend, who was in another room. The study, which adjoined the parents' bedroom, was a room which Leslie had not been allowed to use as a child, but to which she would sneak especially at night, to listen to the noises from the parental bedroom, when the parents were "fighting." Because this room was infrequently used, it always contained spiders, or more spiders than other parts of the house. In Leslie's spider fantasies, the spiders, often in enormous numbers, came from this room. Her parents leaving her had revived her unresolved separation conflict as well as the oedipal conflict and hate (for being excluded from parental intercourse), and had mobilized the regressive wish for inseparable union with mother. Leslie's birth fantasies were mainly anal, the fetus being expelled like feces and discarded into the toilet as worthless and undesirable—like a spider. When she visited a relative who was breastfeeding her baby, she had a recurrence of spider fantasies and expressed fears of holding and nursing a baby. In this connection, Little's (1967) patient, who masturbated by tying himself up with ropes, is of interest. This is a not uncommon and dangerous masturbatory practice of transvestites. The suicides by hanging in Ewers' story and the behavior of Sterba's patient would seem to be related to this.

Returning to the importance of anal fixations in spider symbolism, the fact that it is often combined with phobias and especially with a persistent phobic dependence on mother is of significance. These phobias originate during the anal phase as a result of unresolved separation conflicts and destructive impulses directed against the controlling mother (Sperling, 1967). While the oral features are important in spider symbolism, they seem to overshadow and conceal the more significant anal features in this symbol choice.

The choice of the spider symbol is also an indication of the child's severely injured narcissism, which is especially vulnerable during the anal phase when sphincter and impulse control are to be acquired, and the hatred for this deprivation is projected on the spider-mother. The spider is also, as was pointed out earlier, repulsive, something which not only may but should be destroyed, which can be stepped on and crushed. This is exactly how Leslie felt as a child: crushed and stepped on. The spider reflects the patient's lack of self-esteem, which relates in part to impulses he considers repulsive and dangerous.

This was obvious in all patients, and particularly in Leslie. At age 2, Leslie had been attacked and bitten on her mouth by the neighbor's dog. One might have expected that she would develop a dog phobia under these circumstances. At that time Leslie's parents owned a similar dog. Not only was Leslie not afraid of this dog, she always wanted and had a dog to whom she talked and with whom she liked to sleep. To Leslie, the dog possessed human status and represented her father. This became quite clear in her analysis when she expressed concern lest her dog, who was old, might die. She felt the same way about her father who was considerably older than her mother. Leslie had felt rejected by her mother. She hated her mother and was afraid to express hatred. This preoedipal hate was further intensified by oedipal hatred. Leslie had contempt for her mother. To her, the female genital was repulsive, dangerous, mysterious, and surrounded by hair—like a spider. The correspondence here with Freud's (1922) interpretation of the Medusa head is worth noting. Leslie could not therefore identify herself or her mother with an animal who was loved and treated with affection, as her dog was treated by her family.

Preoccupation with smell is another important characteristic found in these patients. It has to do with their coprophilic and coprophagic impulses, and was present in all patients, particularly in patients 4 and 5, who had colitis. These impulses find indirect gratification in the pregenital practices which these patients prefer to genital activity. Direct gratification of these perverse impulses is warded off as "crazy," and finds expression in the spider symbolism. The frequent fear of such patients of a spider falling into their mouths, also most clearly expressed by Leslie, contains and expresses such coprophagic wishes and destructive (killing) impulses. The spider represents the anally devalued breast and penis and their excretions as poisonous and dangerous. In this connection, a patient described in "Trichotillomania, Trichophagy and Cyclic Vomiting" (Sperling, 1968) is of interest. This patient had an intense insect phobia, especially of insects flying into her mouth. She would eat the hair she pulled and experience the sensation of swallowing live insects, which to her meant sperm-feces. She, too, was anally fixated with many phobias and an intense phobic dependence on her mother.

SUMMARY

Psychoanalytic studies of patients who used spider symbolism for the expression of their repressed (perverse) impulses and conflicts revealed, as important genetic factors, pregenital, particularly anal, fixations and unresolved preoedipal relationships with their mothers. The spider symbolism as well as the symptoms most frequently found associated with it, such as severe sleep disturbances and phobias, are also an indication of unresolved separation conflicts and a high degree of ambivalence which intensifies bisexuality and the problems of sexual identification. The mechanisms of defense employed in spider symbolism and in phobias are denial, externalization, projection, splitting, and displacement. They indicate the primitive, ambivalent, narcissistic ego organization of this phase. The personalities of these patients and of the mothers in cases where it was possible to study them showed marked paranoid trends. They also used psychosomatic symptoms in stress situations, either episodically or more persistently for the immediate (somatic) discharge of threatening impulses. The spider symbolism in most cases remained latent and became manifest in traumatic life situations and in analysis when the phobic and psychosomatic defenses were invalidated. In the analytic situation the spider symbolism was indicative of a specific mother transference.

I have tried to elaborate on some of the factors operating in the genesis and choice of the spider symbolism and to deal more fully with its dynamic and economic functions. I particularly wanted to draw attention to the diagnostic and prognostic significance of spider symbolism in clinical practice.

REFERENCES

Abraham, K. (1922), The spider as a dream symbol. In: *Selected Papers on Psychoanalysis.* New York: Basic Books, 1953, pp. 326–332.

Azima, H., & Wittkower, E. D. (1957), Anaclitic therapy employing drugs: A case of spider phobia with Isakower phenomenon. *Psychoanal. Quart.*, 26:190–205.

Foulkes, S. H. (1943), The idea of a change of sex in women. *Internat. J. Psycho-Anal.*, 24:53–56.

Freud, S. (1919), The uncanny. *Standard Edition*, 17:217–252. London: Hogarth Press, 1955.

——— (1922), Medusa's head. *Standard Edition*, 18:273–274. London: Hogarth Press, 1955.

Gloyne, H. F. (1950), Tarantism, mass hysterical reaction to spider bite in the Middle Ages. *Amer. Imago*, 7:29–42.

Little, R. B. (1966a), Oral aggression in spider legends. *Amer. Imago*, 23:169–179.

——— (1966b), Umbilical cord symbolism of the spider's dropline. *Psychoanal. Quart.*, 35:587–590.

——— (1967), Spider phobias. *Psychoanal. Quart.*, 36:51–60.

Newman, L. E., & Stoller, R. J. (1969), Spider symbolism and bisexuality. *J. Amer. Psychoanal. Assn.*, 17:862–872.

Sperling, M. (1949), Neurotic sleep disturbance in children. *Nerv. Child*, 8:28–46.

——— (1952), Animal phobias in a two-year-old child. *The Psychoanalytic Study of the Child*, 7:115–125. New York: International Universities Press.

——— (1954), Reactive schizophrenia in children. *Amer. J. Orthopsychiatry*, 24:506–512.

——— (1955a), Psychosis and psychosomatic illness. *Internat. J. Psycho-Anal.*, 36:320–327.

——— (1955b), Roundtable on therapy approaches in childhood schizophrenia. Paper presented American Psychiatric Association meeting, Atlantic City, NJ.

——— (1958), Pavor nocturnus. *J. Amer. Psychoanal. Assn.*, 6:79–94.

——— (1960), Symposium on disturbances of the digestive tract, II. Unconscious fantasy life and object-relationships in ulcerative colitis. *Internat. J. Psycho-Anal.*, 41:450–455.

——— (1961), A note on some dream symbols and the significance of their changes during analysis. *J. Hillside Hosp.*, 10:161–266.

——— (1963), Some criteria on the evaluations of the treatment potential of schizophrenic children. *J. Amer. Acad. Child Psychiatry*, 2:593–604.

——— (1967), School phobias: Classification, dynamics and treatment. *The Psychoanalytic Study of the Child*, 22:375–401. New York: International Universities Press.

———— (1968), Trichotillomania, trichophagy, and cyclic vomiting. *Internat. J. Psycho-Anal.*, 49:682–690.

———— (1969), Sleep disturbance in children. In: *Modern Perspectives in International Child Psychiatry*, ed. J. G. Howells. Edinburgh: Oliver & Boyd.

Sterba, R. (1950), On spiders, hanging and oral sadism. *Amer. Imago*, 7:21–28.

CHAPTER 9

The Cat People Revisited

VAMIK D. VOLKAN, M.D.

In my mind's eye, I am sitting next to my mother in a moving truck, holding our cat, Rengin, whose name in Turkish means something like "colorful." When I think of Rengin, I visualize not an animal, but a kaleidoscope of colors. Suddenly, I lose control of the cat: he jumps out of an open window and disappears into the fields like a fading rainbow. I am filled with sadness.

It is not surprising that this episode is one of my earliest memories. I was 4 years old when my family made this move from one town in Cyprus to another. Moving from a familiar place where I was my mother's "darling," to a new town, where a typhoid epidemic struck one of my sisters, probably induced various anxieties—including worries about losing my mother or her love (since she had to spend more time with my ill sister) and about separation–individuation struggles. When pets are in our childhood environment, they can easily function as displacement figures and symbols involved in our internal dramas. Rengin's different colors might, for example, represent different childhood affects pertaining to the "loss" of my mother.

Though my present "relationship" with Rengin's representation is not much more than recollection, there are individuals who, as adults, use cats to respond to the demands of their internal worlds—and, for some of them, cats are no longer just pets. This chapter will consider individuals who use cats to symbolize body and mental images. I will focus especially on those adults who deploy cat images as extensions of their self- and/or internalized object representations, for whom cats function as protosymbols (Werner and Kaplan, 1963): for whom a cat is what it in reality represents. Since they identify themselves to one degree or another with cat images, I call such individuals "cat people."

In the psychoanalytic literature, the term *cat person* was first used by Sanford (1966) in her engaging account of Elsie, who was so enmeshed with her pet cats and so involved in living through them that she always appeared in her analyst's notes as "the cat girl." While Sanford did not provide an in-depth description of Elsie's internal world, it is clear that this patient not only displayed feline qualities herself, but also cast her analyst in a feline role, reflecting her cat protosymbolization. Ten years later, I described my first "cat person" patient (Volkan, 1976); in 1978, James Kavanaugh and I reported three additional cases. This chapter updates these early reports, provides further case studies, and expands our understanding of the internal worlds of various types of "cat people."

CATS AND HUMANS: A LONG HISTORY OF SIGNIFICANCE AND SYMBOLISM

The importance of cats and other pets in people's lives should not be underestimated: there are currently 229 million pets living in U.S. households alone. Pollock (1996) suggests that our attachment to pets derives from our prehistoric ancestors' use of animals to alert them to potential dangers. Silvester (1995) hypothesizes further that cats might have become especially common pets throughout the world because of their usefulness in the human war against rodents. In rural areas, he argues, cats keep the proliferation of mice and rats under control and thus help to facilitate the production and storage of food supplies. Because ships' cargoes were particularly susceptible to rodent infestation, navigators began to keep cats on board. Because cats do not like living on the water, however, many probably jumped ship, thereby populating the world with felines.

But the importance of cats in human life has long transcended such mundane practicalities as well. The Egyptians—said to be the first to domesticate *Felis catus,* a descendant of the Abyssinian cat native to the African deserts—evolved a broadly influential cult of cat worship before the 12th Dynasty (c. 2000 B.C.E.). Ancient Egyptians gave cats the greatest respect: it was a capital offense to kill one, and cats were mummified and mourned in extravagant funeral rituals occupying a unique place in the religion of Egypt for more than two thousand years. (Mourning the deaths of cats and other pets is still done in sometimes extravagant ways, and complications in such mourning processes are still very much with us [Pollock, 1996].) The goddess Bastet, who was depicted with a human body and a feline head, was loved and revered as the highest expression of femininity and maternity. Classical Greek historian Herodotus (c. 485–425 B.C.E.) left vivid descriptions of the great red granite temple sacred to the cat at Bubastis, Egypt (Godolphin, 1942) and equated Bastet with the Greek Artemis, virgin goddess of the hunt and moon. Cats appear on many ancient Greek vases.

Cats' cultural significance has not always been as positive as it was in ancient Egypt, however. In medieval Europe, the cat was often considered an emblem of evil whose glowing eyes not only penetrate darkness but also glimpse a sinister other world: an omen of bad luck, even a messenger of the devil. As the supposed cohorts of witches and demons, cats were regarded as agents of dark powers and nameless horrors (Russell, 1972). A dread of cats was reflected in both religious practice and secular law. Many a forlorn old woman was tortured to confess that her cat was her link to Lucifer, an instrument of her malevolent charms and spells. Throughout the sixteenth and seventeenth centuries, cats were routinely cast into bonfires, particularly during the Lenten season of fasting and purification.

Because of the long history of close association between humans and felines, and because of the ambivalence that has frequently characterized that association, it is not surprising that cats appear frequently in children's literature and games (Opie and Opie, 1959, 1969) and in popular culture. Referred to in advertising slogans, caricatured in cartoons, and invoked as team "totems," cats are to be found across our cultural lexicon. In the late 1990s, many newspapers—especially gossip columns—reported on a New York socialite who had endured ten years of plastic surgery to make herself look more feline. Dubbing her "Cat-Woman," newspapers printed and reprinted photographs of Jocelyne Wildenstein before and after her many plastic surgeries. Many of the accompanying stories focused on Wildenstein's envy of her billionaire ex-husband's love for his pet big cats as a possible reason for her attempts at surgical transformation. Though I obviously have no knowledge of her more hidden motivations, she represents a quite concrete identification with cat images—a literalization we also see in the classic thriller film *Cat People* (1942) and the highly sexualized 1982 remake of the same title.

Indeed, in clinical practice as well as in everyday life, we frequently observe cats used as sexual symbols. From Tennessee Williams' *Cat on a Hot Tin Roof* (1955) to the B-movie *Cat Women of the Moon* (1953), female sexuality is often associated with the feline. American slang includes the term *cat house* (brothel) and sexualized references to *pussycats*. In free associations, fantasies, and dreams, we note, a cat may stand for a soft and loving mother, a seductive mother, a vicious mother, a mother's pubic hair or vagina, or vaginas in general. For example, Gary, a neurotic man in his late twenties experiencing premature ejaculation, hated and avoided cats. Suffering from extreme castration anxiety, he experienced *vagina dentata* fantasies. When he had come to understand that cats unconsciously stood for the dreaded female genitalia, he dreamed of a woman with the same color hair as his mother who lay naked in a bed with a cat between her legs; the cat's mouth was open, and Gary could see its sharp teeth.

Cats as sibling representations are also common (Volkan and Ast, 1997a). Christine, for instance, a 38-year-old single woman, had a peculiar relationship with her two cats. She allowed them to run around in the house, but she was also sure that she would never allow the animals to "intrude" into her life. When she began her treatment, she "introduced" them to her therapist as if they were family members. Initially, too, she often wanted to cut her therapeutic sessions short so that she could go home to feed her cats.

Analysis of her demands revealed she was exhibiting not only a reaction formation against aggressive feelings toward her siblings but also resistance to understanding these feelings. The oldest child in a poor family, Christine had shared a room during much of her childhood with a brother three years younger, who was her father's favorite. When she was 9 years old, her mother gave birth to a premature baby sister who required a great deal of attention, and whom Christine referred to as an "intruder." For about a year and a half during her youth, Christine had been required to sleep in the same bed with her sister. Because the mattress was so soft, they would often roll together in the middle of the bed, and Christine felt that her own "territory" was literally invaded.

As an adult, Christine kept two cats, one male and one female, who represented her two siblings: now she could control them. By interrupting her sessions to feed the cats, she was showing her analyst how much she cared for the cats (for her siblings) so that the analyst would not investigate her aggression against her brother and sister. Since Christine's mother was allergic to cats, she would not touch them or otherwise pay them any attention when she came to visit Christine's home. Thus these visits reenacted Christine's unconscious fantasy of being her mother's sole "child" (Volkan and Ast, 1997a).

There are, of course, many other ways in which cats and their images are utilized as symbols. For example, I treated a pregnant woman whose childhood experience of her mother was very poor. During her pregnancy, this woman treated her pet cat as if it were a baby in order to "train" herself for motherhood. Sometimes, cats become "linking objects" (Volkan, 1981; Volkan and Zintl, 1993) and are contaminated in the mind of a mourner with the image of the dead loved one. We may see a parent who has lost a child turning his or her attention, at least temporarily, to a pet cat, as if the cat represents the lost child. We also observe cats used to symbolize hurtful or angry childhood self-images: a dream of a crying or snarling cat may represent the patient as a frustrated infant who wished to bite her mother's nipples.

What, crucially, is common to all of these examples is that the cat or its image remains a symbol. For individuals who utilize a cat or its image as a symbol—at all times or soon after hearing the analyst's interpretation of the meaning of the symbol—"a cat is a cat." For those I call "cat people," however, there is confusion about where aspects of the person or his or her self-images and internal object-images end and where the cat's image begins.

THREE TYPES OF CAT PEOPLE

In order to become a "cat person," an individual has to be among those whose self-representations lack cohesion, who experience blurred or lost reality testing, and who suffer from object-relations conflicts. Cat people thus possess borderline or psychotic personality organizations, or suffer from focalized psychosis. For practical purposes, I divide adult cat people's use of cats or cat images as protosymbols into three categories: (1) cats as reactivated transitional objects; (2) cats as differentiated but unintegrated self- and object-representations; and (3) cats as undifferentiated psychotic cores (infantile psychotic selves).

Cats as Transitional Objects

Winnicott's (1953) description of the transitional object is well-known. The child's first "not-me" object, it is nonetheless never totally "not-me," since it is a bridge between "not-me" and "mother-me" (Greenacre, 1969), Like Modell's (1975), my own work has focused on the Januslike quality of the transitional object (Volkan, 1976), which can be likened to a lantern with one opaque and one transparent side; when the opaque side faces the outside world, the world is "wiped out" by darkness, but, turned, the lantern's other side illuminates the world so that it can be known. Adult borderline patients' characteristic use of nonhuman objects (animate or inanimate) as *reactivated* transitional objects manifests the same combination of progressive and regressive elements. The illusion that such an object is under the patient's absolute control (Volkan, 1976; Volkan and Akhtar, 1979) maintains his or her borderline personality organization (Kernberg, 1976; Volkan, 1976). In treatment, however, the patient can also use the object progressively as he or she becomes ready to know the outside world and to appreciate its separateness from the self.

When an individual experiences a cat as a reactivated transitional object (a not-me and mother-me combination), he or she feels far more obliged to maintain an illusion of *absolute* control over the cat at all costs than does a neurotic patient such as

Christine, whose case I mentioned in the last section. When the borderline patient cannot control the cat, as inevitably must happen, he or she may experience anxiety so extreme that it loses its signaling function and becomes overwhelming. The patient may strike out at or beat the cat, much like a child who wildly abuses a teddy bear. At the same time, the patient may also use the cat as a "cushion" (a sort of living teddy bear) and may appear "addicted" to it; for instance, the patient may only be able to fall asleep after the cat is snuggled into bed with him or her. Sometimes a patient with borderline personality organization may feel compelled to place the cat between him- or herself and a bed-partner's body; through this concrete link, the patient "controls" the physical and—more importantly—the psychic distance between the patient and the partner, who can be "good" but might also suddenly turn "bad." It is important to note, however, that the clinical picture may be confusing since the adult patient using a cat as a reactivated transitional object (a protosymbol) can also condense higher-level meanings in it; the cat also may become an adult fetish (Freud, 1927), for example, or a linking object.

Margaret: A 19-year-old white, middle-class Southerner, Margaret found herself seated on an overnight bus trip beside a man who repeatedly ran his hands over her body in the darkness. Since there were others on the bus, any noisy protest would have stopped him, but she felt she could not say no to his advances because she perceived him, a middle-aged black man, as underprivileged and needy. Indeed, Margaret exhibited an acute inability to say "no" to needy people generally (Volkan, 1982). As her five-year analysis progressed, I uncovered that this personality trait was related to the fact that her mother had been depressed during Margaret's first years of life. For Margaret, needy people represented her depressed mother, whom she hoped to repair and make whole so that she herself could break out of the symbiotic relationship that bound the mother and daughter together.

Margaret's maternal grandmother had allegedly been injured while giving birth to Margaret's mother and her twin sister, and—in spite of the fact that she did not die until ten years later—her death was attributed to this injury in childbirth. Margaret's mother never fully accepted her own mother's death and endlessly sought her return. Further, she always felt "incomplete" without her sister, and chose to live near her, even after both were married. Margaret was conceived during a time when her mother was obliged to live apart from her twin, however, a separation that induced the depression that continued through Margaret's early life. When Margaret was born, her mother consciously thought of her not only as her own dead mother but also as her "lost" sister.

Margaret's mother's inability to achieve true individuation in spite of her many achievements accounted for a number of peculiarities in her daughter's object relationships, exacerbated by the fact that Margaret's four siblings (two older and two younger than she) paired off, leaving Margaret alone with her mother. When Margaret was ill, mother and daughter often rested on the bed side by side with their bodies curved reciprocally, emblematic of their psychologically symbiotic relationship; when Margaret entered psychoanalysis, she felt that she could communicate with her mother and her analyst by means of "waves," "osmosis," or "a third eye." It should be noted that, outside the area of intimacy with the representatives of her depressed early mother (as in the transference), Margaret was able to differentiate her self-representation from object-representations and one external object from another in her daily life. When under stress or relating to "needy" people, however, she tended to regress to more symbiotic modes of relationship.

At the age of 4 or 5, Margaret had developed a practice that, as an adult, she still used to protect herself from difficulties in her object relations: she habitually rolled lint between her fingers into what she called "fuzz balls," which she fingered to soothe herself when anxious. She had begun this habit when the blanket she had carried about with her everywhere had disappeared; now, these tangible reminders of her soothing blanket were under her absolute control. She even brought fuzz balls to her psychoanalytic sessions, concealing them at first in her purse or between her fingers.

A few months before entering analysis, Margaret had stolen a cat from a child on the street; eventually, the cat became for

Margaret a living "fuzz ball." Though the cat was female, Margaret named it after her father, contaminating the stolen pet with bisexual fetishist elements. It was not until a year of analysis had passed, however, that the cat became a truly reactivated transitional object. By this stage in Margaret's treatment, the analyst had come to represent the early depressed mother, and introjective–projective relatedness with the analyst intensified as the patient merged with the analyst-mother, separated, and merged again. It was at this point that the cat became a specially intense combination of mother-me and not-me. She became not only addicted to the cat, but also excessively preoccupied with it in her hours on the couch as the cat became a magical object for her. At home she could not sleep without it. In bed, she made the cat curl around her body as her mother had done when they "twinned" (Volkan and Ast, 1997b) together, surrendering the boundaries between them. Margaret began to see the cat as having human characteristics. In its absence, Margaret was at times uncomfortable, even frightened.

Aware of what she was doing, Margaret tried to advance from this sort of object relation. Her struggle to separate from the representation of her mother-analyst—and the concomitant pull back to symbiosis with the mother-analyst's representation—manifested itself in a series of dreams. The significance of the cat as a reactivated transitional object came to light after Margaret dreamt first of killing her mother, and then of searching for the meaning of "integrity." In a previous analytic session, Margaret had spoken of herself as having no integrity when she meant to say she had no *integration*. These dreams were followed by others of which she was unable to recall the contents but to which she felt tied "by an umbilical cord." On the couch she felt the sensation of "floating in the air"; the couch itself seemed to float into position beneath her. During her sessions, she expressed the desire to move away from the couch (and analyst), but at the same time she wanted to cling to it. She fingered her fuzz balls more—and more aggressively—than ever; at home, she kicked her cat as if intending to kill it.

Though she was not conscious of doing so, Margaret began to leave a little heap of fuzz balls behind after each analytic session. I collected them in an ashtray for more than a month before

she realized what she had been doing. She said the fuzz balls were
no longer a solace, that she no longer needed them or the cat.
"For safety's sake"—in case she would need them again—she
kept some on hand, and a month later reported trying to relax
by masturbating with the fuzz balls between her fingers. This effort was unsuccessful, so she collected all the fuzz balls in her
possession, flushed them down the toilet and said "good-bye" to
her mother's representation out loud. Of course, this dramatic
event did not bring about a psychic separation from her mother
once and for all but it did represent a major turning point in her
analysis. Soon, she took the fuzz balls from my ashtray and threw
them in the trash on her way home. Shortly thereafter, her cat
returned to being a cat, a nonmagical pet.

Annabel: As Annabel, a college student in her early twenties with a borderline personality organization, was working
through separating intrapsychically from her mother-analyst's
representation, she went about her daily life as if her activities
were exercises in doing things on her own, without need of an
external ego (her early mother). This practice caused Annabel
anxiety, and she would often fall back into symbiotic object relationships only to redouble her efforts. After I thought she had
"exercised" long enough, I recounted to her the story of Tarik,
the Muslim conqueror of Spain after whom the Rock of Gibraltar
was named, as an analogy for the psychic problem she was facing
at that time in her analysis. When Tarik and his men reached the
shores of Spain from North Africa in 711 c.e., he ordered the
ships in which they had made the passage burned so that any
possibility of retreat (regression) would be cut off. This move left
only two possible outcomes: the invaders either would be engulfed by the sea (symbiosis) or would earn new territories (new
ego functions) through conquest.

A few months after hearing this story, Annabel began to
speak of wanting a cat; eventually she found a kitten, which she
named "Tarik." For a few months she was greatly preoccupied
with it, spent time with it before going to bed at night, and kept
it by her side when she had visitors, particularly a young man
who had entered her life. She seemed to need it in intimate

relationships with others and experienced a sense of terror instead of anxiety when it climbed a tree and was lost to her until rescued by neighbors. At this time, the cat was utilized as a proto-symbol. After a few months, Annabel confided that, before she had named the cat "Tarik," she had gone to the library to research the historical figure further. The cat represented her wish to struggle forward toward new territories of reality after giving up the regressive possibility of retreat and surrender, after "burning her bridges behind her." When she understood the role her cat played in this forward effort and could actually take steps toward further individuation, her investment in the cat diminished, and most of its "magic" disappeared and she began using the cat as a symbol.

Jane: Jane was a 21-year-old college student when she began her treatment (see Volkan [1995] for a detailed examination of Jane's case and her six-year analysis). In treatment, Jane initially presented a psychotic condition, a rather generalized inability to differentiate between her self-images and her object-images. Later, when her condition improved, she evinced a borderline personality organization dominated by a stable splitting of her self- and object-images: she pronounced all objects, animate and inanimate, either "benign" or "aggressive." During this period of borderline personality organization, Jane became significantly preoccupied with the family cat; like Margaret's and Annabel's feline fixations, Jane's preoccupations marked an attempt in the transference to find a distinction between herself and mother-analyst representations and to get to know the world more realistically.

Jane was the second child of a couple whose first-born, eighteen months older than Jane, was congenitally deformed and expected to die in infancy. Indeed, before Jane reached age 2, her sibling did die—in the mother's arms, on the way to the hospital, with Jane in the car. The mother, who had expressed great anxiety at the frailty of her first child, was unable either to grieve appropriately over the baby's death or to give her surviving daughter adequate mothering. When Jane was 5, her father began to play sexual games with her. Though there was no actual intercourse, he repeatedly showed her his erect penis, made her touch and fondle it, and kissed her genital area. Their "secret," at the oedipal level, resulted in Jane's regression and helped to preserve the earlier symbiotic core with its primitive object relationships. This incestuous relationship continued until the patient had her first menstrual period, whereupon Jane's father approached her in her bedroom and kissed her breast so hard that she screamed. He never touched her sexually again.

Jane's family lived in a traditional Southern community in which class differences were rigidly upheld, and Jane's mother pressured her daughter to submit to her own social climbing. Thus Jane was sent to a college traditionally acceptable to families of wealth, but had to work as a waitress to meet her expenses. The psychotic episode, which appeared a few months before she graduated from college, was initiated because Jane made a bid at inner independence and individuation for which she was psychically unprepared.

Three years into her treatment, Jane was beginning to think of leaving her parental home, where she still lived, and finding an apartment of her own. She feared being poisoned by her mother as she attempted to separate from her physically and psychically, and also saw the analyst as dangerous. It was at this point that the family cat, called Miss Kitty, became a most important object, as talk about the pet filled Jane's analytic sessions. At times she totally identified with the cat, and thought her mother might be poisoning it too. More frequently, however, the cat functioned as a bridge between Jane-mother, or Jane as an individuated person, and the external world, mainly her mother. Although Jane symbolically figured the cat as a penis by describing it as "a root into my mother," its principal significance, as events demonstrated, was as a reactivated transitional object, a protosymbol. She continued to be preoccupied with the cat, which she took to her apartment several months after leaving home. At night Miss Kitty joined her in bed; in fact, Jane could not sleep without the cat.

As Jane worked through her attempt to differentiate herself further from the mother-analyst and to achieve individuation, the magic of the cat as a bridge between internal and external worlds dimmed. Concerned the cat was ailing, she took it to a veterinarian and talked him into performing a hysterectomy in spite of the fact that she knew, even without warning, that the cat would not survive. Her associations to the cat at this time were reduced to breasts and nipples. An artist, she drew a picture of Miss Kitty lying on her back, displaying conspicuous udders with swollen teats. When, as expected, the cat died in surgery, she asked me, "Did you know that part of me wanted Miss Kitty to die?" I replied softly, "Yes." "She experienced sadness but could not yet mourn in the adult sense.

Some months later, Jane acquired another cat, which she placed in bed between herself and the young man with whom she had become intimate. She consciously thought of the cat as a symbolic penis which could belong to both her and her partner, but, on a lower level, she continued to treat the cat as a kind of reactivated transitional object. For months, she "played" with her relationship with the young man via the cat, and slowly began not only to find her sexuality but also to achieve a solid view of herself as an entity apart from the external world around her.

Cats as Self- or Internalized Object-Representations

Another characteristic of persons with borderline personality organization is that they typically use the mechanism of splitting to separate libidinally invested self- and object-representations from aggressively invested self- and object-representations. Cats are, for a number of reasons, suitable targets for an externalization of both "good" and "bad" self- and object-representations and, in such individuals' minds, can actually *become* those representations.

A pet cat is typically sociable and aloof by turns. As a kitten it is very appealing; in maturity it often seems tantalizingly remote and self-absorbed. Unpredictable and somewhat fickle in its behavior, it gives affection on its own terms alone. It is soft, but it can scratch. It is a solitary hunter, but sometimes demands attention. Further, cats' daily rhythms do not match those of humans; cats quickly alternate between napping and alertness, for example. And a pet cat, unlike a pet dog, usually refuses to be dominated. As we observed borderline patients' own perceptions of their pets, Kavanaugh and I (Volkan and Kavanaugh, 1978) concluded that the feline nature especially well suits the young child's (or adult borderline patient's) need for a reservoir for unmended "good" and "bad" self- and object-representations.

Samantha: Samantha was a 31-year-old married woman when I began seeing her as an inpatient; her hospitalization lasted about nine months, after which she continued in therapy as an outpatient (for further details of her story and treatment, see Volkan [1976]). At the beginning of treatment, she described a fragmentation of her personality. She had many "selves" that came and went, none remaining for any length of time. They were, she said, under two "main controls"—her left "side" and her right—and she referred to these "sides" as components of her "double personality." She described a division between her two "main controls" and named it "the bar." "There is no place to land on it," she explained, communicating her perception of the "bar" as a gap between the two "sides." She also reported that at times she would lose this "double personality" and regress to what she named a "complete backwards" state. Before her extreme regression and hospitalization, Samantha had behaved like a person with a stable borderline personality organization. During that time, she had used her pet cats as externalized representations of her split inner world. When she could no longer maintain this externalization, Samantha became psychotic, leading to hospitalization and to my care.

In therapy, it became clear that when Samantha was controlled by her "left side" she spoke softly, and behaved seductively and gently. When the "right side" dominated, she spoke roughly and exhibited temper to the point of throwing things at me. The "bar," perceived as a chasm, represented the splitting that separated her two "main controls"; one of the two "sides" represented her aggressively determined self- and object-representations while the other represented its libidinally determined counterparts. When she began her treatment with me, however, Samantha was not functioning at a borderline level, for neither of her "sides" could be maintained long enough; further, her two "sides" were themselves fragmented. Early in treatment, she frequently regressed to a condition in which she could not differentiate at all between self- and object-images. When in her "complete backwards" state, Samantha lay speechless and motionless in the fetal position, eyelids heavy, oblivious of others. One might expect that an adult woman attempting to recapture a state of such extreme regression would retain an observing ego, however shaky, but as long as she remained in a "complete backwards" state she was incapable of verbal reporting. Though later she would be able to articulate something of what had happened to her, as long as she was in this condition she had no words; her thoughts, she said, came only "in music."

Samantha was the firstborn in a musical and "temperamental" family in which the father was only marginally involved, passive and rather colorless. Her mother was contemplating a professional career as a concert pianist when she became pregnant with Samantha. Emotionally unprepared for motherhood, she raised her daughter according to the advice of a book that recommended leaving babies alone and refraining from unnecessary handling and affectionate play. To Samantha's mother, the child was a lovely doll who would, in the course of time, gratify her mother by becoming a famous musician. As Samantha lay in her crib or played in her playpen without tactile stimulation or other bodily contact, her mother played the piano endlessly. The mother's practical competence was so lacking that Samantha developed long crying spells at the age of only a few months. The physician who had to be called declared the infant "hungry" and advised bottle-feeding.

Samantha's mother persisted in her efforts at "musical communication" with her daughter and tried to teach the child to play the piano at an early age. Samantha's limited musical accomplishment disappointed her mother's hopes, however, and when another girl was born, 13 years after Samantha, the mother transferred her musical interests and ambitions to the younger child. By this time, however, Samantha was caught in hostile dependency on her mother and a partly symbiotic relationship with her mother's representation. When Samantha married at the age of 17, she had difficulty handling the ordinary responsibilities of wife and mother, and from time to time retreated under stress to her mother's home, which was near her own home.

Seven years before she began treatment with me, Samantha had moved to Europe with her husband and young daughter because of her husband's business. The necessity of living at a great distance from her mother represented an intrapsychic separation from the representation of her mother, creating extreme anxiety. In addition, however, the European move also placed her in what she called "the most musical countries of the world"; even her neighbors, as it happened, were musically inclined and often played the piano. The "musical environment" in this distant land represented her own very early "musical environment" at home with her mother; it was here that she regressed into psychosis.

The family had taken their cats—Maxie, a male, and Marie Jane, a female—to Europe with them. Samantha anthropomorphically endowed Marie Jane with gentleness and Maxie with strength and power, representing her own two "sides." As Samantha described them to me, I was struck not only by her identification with them, but also with her own catlike behavior in sessions. When she felt gentle, she worked her hands like the paws of a kitten kneading its mother's belly while nursing; aggression, on the other hand, was expressed with clawing gestures. She once made a significant slip of the tongue, saying that she had "tasted" her cats when she meant to say she had "chased" them, revealing her introjective relationship to them. As her treatment progressed, it came out that Marie Jane had met her end after falling from a window and going into convulsions (it was unclear whether Samantha had actually pushed her, though she blamed the maid for the accident). When it happened, Samantha reported, she had not wept, but assumed the stillness and composure she had attributed to Marie Jane. Now the balance between the "libidinal" cat and the "aggressive" one was disturbed. She became greatly concerned about and fearful of the "wildness" she saw in Maxie after his mate died. She wondered whether he should be destroyed, feeling that she would be liberated from her own aggression if the animal that reflected that feeling in her environment were eradicated. Finally, she persuaded her husband to have Maxie euthanized, and afterwards felt "killed inside," as she said, for she had lost her split self- and object-representations. It was at this point that she first regressed to the state she designated "the complete backwards": fused, undifferentiated self- and object-representation.

Cat as a Psychotic Core

Three decades of intensive therapeutic work with adult schizophrenic patients have led me to the conclusion that no adult truly becomes schizophrenic simply because of a massive regression. Rather, adult schizophrenia occurs because of the existence, from childhood on, of an undifferentiated core self-representation that is saturated with "bad," aggressively invested affects and that has object relationships through fusion-defusion or rapid introjective–projective relatedness. In the person who has the potential to develop adult schizophrenia, this core, "the infantile psychotic self" (Volkan, 1995, 1997; Volkan and Ast, 1997b), is enveloped by a healthier self-representation, also developed in early life. Adult schizophrenia is initiated when the encapsulated infantile psychotic self can no longer be effectively controlled and managed by those ego mechanisms associated with the enveloping healthier self (see also Ast, 1997). Further, my work on the infantile psychotic self has established that this core may have various fates besides its role in the initiation of adult schizophrenia (Volkan, 1995; Volkan and Akhtar, 1997). Here I will focus on one of these fates: the development of a psychotic personality organization.

In a psychotic personality organization, the infantile psychotic self is only *partially* encapsulated. Thus, from childhood on, the enveloping healthier self absorbs aspects of the infantile psychotic self and becomes its "voice." In other words, the infantile psychotic self constantly influences the ego mechanisms associated with the healthier self. The most typical of these mechanisms involves obsessive repetition that promotes two illusions: (1) an illusion of "fit" between external reality and the infantile psychotic self; and (2) the illusion of "starting again" with a core self saturated with libido/"good" affects. (If an individual's initial core or self is libidinally saturated, it evolves and he or she does not develop an infantile psychotic self. People with infantile psychotic selves often attempt to go back to such a healthy beginning.) Outside of his or her compulsive reenactments, the patient is often capable of carrying out the routines of day-to-day living, and may seem "normal" on one functioning level. Examining his or her obsessive activities, however, reveals a life dominated by "killing" or repairing, fusion-defusion, introjective–projective relatedness, paranoid fears or extreme idealization, and sexual or aggressive perversions and psychosomatic expression hidden beneath the surface of the patient's "normality."

Greer and I (1996) have described activities related to the infantile psychotic self among transsexuals: they repeatedly search for surgical alterations in order to create the two illusions mentioned above. The transsexual's infantile psychotic self reflects the infant's fused representation with the depressed mother. Though the child later evolves more mature self and object relations, the initial fused mother–infant representational unit remains partly encapsulated and saturated with "bad" affects. The adult transsexual, by repeatedly demanding surgery, seeks to find a fit between the infant psychotic self and external reality as well as to saturate the core self with "good" affects. For example, the surgery that transforms a male transsexual into a "woman" produces the illusion that the male child–mother unit can *really* be created. If a female transsexual becomes a "man," the created penis is imagined to satisfy the depressed mother so that the early mother-child interaction becomes infused with "good" feelings—the prerequisite for developing a positive core self.

For "cat people" with psychotic personality organization, the cat stands for the patient's infantile psychotic self. Sometimes the patient totally identifies with the cat and feels the infantile psychotic self within himself or herself. At other times, the cat remains as an externalized version of the infantile psychotic self, allowing the patient to appear psychologically "healthier" than he or she actually is.

Sarah: At the age of 36, Sarah sought treatment because of loneliness, headaches, and a wish, as she put it, to "be fixed." For the last decade, she had been visiting plastic surgeons to be "fixed" physically; like a transsexual, she was preoccupied with her body image and its "correction." Even during her sessions she would often become preoccupied with a pimple or put drops in her eyes and Vaseline on her lips. Unlike a transsexual, though, she did not focus on changing her genital area but had demanded surgery on her nose, chin, and the high bones of her face; when she entered treatment, she was considering a change in the appearance of her hips as well. Sarah's first plastic surgery had come just after her mother's death, when Sarah was 26. With the money she received from the sale of her mother's property, she procured her second operation. Subsequent surgeries were paid for by her mother-in-law. And although she contemplated still more surgery, Sarah delayed, fearing that a request for more money would upset her husband's mother. It was postponing further surgery that initiated the internal disturbances that led her to seek treatment.

Sarah's other preoccupation, when she began treatment, was her "family" of many cats. Sarah had graduated from college with a professional degree, but had never practiced her profession, having married an independently wealthy man while in college. After Sarah's graduation, the couple moved into a house in the country where Sarah's daily life revolved, for all practical purposes, around the cats, most of which suffered from feline leukemia or Addison's disease; like her infantile psychotic self, the cats were saturated with "bad" elements.

Sarah, an only child, was born by cesarean section when her mother and father were in their early forties. Her mother had suffered a number of miscarriages before Sarah was born and had more after her arrival; in a sense, it was as if Sarah had survived by accident. Soon after Sarah was born, her mother became ill, so one of her mother's friends became Sarah's primary caregiver during her first months of life. (I assume that Sarah's infantile psychotic self resulted from her earliest experiences of "bad" mothering by her sick biological mother. It is also possible that "good" mothering by her mother's friend [after whom Sarah had been named] created a healthier core which encapsulated, but only incompletely, the psychotic one.) Sarah's family lived in a farming community where her parents ran a country store in which they spent most of their time. There were no other children for her to play with regularly, so she had little social interaction beyond the family.

Sarah slept in a crib in her parents' bedroom until she was 4 years old, when her mother's widowed stepmother moved in with the family and bedroom arrangements changed. The older woman moved into the big bedroom where Sarah and her parents had slept. Sarah and her mother moved into another room, where Sarah slept in the same bed with her mother until she was 15 years old, a reflection of their symbiotic relationship. Meanwhile, Sarah's father moved into a very small bedroom all by himself. Clearly, however, Sarah's mother visited him there periodically as she continued to become pregnant and to suffer miscarriages throughout Sarah's childhood. When Sarah was 15, her maternal stepgrandmother died, and bedroom arrangements were changed again: for the first time, Sarah was given her own room.

When Sarah was 19, her father died. Soon after, she left for college in a big city some distance away and took the family cat, which had feline leukemia, with her. Sarah believed that this cat was the origin of the epidemic of fatal illness that was rampant among her pets. As she collected more and more cats, one would infect the next new one and so on until, when she entered treatment, she had dozens of sick cats. Eventually, Sarah became a member of the Day Lily Club, where members join in mourning their pets' deaths.

Gradually I reconstructed Sarah's unconscious fantasy, which centered around the notion that she was both dead and alive. She had been told that her mother became pregnant with her soon after suffering a miscarriage. The mother probably believed that Sarah would also die and passed this belief on to her daughter; Sarah's infantile psychotic self reflected an early relationship with her mother's representation that was filled with "bad" affect and contaminated with the mother's unconscious fantasies about the infant and later the child's corresponding unconscious fantasies. Complicating this situation, Sarah's mother had been mostly unavailable to her in the early months of her life, and Sarah had been given the name of her mother's friend as if that woman were her mother. Then, after three months of life, she was taken completely away from this "mother" to be placed at the mercy of a woman whom she came to experience as a "killer." Though Sarah retained few memories of childhood, she did often recall her mother beheading chickens and had a single vivid memory of watching her mother kill a sick kitten by hitting the cat again and again against a tree until its head was smashed. After this episode, Sarah began to have "imaginary cats"; when, at the age of 5, she saw her mother brutally murder the kitten, she unconsciously perceived that she herself might face a similar fate, and thus cats came to be protosymbols of her infantile psychotic self. As a child, Sarah felt that she was not "good enough" in any respect: intelligence, beauty, and so on. (In reality, Sarah is an intelligent and very beautiful woman, even after her surgeries.) Though her mother had actually validated her worth, Sarah never believed that her mother meant what she said. She was the child fated to be not "good enough" to live. Having to sleep with the "killer" mother in the same bed until she was 15 "forced" Sarah to maintain a partially enveloped infantile psychotic self and its externalized representation as a smashed cat.

In addition to representing her externalized psychotic core, cats assumed other meanings in Sarah's unconscious fantasy as well. On one level, significantly, the cats represented her mother's miscarried fetuses (a representation of Sarah's nonexistent siblings), and she accordingly related to them with ambivalence; she wanted to repair them and to keep them alive, but at the same time wanted to kill them. A vegetarian, she expressed a desire for all her animals to have dignity, saying "cats are kids." Each of her cats had a name, and she knew each one's personality and physical condition. At the same time, she would complain that the human race had allowed a "pet overpopulation" to occur, reflecting her wish to kill the "excess" fetuses/siblings.

Sarah's headaches were connected to an identification with the cat whose head was smashed by her mother. The manner in which Sarah typically talked about herself in the third person—saying, for instance, "Everybody is grown-up and she [Sarah] has no one to play with"—also reflected her partially enveloped infantile psychotic self. Deep down she felt that she was a "thing" and that her mother treated her on the one hand as a "thing," half-dead and half-alive, and on the other hand as someone else's baby. In her preoccupation with sick cats, she would constantly "kill" and "repair" her own "bad" infantile core as well as the representation of her mother's fetuses. But, in spite of her and her veterinarian's interventions, the cats kept dying, and she kept collecting new ones who in turn sickened and died; she felt doomed to repeat in action her life and death fantasies.

This account of her unconscious fantasy and infantile psychotic self emerged as I began to understand the meaning of Sarah's surgical attempts at physical alteration. Listening to her descriptions of how she wished her body to look after surgery, I sensed that Sarah wanted to turn herself into a repaired cat, not the smashed cat representing her core aggression saturated by her traumatic early life experiences. Like a transsexual, Sarah wanted bodily change that would allow a new relationship to develop between an undamaged Sarah and a mother who was not a destroyer. Sarah wanted a chance at a new beginning, a psychic core infused with more libido than aggression. As she "heard" my interpretation of the meaning behind her "need" for continued surgery, Sarah's desire for more bodily change slowly disappeared, and other changes followed. Now she was able to describe to me "the horrors" that existed in her infantile psychotic self. Some nights she would experience "the horrors" and take any available medications to control them. She spoke of her infantile self as a "buffered land," reflecting how it was at least partly enveloped. She also began to understand why she reached orgasm during intercourse literally in seconds: it was as if pleasure must be experienced right away, otherwise it might not be given to her at all, and "the horrors" might swallow up the pleasure.

In the fifth year of her treatment, Sarah began to make therapeutic modifications in her infantile psychotic self. In one memorable dream, she saw herself in a dirty pond representing a fused state with her "bad" mother's aggression-filled representation. In the dream, I, her therapist, stood at the shore, but did not throw a rope to Sarah in order to save her. Sarah knew that she had to learn to swim to safety. At the dream's end, she swam to the shore, where I looked at her and said, "Your complexion is fine." She felt triumphant, and after this period of her treatment, took on a new hobby: welding. In a symbolic sort of "play," Sarah had begun to repair her core.

As her attempts at differentiation and separation from her mother–therapist representation progressed, Sarah experienced a series of dermatological problems, as if she were developing a new (psychological) skin. At the same time, she was in many ways demanding that her therapist be a "good" mother so that she could succeed in differentiating, individuating, and developing a core saturated with libido. All along, however, she was afraid that her face would somehow be disfigured (like the smashed cat)—that her "new" infantile self would be modeled after the original one. She developed blisters on her tongue and went to see a doctor who diagnosed her as having a "tongue allergy." I recognized that her skin and tongue problems had both regressive and progressive sides. The patient might be experiencing "new" mothering experiences with the therapist that were as "bad" as her original mother-experience. But, as I explained to Sarah, the blisters in her mouth were also like a wound, indicating a separation from her mother. I suggested that Sarah focus on this progressive (separation-individuation) aspect of her internal processes, and soon the blisters disappeared.

Sarah was feeling better and it was now obvious that her preoccupation with cats was diminishing. Sarah began to have fantasies about ice skating around a deep hole in an ice-skating rink. She knew that if she did not learn to skate properly, she would fall into the hole (i.e., she would regress). Her skating daydreams continued as she reported learning, in real life, how to skate better and better. To one session she brought a Thomas Wolfe book, declaring, along with its title, "You can't go home again!" But, of course, her fears that the "new" core self would also be killed and that her therapist would be like her original mother continued for some time.

As her investment in cats receded, Sarah bought two llamas and turned her attention to these new and different pets. Sessions were filled with comparisons of llamas and cats. Llamas lived outside of her house (i.e., they were, symbolically speaking, differentiated objects). She could make money by breeding llamas; they were "contaminated" with the reality of adult life. Alongside these comparisons, she unearthed more childhood memories of aggression and death in her relationship with her mother. She recalled the anxiety she felt watching her mother's breathing as they slept side by side: she expected her mother to die. Now, with the modification of her infantile psychotic self and her separation-individuation from her mother more advanced, Sarah, for the first time, began to bring genuinely oedipal material to her sessions.

The "cat people," as I have termed them, relate to cats in their environments as protosymbols and may use them as reactivated transitional objects, as externalized self- and object-representations, or as embodiments of their infantile psychotic selves. Such patients possess borderline or psychotic personality organization and exhibit focalized psychosis. Only when their treatment is successful, can they begin to perceive their pets as symbols, or even just cats.

REFERENCES

Ast, G. (1997), A crocodile in a pouch. In: *The Seed of Madness*, ed. V. D. Volkan & S. Akhtar. Madison, CT: International Universities Press, pp. 133–154.

Freud, S. (1927), Fetishism. *Standard Edition*, 21:147–157. London: Hogarth Press, 1961.

Godolphin, F. R. B. (1942), *The Greek Historians*, Vol. 1. New York: Random House.

Greenacre, P. (1969), The fetish and the transitional object. In: *Emotional Growth*, Vol. 1. New York: International Universities Press, 1971, pp. 315–334.

Hilton, A. (1953), *Cat-Women of the Moon*. T. Williams, [director].

Kernberg, O. F. (1976), *Object Relations Theory and Clinical Psychoanalysis*. New York: Jason Aronson.

Modell, A. H. (1970), The transitional objects and the creative art. *Psychoanal. Quart.*, 39:240–250.

Opie, I., & Opie, P. (1959), *The Love and Language of School Children*. Oxford, U.K.: Clarendon Press.

——— (1969), *Children's Games in Street and Playground*. Oxford, U.K.: Clarendon Press.

Pollock, G. H. (1996), Saying farewell to a friend. In: *The 1996 Medical and Health Annual*. Chicago, IL: Encyclopedia Brittanica, pp. 192–201.

Russell, J. B. (1972), *Witchcraft in the Middle Ages*. Ithaca, NY: Cornell University Press.

Sanford, B. (1966), A patient and her cats. *The Psychoanalytic Forum*, 1:170–176. New York: International Universities Press, 1972.

Silvester, H. (1995), *Cats in the Sun*. San Francisco, CA: Chronicle Books.

Volkan, V. D. (1976), *Primitive Internalized Object Relations: A Clinical Study of Schizophrenic, Borderline, and Narcissistic Patients*. New York: International Universities Press.

———— (1981), *Linking Objects and Linking Phenomena*. New York: International Universities Press.

———— (1982), A young woman's inability to say no to needy people and her identification with the frustrator in the analytic situation. In: *Technical Factors in the Treatment of the Severely Disturbed Patient*, ed. P. L. Giovacchini & L. Bryce Boyer. New York: Jason Aronson.

———— (1995), *The Infantile Psychotic Self and Its Fates: Understanding and Treating Schizophrenics and Other Difficult Patients*. Northvale, NJ: Jason Aronson.

———— (1997), The seed of madness. In: *The Seed of Madness*, ed. V. D. Volkan & S. Akhtar. Madison, CT: International Universities Press, pp. 3–16.

———— Akhtar, S. (1979), The symptoms of schizophrenia. In: *Integrating Ego Psychology and Object Relations Theory*, ed. L. Saretsky, G. D. Goldman, & D. S. Milman. Dubuque, IA: Kendall/Hunt, pp. 270–285.

———— ———— (1997), *The Seed of Madness: Constitution, Maternal Environment, and Fantasy in the Organization of the Psychotic Core*. Madison, CT: International Universities Press.

———— Ast, G. (1997a), *Siblings in the Unconscious and Psychopathology*. Madison, CT: International Universities Press.

———— ———— (1997b), A room without a room: Clinical observations of a "made" core. In: *The Seed of Madness*, ed. V. D. Volkan & S. Akhtar. Madison, CT: International Universities Press, pp. 111–131.

———— Greer, W. (1996), True transsexualism. In: *Sexual Deviations*, ed. H. Rosen. London: Oxford University Press, pp. 158–173.

———— Kavanaugh, J. G. (1978), The cat people. In: *Transitional Objects*, ed. S. Grolnick & L. Barkin. New York: Jason Aronson.

———— Zintl, E. (1993), *Life After Loss: Lessons of Grief*. New York: Charles Scribner's Sons.

Werner, H., & Kaplan, B. (1963), *Symbol Formation*. New York: Wiley.

Winnicott, D. (1953), Transitional objects and transitional phenomena. *Internat. J. Psycho-Anal.*, 34:89–97.

———— (1955), *Cat on a Hot Tin Roof*. New York: New Directions.

NAME INDEX

SUBJECT INDEX

For Product Safety Concerns and Information please contact our EU
representative GPSR@taylorandfrancis.com
Taylor & Francis Verlag GmbH, Kaufingerstraße 24, 80331 München, Germany